Ernest Alexander Cruikshank

The documentary History of the Campaign upon the Niagara Frontier in 1814

Ernest Alexander Cruikshank

The documentary History of the Campaign upon the Niagara Frontier in 1814

ISBN/EAN: 9783337148782

Printed in Europe, USA, Canada, Australia, Japan

Cover: Foto ©ninafisch / pixelio.de

More available books at **www.hansebooks.com**

THE DOCUMENTARY

HISTORY OF THE CAMPAIGN

— ON THE —

NIAGARA FRONTIER IN 1814.

EDITED FOR THE LUNDY'S LANE HISTORICAL SOCIETY

BY CAPT. E. CRUIKSHANK.

WELLAND:
PRINTED AT THE TRIBUNE OFFICE.

The Documentary History of the Campaign on the Niagara Frontier in 1814.

LIEUT.-COL. JOHN HARVEY TO MAJ.-GEN. RIALL.
(Most Secret and Confidential.)

Deputy Adjutant General's Office.
KINGSTON, 23rd March, 1814.

SIR,—Lieut.-General Drummond having had under his consideration your letter of the 10th of March, desiring to be informed of his general plan of defence as far as may be necessary for your guidance in directing the operations of the right division against the attempt which there is reason to expect will be made by the enemy on the Niagara frontier so soon as the season for operations commences, I have received the commands of the Lieut.-General to communicate to you the following observations and instructions:

The Lieut.-General concurs with you as to the probability of the enemy's acting on the offensive as soon as the season permits. Having, unfortunately, no accurate information as to his plans of attack, general defensive arrangements can alone be suggested.

It is highly probable that independent of the siege of Fort Niagara, or rather in combination with the attack on that place, the enemy will invade the District of Niagara by the western road, and that he may at the same time land a force at Long Point and perhaps at Point Abino or Fort Erie. An attack of such a general and combined nature, if made, as it doubtless will be, in force, you can have no hope of successfully resisting by any other means than a concentration of your whole force at Burlington or Ancaster, leaving for the moment the garrisons at Fort Niagara and Fort George to themselves and those means of defence which it is expected that they possess and will most strenuously exert.

With your whole force thus concentrated in an advantageous and open position, the Lieut.-General has no apprehension of your not being equal or superior to anything the enemy can bring against you. On the contrary, if correct information of the enemy's movements be fortunately obtained by you in time to enable you to effect your own concentrative movements with that precipitation (that rock which has so often been fatal to the success of our operations) Lieut.-General Drummond feels confident that, notwithstanding the proverbial caution of General Harrison, an opportunity will be afforded you of effecting, by one action, the defeat, capture, or destruction of a considerable part of the enemy's disposable force.

It is clearly to be understood that the abandonment, even for a moment, by the troops under your command, of their advanced position on the frontier for the purpose of concentrating at Burlington, is a measure which the Lieut.-General would approve only in the event, clearly ascertained, of the actual advance of the enemy in great force from the westward.

If the enemy's principal force be assembled on the Niagara frontier and smaller bodies advance from the westward and from Long Point for the purpose of threatening your rear, it will be sufficient (as no serious attack will in that case be apprehended) if you order the troops at Burlington to make a forward movement for the purpose of taking a position, say at Burford or Ancaster, or to dispute the passage of the Grand River, where the detachments at Long Point and Oxford can fall back on them, and the whole, with such Indians and militia as can be assembled, form a corps of observation sufficient to keep in check the enemy's force and cover your rear.

The whole of the troops on the frontier will then become disposable, and may, it is hoped, prove sufficient with the powerful *appui* they will have in Fort Niagara and Fort George and the aid which the squadron will afford them, to prevent the enemy's covering army (for it must be recollected that the siege of Fort Niagara will, in all probability, occupy a considerable part of his force) from being able to force back your division from the frontier and by that means greatly facilitate his operations against Fort Niagara by the possession of both banks of the river.

In the distribution of so comparatively small a force as you are likely to have for the defence of the Niagara frontier, the arrangement which would naturally strike a military man unacquainted with the character of the enemy he has to contend with, or with the events of the two last campaigns on that frontier, would be to concentrate the troops in some central position from whence they could be moved to either extremity or whatever point was invaded.

Such an arrangement, however, would leave the extremities of the line open to attack and would actually invite invasion, and the persons and property of the inhabitants would be left exposed to the smallest parties of the enemy's marauders. Experience, moreover, has proved that a small force may be distributed along the frontier without any great risk of being cut off. It is, therefore, Lieut.-General Drummond's wish that the distribution of the force should be made with reference to that of the last and preceding campaigns (previous to the attack of the enemy on Fort George on the 27th May last) and that all the stations that were then occupied from Fort George to Fort Erie (but not further) should be now occupied. Change of circumstances has prescribed a change of strength of several detachments—that at Fort Erie, for instance, the Lieut.-General conceives need not consist of more than one strong company of infantry, with a small party of artillery sufficient to man the 24 pounder proposed to be mounted in the southern demi-bastion, and this detachment (if the arrangement pointed out by the Lieut.-General to the acting-deputy-quartermaster-general be made) would be well covered and in perfect security against anything short of an invasion in force—and even in the latter case a small party so posted might not only very much annoy any craft or vessels which might approach the head of the river, but would operate with infinite advantage in the rear of any force which might venture to place itself betwixt two fires by landing between Fort George and Chippawa, and even if cut off its loss would be of no importance comparatively with the services which, under an intelligent officer, it might render. Chippawa should be *strongly* occupied (the *expression* is of course relative) and a detachment placed intermediately betwixt Chippawa and Fort Erie—say at Frenchman's Creek—and a rapid movement should be made from Chippawa to support the detachments on the right and to oppose any descent made above Chippawa.

I now come to a proposition made by you in a former letter to Lieut.-General Drummond for reducing the extent of the works of Fort Niagara, with a view to the reduction of the garrison. Your proposition will be referred to His Excellency the Commander of the Forces, but in the meantime I am directed to observe to you that, considered in a point of view which does not seem to have struck you, Lieut.-General Drummond is so far from being inclined to diminish the defences or the garrison of Fort Niagara (still less wholly to destroy or abandon that fort) that it appears to him that 500 or 600 men of your division cannot be better occupied than in occupying, as they in all probability will, at least ten times their number, and *that*, it is confidently hoped, for no inconsiderable period.

Strengthened indeed as your division will be by the accession of a regiment of upward of 700 strong, (the 103d,) which will join you as soon as the navigation opens, the Lieut.-General is disposed to indulge the hope that much may be done even in the open field against an enemy the greatest part of whose force will probably be directed against Fort Niagara.

In the reduced state contemplated by your proposal you are aware that that place could not possibly hold out for a single day against the powerful means which the enemy will be able to bring against it. By the adoption of that suggestion, therefore, it appears to the Lieut.-General that we should be voluntarily resigning for a possible but contingent good, all the solid advantages which the acquisition and possession of this fort is capable of affording us, and of which, besides the important one above alluded to, of occupying so large a portion of the enemy's force in its reduction, the benefit to the squadron of a secure harbor in which to take shelter, either from the weather or a superior enemy, is far from being the least—to say nothing of the negative advantage of the loss of that harbor to the enemy.

The occupation of Fort George as a flank to Fort Niagara is essential to the defence of the latter. A battery of a few heavy guns to bear upon the esplanade of Fort Niagara should, therefore, be immediately completed in Fort George. A small detachment, even in the event of its becoming necessary to withdraw the whole of the troops from the Niagara frontier for the purpose of concentration at Burlington, would be sufficient to place in that for- (George), which in its turn is protected by, as it is commanded by, Fort Niagara.

A battery at Missassauga Point (Flagstaff) is highly necessary, and an enclosed one on Queenston Heights if time, &c., permit its completion.

In concluding these observations Lieut.-General Drummond has particularly directed me to invite you to communicate such remarks as may suggest themselves to you, and to beg that you will on all occasions freely and fully communicate your ideas on all subjects connected with your most important command, but especially on those herein discussed.

I am further commanded to take this occasion of assuring you of the very great satisfaction and consolation which Lieut.-General Drummond experiences in the reflection that the arduous trust connected with the command of the Right Division at this critical juncture is reposed in an officer of such tried zeal, activity and ability as yourself. I have the honor to be, Sir,

J. HARVEY, Lt.-Col., D. A. G.

Lieut.-General Sir Gordon Drummond to Sir George Prevost.

KINGSTON, April 7th, 1814.

SIR,—I have the honor to report to Your Excellency that Major-General Riall's last letter to me states that no regular force has as yet made its appearance on the American side of the Niagara River, and that consequently he supposes no part of the column which left Sackett's Harbor some time since had arrived in that neighborhood, conceiving, from the display the enemy used to make formerly, they will not be long in showing themselves when they do arrive, at the same time expressing his hope and belief that in the hands of the garrison (the 100th regiment), who so gallantly gained possession of it, Fort Niagara is, for the present, safe.

A Mr. Bell, a respectable man, and two others, lately made their escape from Malden, and report that there is not the slightest appearance there for a forward movement, nor did they hear it spoken of. They were totally unacquainted with occurrences at Presqu' Isle. On their way to Port Talbot they discovered the two guns left by the enemy in the woods near Point Aux Pins, and hid them so carefully as to prevent them from being found again except by themselves. Two gun carriages and two ammunition carts, discovered at the same time and place, Colonel Talbot has sent a party to destroy.

I am happy to inform Your Excellency that Assistant-Commissary Coffin, in the absence of Mr. Dance, has reported to me that the three months' supply of provisions, ordered to be deposited in Fort Niagara, will have been laid in there in the course of a week from the 27th ultimo.

Major-General Peter B. Porter to Governor D. D. Tompkins.

CANANDAIGUA, 8th April, 1814.

SIR,—I returned yesterday from Buffalo, where I met Mr. Parrish, with a talk from the Secretary of War to the chiefs and warriors of the Six Nations, inviting them to take up arms and form a corps to be attached to my command.

We met the chiefs of Buffalo on Sunday, and altho' they decline giving an answer to so important a proposition until they consult the chiefs of other villages, Red Jacket, who was the speaker, expressed his full conviction that they would all turn out. They have sent runners to the west and are to give us an answer at this place in four or five days from this time. Mr. Parrish is of opinion that we shall have 500 warriors ready to act with us by the first of May.

Our prospects for volunteers in this county and to the west are very flattering. There is every reason to calculate that from the counties of Ontario, Genesee and Niagara we shall raise from 800 to 1,000 men. In the more remote counties I have less faith. The zeal and patriotism of those who are not in immediate danger is not so much to be calculated on, and the most discouraging circumstance is that the pecuniary inducements offered to volunteers is so much below those offered to other troops. If the five dollars were added we should find no difficulty. We have encouragement, however, that Steuben, Seneca, Cayuga, Onondaga, Otsego, Broome and Tioga counties will average at least one company each, and a company is expected from Tioga in Pennsylvania. From the counties more to the east we have not heard, owing to the badness of the roads and the snail-like movement of the mail. Colonel Dobbins and several other valuable officers are engaged in recruiting among the detached militia on the frontier.

* * * * * * *

Colonel Swift is very active in engaging volunteers and will enter heartily into all the views of the Government in authorizing this force.

Sir Gordon Drummond to Sir George Prevost.

KINGSTON, April 10th, 1814.

SIR,—I have the honor to acquaint Your Excellency that Major-General Riall has reported to me his having been requested to attend a grand council of the Indians at the head of the lake. The Prophet has been chosen the principal chief of all the western nations. His having been presented with the sword and pistols from His Royal Highness the Prince Regent gave very general satisfaction. He has promised the most cordial co-operation, and says that their smallest boys capable of bearing arms shall be ready to march at a moment's notice.

I am much concerned to communicate to Your Excellency that the Major-General states three of the Six Nations, speaking through their principal chiefs, have requested the Major-General to represent to Your Excellency their dissatisfaction at the appointment of Captain Norton to be their leader. They say they will not acknowledge him as such, will pay him no respect or obedience, nor look to him for anything they want: that they know him not, except as a disturber of the peace and harmony that ought to exist amongst them: they have a head man whom the King has appointed, and they want no other (Colonel Claus): the representation made to Colonel Drummond was the work of a few who had no authority to do so and it was not the opinion of the nations. The Major-General inquired if such was the general opinion. The chiefs of three, viz., the Mohawks, Oneidas and Tuscaroras, said it was theirs decidedly; the others, viz., the Cayugas, Onondagas and Senecas, refused to answer.

Lieut.-Colonel Robert Nichol to Sir Gordon Drummond.

YORK, April 22, 1814.

SIR,—A man of the name of Constant Bacon came over from the enemy the day before yesterday and has been sent to this place by Major-General Riall on suspicion of being a spy. I have examined him, and as I conceive the information he has given to be of the greatest consequence, and as it appears from a full consideration of all the circumstances to be correct, I have requested Colonel Stewart to despatch an express with it that you may have it in your power to act upon it.

I was always of the opinion that the enemy's troops on the Niagara frontier must be supplied on the opening of navigation by water, and that they would form depots in different places along the south shore of Lake Ontario, to be transported under the protection of their fleet so soon as it should put to sea.

To destroy these is an object, as I conceive, fully within our power, and which, if effected, must have the happiest effects on the future operations of the campaign, and, with the greatest deference, I beg leave to propose it. Great quantities of provisions, of which we are much in want, may be brought off, and what we cannot bring away can be easily destroyed. To succeed in this business, however, no time must be lost, for if the American fleet gets out, unless we should defeat them in a decisive action, the attempt should not be made. I am only waiting for a batteau to go to Kingston, when, if you see fit to undertake the business, I will be happy to give every assistance.

Bacon says the Americans intend attacking us on this side, which I think probable, but I firmly believe their principal object will be Burlington, and that a joint attack from both lakes will be made upon it. A blow of this kind, which if well arranged must succeed, would ruin us, and I fear unless Long Point is soon occupied in force it will be attempted and carried into effect.

Deposition of Constant Bacon.

YORK, April 2nd, 1814.

Examination of Constant Bacon, late a sutler with the division of the American army on the Niagara frontier, born in the town of Scipio, County of Cayuga, State of New York—left the American advanced posts on the 20th inst. and arrived at Fort Niagara about 2 o'clock in the afternoon of the same day—gives the following information:

The troops on that line are stated by the officers and men to amount to 7,000, of whom (25th regiment) 500 at Hardscrabble, five miles in rear of Lewiston, 100 at Black Rock, and 6,400 at Eleven Mile Creek. There is an arsenal (log building) at Hardscrabble containing 500 stand of arms, deposited by the militia, who were all dismissed on the 11th inst.; there is also a quantity of ammunition and four wagon loads of entrenching tools. There were no field pieces. There is a depot of provisions on the Ridge Road at the widow Forsyth's, about nine miles from Hardscrabble. It consists of beef, pork, whiskey and flour, of all of which there is a large supply. There is a road leading from the mouth of the Eighteen Mile Creek on the west side. The distance is ten miles, but the road is very bad. Thinks there is at least 2,000 barrels of provisions at this depot. There is no force nearer to Hardscrabble than the Eleven Mile Creek and Buffalo, which are equi-distant (about 32 miles.) There are at the Eleven Mile Creek some heavy guns, viz., a long 24 pounder, an 18 pounder, one 9 pounder, two 6 pounders, two mortars, and a large depot of provisions. General Harrison is expected in about three weeks with a strong reinforcement from Detroit. The nearest depot of provisions to those already mentioned is at the mouth of the Genesee River and at the upper landing, exactly four miles, up to which place large schooners can sail. There are there large quantities of beef, pork, salt, and whiskey, and no batteaux, guns, or troops for their protection. The next, consisting of flour, pork, and whiskey, is at Irondiquet, a few miles further to the eastward. It is exactly four miles from the falls of the Genesee to the Irondiquet storehouse, and three miles from the upper landing to the falls. The country here is not well settled. The next depot is at Putney, which is between the Genesee River and Big Sodus—this depot is on the lake shore. It consists, as before, of a large quantity of provisions and salt, and there are no men stationed here, unless they have come very lately. There is also a large depot at Sodus. There is also a large depot at Oswego, but there is a strong force stationed there. A schooner of 40 or 45 tons is building at Irondiquet. He says the army on the frontier has no boats, was in this province at Swagatchee (Ogdensburg), but has no acquaintance with any person there. His object in coming here was to get rid of paying some money which he owed for a cargo of liquors which he had bought on credit, and which had been plundered from him by the American troops.

Bacon further says it is intended to attack on this side.

ROBT. NICHOL.

Sir Gordon Drummond to Sir George Prevost.

KINGSTON, April 25th, 1814.

SIR,—I have the honor to transmit for Your Excellency's information a copy of a deposition of Constant Bacon, who was sent to York from Fort Niagara, having left the advanced posts of the enemy on the 20th inst., and arrived at that place on the evening of the same day.

Should this man's report be true, and should not the most ample supplies of provisions particularly flour, be sent from the lower provinces, I feel strongly apprehensive that the right division will not be able to hold its ground, even though the entire resources of the country should be at our command.

Major-General Riall, I am concerned to report to Your Excellency, states to me that he has received a very strong representation from Deputy-Assistant-Commissary-General Dance of the absolute necessity of decreasing the issue of flour to the Indians. Mr. Dance says that "without losing time by the consideration of the necessity or policy of this, I must repeat my positive conviction that at the rate of our present issues to them (nearly 1,200 barrels to the Indians alone per month) no effort of human exertion can supply this army many months longer, for the flour is not in the country." The total consumption he states at nearly 2,000 barrels per month, without including the garrison of York or the militia. The average consumption of the Indians of all descriptions being about 40 barrels per day. The consumption on the immediate frontier being about 20 barrels per day.

Major-General Riall feels much at a loss how to act with respect to the issues to the Indians, being very certain, in which I agree with him, that the reduction of any portion of the usual ration of flour will excite considerable discontent, and even defection, unless some other article is substituted for it. Fresh meat is not to be had, and very little, indeed, can be expected from fishing. Salt meat, therefore, is the only alternative, and this must be procured with immense difficulty from the lower province, and the transport of it by the squadron we cannot always depend upon.

From the enclosed information and the circumstances before detailed, I therefore consider that the safety of the province, in a great measure, depends as well upon the naval superiority as upon the destruction of the enemy's vessels, etc., at Sackett's Harbor, and there does not appear to me a more favorable opportunity than the present, could Your Excellency afford the means of undertaking the enterprise, which, to ensure a reasonable hope of success, cannot consist unquestionably of less than 4,000 effective men.

Return of the Resources of the Niagara and London Districts, Including the West Riding of the Home District.

1st Lincoln—442 cwt. of flour, 7,997 bushels wheat, 1,299 bushels rye, 1,387 bushels oats, 134 bushels corn, 38 bushels barley, 184 bushels peas, 6 fat cattle, 33 to fat, 257 oxen, 1,206 cows, 1,057 young cattle, 3,222 sheep, 1,705 hogs, 835 tons of hay, 733 horses, 254 sleighs, 105 wagons, 2,129 acres of wheat, 2 of barley, 101 of rye.

2nd Lincoln—337 cwt. flour, 7,881 bushels wheat, 301 bushels rye, 1,749 bushels oats, 180 corn, 511 peas, 11 fat cattle, 50 to fat, 403 oxen, 1,325 cows, 930 young cattle, 3,980 sheep, 1,676 hogs, 950 tons hay, 716 horses, 236 sleighs, 99 wagons, 3,228 acres wheat sown, 128 acres of rye.

3rd Lincoln—392 cwt. flour, 6,043 bushels wheat, 267 rye, 3,417 oats, 466 corn, 580 peas, 6 fat cattle, 50 to fat, 362 oxen, 1,087 cows, 894 young cattle, 3,028 sheep, 1,665 hogs, 1,073 tons hay, 598 horses, 174 sleighs, 106 wagons, 2,659 acres of wheat sown, 152 of rye.

4th Lincoln—400 cwt. flour, 6,000 bushels wheat, 350 rye, 3,000 oats, 520 corn, 280 peas, 12 fat cattle, 52 cattle to fat, 350 oxen. 1,236 cows, 1,080 young cattle, 3,205 sheep, 3,706 hogs, 975 tons hay, 500 horses, 200 sleighs, 80 wagons, 3,217 acres of wheat sown, 200 of rye.

5th Lincoln—2,000 cwt. flour, 12,700 bushels wheat, 1,637 rye, 2,455 oats, 419 corn, 15 barley, 213 peas, 1 fat animal, 13 cattle to fat, 359 oxen, 1,318 cows, 677 young cattle, 3,110 sheep, 1,155 hogs, 543 tons of hay, 605 horses, 253 sleighs, 54 pungs, 85 wagons, 18 carts, 3,594 acres of wheat sown, 310 of rye.

2d York—2,022 cwt. flour, 9,797 bushels wheat, 589 rye, 2,062 oats, 157 corn, 96 barley, 142 peas, 102 cattle to fat, 472 oxen, 982 cows, 897 young cattle, 1,969 sheep, 1,308 hogs, 409 tons hay, 467 horses, 215 sleighs, 68 wagons, 3,365 acres of wheat sown, 1 acre of barley, 130 of rye.

1st Norfolk—473 cwt. flour, 3,211 bushels wheat, 2,495 rye,

1,587 oats, 446 corn, 55 peas, 48 cattle to fat, 288 oxen, 520 cows, 475 young cattle, 1,180 sheep, 954 hogs, 249 tons hay, 265 horses, 84 sleighs, 37 pungs, 49 wagons, 20 carts, 1,257 acres of wheat sown, 551 of rye.

2nd Norfolk—407 cwt. flour, 4,093 bushels of wheat, 3,199 rye, 2,093 oats, 487 corn, 4 peas, 5 cattle to fat, 280 oxen, 651 cows, 583 young cattle, 1,472 sheep, 1,050 hogs, 208 tons of hay, 373 horses, 101 sleighs, 19 pungs, 65 wagons, 3 carts, 1,483 acres of wheat sown, 620 of rye.

Oxford—226 cwt. flour, 2,798 bushels wheat, 983 rye, 1,861 oats, 831 corn, 129 peas, 8 cattle to fat, 278 oxen, 649 cows, 623 young cattle, 1,395 sheep, 1,050 hogs, 232 tons hay, 242 horses, 41 wagons, 63 sleighs, 872 acres of wheat sown, 132 of rye.

Recapitulation—Flour, 6,699 cwt., equal to 3,828 barrels: 60,520 bushels wheat, 11,031 bushels rye, 19,611 bushels oats, 3,640 bushels corn, 149 bushels barley, 2,099 bushels peas, 36 fat cattle, 361 cattle to fat, 3,046 oxen, 8,974 cows, 7,219 young cattle, 22,561 sheep, 12,329 hogs, 5,474 tons of hay, 4,529 horses, 1,580 sleighs, 110 pungs, 698 wagons, 41 carts, 21,756 acres of wheat sown, average yield 12 bushels per acre, 3 acres of barley, 2,330 acres of rye, average yield 15 bushels per acre.

Dated February 24th, 1814.

General Peter B. Porter to Governor D. D. Tompkins.

CANANDAIGUA, 3rd May, 1814.

SIR,—The first of the month, Your Excellency knows, was appointed for the rendezvous of the volunteers at this place, when I had reason to hope, as well from the assurances I received before leaving Albany as from the obvious necessity of the thing itself, there would be some tents and other camp equipage provided for our accommodation.

About ten days ago, seeing no prospect of the arrival of these articles and dreading the embarrassments which the want of them would occasion, I sent directions to the recruits in various parts to remain where they were until further orders. A considerable number, however, whom the order did not reach, have come in. These I can made shift to dispose of.

On the first and second inst., about forty officers came in for instructions. The difficulty of the situation was great. I had no alternative consistent with my reputation and that of the government but to dismiss the recruits and wholly abandon the undertaking, or to prosecute it with all the energy and effect which a total destitution of the necessary means would allow. Not feeling authorized to do the first, I resolved of course on the latter.

From the information of the officers I calculate that we have now about 1,000 recruits engaged. Having now so many assistants, we can recruit with great rapidity. The officers all went home in high spirits, and we calculate to collect the troops at this place about the 18th or 20th inst., provided we shall in the meantime receive the necessary supplies of camp equipage, &c.

There is not a tent, camp kettle, axe or spade in the arsenal of this place.

Red Jacket and five other chiefs came in on Saturday to inform me that the Indians had all agreed to accept the invitation of the President, and they will join me here or in Buffalo any day I may name. There will probably be 500 warriors. The Oneidas receive an indemnity from the State about the first of June. Would it not be convenient to send it a little earlier this year, that they may have the benefit of it to prepare them for the campaign?

If I were furnished with the proper supplies I have little doubt but I could complete my corps in the course of the month. Colonel Swift and I shall set out for Onondaga and other counties to the east to-morrow.

Major-General Riall to Sir Gordon Drummond.

FORT GEORGE, May 19th, 1814.

SIR,—I have the honor to transmit to you a report made to me by Colonel Talbot, commanding the militia in the London district, that on the 14th inst. a party of the enemy, consisting of about 1,800 men, had crossed Lake Erie from Presqu' Isle and landed near Dover, which place, together with the mills and stores in its neighborhood, they destroyed, and after having committed every other excess possible re-embarked. They showed a disposition to land again at Turkey Point, but were, it is supposed, deterred from doing so by the appearance of a body of militia and a detachment of the 19th Dragoons, whom Colonel Talbot had assembled at that place. When Colonel Talbot had despatched his report the enemy's vessels were at anchor at the extremity of Long Point. Should they again attempt to land I hope they will be received by a detachment of troops and Indians which I ordered from Burlington, under the command of Lieut.-Colonel Parry, 103d Regt., upon receiving the first intelligence of their attempt.

Sir Gordon Drummond to Sir George Prevost.

KINGSTON, May 27th, 1814.

SIR,—In my letter which I had the honor to address to Your Excellency on the 21st inst., I stated that a force of the enemy, at that time supposed to be about 300, had landed near Dover on Lake Erie. I have now the honor to transmit a letter from Major-General Riall conveying a report of Colonel Talbot, commanding the militia of the London District, on the subject. Your Excellency will, however, perceive that the force of the enemy has since been computed to consist of about 800 men, whose conduct has been disgraced during their short stay ashore by every act of barbarity and of illiberal and unjustifiable outrage. Not only a large store, fitted as a barrack for the militia, but every private house and other building belonging to the peaceable inhabitants of the village and neighborhood of Dover has been reduced to ashes, together with Ryerse's and Finch's mills between that place and Turkey Point. The court house and public buildings at Turkey Point were only saved by the appearance of the militia and a detachment of the 19th Light Dragoons, both of which corps, I have very great satisfaction in acquainting Your Excellency, evinced the strongest anxiety to come in contact with the enemy.

I have likewise received from Lieut.-Colonel Parry of the 103d Regiment the most satisfactory accounts relative to the conduct of the grenadier company of that corps and the light company of the 89th, placed under his immediate orders. The latter, he says, are wild, but with attention and management perfectly tractable and orderly, and Lieut.-Colonel Parry bestows much commendation on the zeal and alacrity with which the militia assembled, considering the distance from whence they were to be collected. The Lieut.-Colonel from all these circumstances feels convinced that had not the enemy retired to his shipping before his arrival, his little band, increased by a few of the rangers and Kent volunteers as well as some persons and some Wyandot Indians who joined him from Amherstburg, would have made the enemy pay dear for their outrages. He states that but one house, in which a sick woman resided, was left standing between Paterson's Creek and Turkey Point, and the enemy on retiring avowed their intention to destroy Port Talbot in a similar manner. And as their officers appear determined to pursue the same system throughout the whole of the western frontier, I feel convinced that nothing but the most vigorous opposition to such disgraceful proceedings will prevent a recurrence of them. The accompanying declaration made by Colonel Holmes, commanding at Amherstburg, to the inhabitants of the new settlement, is a proof of the enemy's nefarious intentions.

Lieut.-General Drummond to Sir George Prevost.

KINGSTON, May 31st, 1814.

SIR,—I have the honor to transmit herewith for Your Excellency's information the deposition of Mr. Mathias Steele of Woodhouse, in the District of London, agent to the property of Lieut.-Colonel Nichol at Dover, who was on the spot at the time the enemy landed there on the 14th inst., and which I feel satisfied is correct.

I have had a communication from Major-General Riall of the 25th, wherein he states that on the 23d three large vessels were standing in for Turkey Point, but that Lieut.-Colonel Parry with his small force, the militia and Indians, had no apprehension whatever of any numbers which could be conveyed in them.

It having been considered necessary, however, to reinforce the detachment of the Royals at Burlington, and as this latter place could but ill spare any drafts from its garrison occupied in the protection of its depot and in guarding a number of civil prisoners at present under trial for treasonable practices at Ancaster, the Major-General considered it necessary to move forward two companies of the 41st Regiment from York, until the arrival of the 103d Regiment at the head of the lake.

The Wyandot Indians, who lately arrived at the beach, amount to 90. They say that many more would join them, but that they are too closely watched by the Americans.

The Chiefs Blackbird and Splitlog, who were with us last year, have joined the enemy.

DEPOSITION ENCLOSED.

MIDLAND DISTRICT.

Personally appeared before me, the Hon. Richard Cartwright, one of His Majesty's Justices assigned to keep the peace in and for the said district, Mathias Steele of Woodhouse, in the London District of Upper Canada, Gentleman, who, being duly sworn on the Holy Evangelists, saith: "That on Saturday, the fourteenth of the present month, an American force computed at about 800 men, and consisting of regulars, militia and seamen, the whole under command of a Colonel Campbell, disembarked at the mouth of Paterson's Creek from six schooners, where they encamped for the night. That, having met with no opposition, they on the following morning advanced and took possession of the village of Dover, and having plundered the houses of all the inhabitants and carried off all their provisions, set fire to the village and entirely destroyed it. They then proceeded to Ryerson's mills, situated a little further up the lake, and set fire to them, with several other buildings, and proceeding still further up the lake destroyed another set of mills, belonging to Mr. Finch. He further deposeth and saith that, to the best of his knowledge and belief, they destroyed altogether twenty dwelling houses, three flour mills, three saw mills, three distilleries, twelve barns and a number of other buildings. He further deposeth and saith, that they shot all the cows and hogs which they could find, leaving them to rot on the ground. And further, that on the said Colonel Campbell being asked the reason of this wanton and barbarous conduct, where he had met with no opposition, he answered that it was done in retaliation for the burning of Havre de Grace, Buffalo, and Lewiston, and further this deponent saith not.

(Sgd.) MATHIAS STEELE.

Sworn before me at Kingston, this 31st day of May, 1814.

RICHARD CARTWRIGHT, J. P.

Major-General Riall to the Officer Commanding at Presqu' Isle (Erie, Pa.)

HEADQUARTERS, NIAGARA FRONTIER, June 19, 1814.

SIR,—The detachment of the United States army which lately made a landing at Dover on Lake Erie, having committed acts of outrage on the private property of the unoffending inhabitants by burning and destroying that village and the mills in the vicinity, I have it in command to request from you an explicit declaration whether those acts were authorized by the government of the United States.

Colonel John B. Campbell, 11th U. S. Infantry, to Major-General Riall.

June 16th, 1814.

SIR,—I have had the honor to receive your communication of the 9th current. I commanded the detachment of the United States army which lately made a landing at Dover on Lake Erie. What was done at that place and its vicinity proceeded from my orders. The whole business was planned by myself and executed upon my own responsibility.

Opinion of a Court of Enquiry on the Conduct of Colonel Campbell at Port Dover, Held at Buffalo, the 20th June, 1814, Composed of Brigadier-General Scott, Major Jesup and Major Wood.

That considering the important supplies of breadstuffs, which from the evidence it appears the enemy's forces derived from the flour manufacturing mills at and near to Dover, Colonel Campbell was warranted in destroying those mills according to the laws and usages of war, and for a like reason the court think him justified in burning the distilleries under the said laws and usages. The saw-mills and carding machine, from their contiguity to the other mills, were, as the court conceives, necessarily involved in one and the same burning.

In respect to the burning of the dwelling and other houses in the village of Dover, the court are fully of opinion that Colonel Campbell has erred, that he can derive no justification from the fact that the owners of these houses were actively opposed to the American interests in the present war, or from the other facts that some of them were at the conflagration of Buffalo. In their partizan services it does not appear to the court that the inhabitants of Dover have done more than their proper allegiance required of them, and the destruction of Buffalo by a Lieut.-General of the enemy's regular forces was emphatically the wrong of the British Government itself, rendered such by its subsequent adoption of the measure, and ought not to be ascribed to a few Canadians who were present at the time.

Sir James Lucas Yeo to Lieut.-General Drummond.

Prince Regent, at anchor off Sackett's Harbor,
June 3d, 1814.

SIR,—The enemy's squadron being now nearly ready for sea, and it being too late for any joint attack on the enemy's force at Sackett's Harbor, I conceive it necessary to determine in what way His Majesty's naval force can best be employed to defeat the enemy's views and protect this province. I transmit you herewith a statement of their force, on which it is unnecessary for me to make any comment.

There are two things to be considered: 1st, what the enemy's squadron can effect before our large ship is ready? 2nd, what object have we for risking an action with our present force, when we will so soon have the superiority?

From the large reinforcements government are sending to this country, it appears to me to be their wish that a respectable naval force should be established to meet the enemy, and that any rash, ill-timed or unnecessary risk would defeat their views. The enemy are not in sufficient force to undertake any expedition in the face of our present squadron, but any disaster on our side might give them a serious ascendancy.

In making this communication I trust you will give me credit when I assure you I do not write from the feeling of a captain of a ship, but consider myself placed here in a highly responsible position as commanding the naval force in this country, on which most materially depends the safety or loss of this province.

I therefore require of you, sir, as the general officer with whom I am acting, your opinion on the several points in my letter. I shall at all times be ready to take the squadron into action whenever the general officer with whom I am acting represents to me that he thinks it necessary for the good of the service and safety of the colony, but such sanction or authority, under existing circumstances, I will require, as I never can take the whole responsibility on myself.

Lieut.-General Drummond to Sir James L. Yeo.

Headquarters, Upper Canada,
KINGSTON, 6th June, 1814.

SIR,—Your letter of the 3d inst. has received my most serious attention. So long as your position off Sackett's Harbor was found to distress the enemy and to retard the armament and equipment of his new ships, so long it appeared to me that the blockade ought to be maintained, and so long in fact no risk whatever could attend it.

It appearing, however, from your letter that the enemy's squadron, including his new ship (Superior) and brigs, is now ready for sea, it is evident that the blockade has not had all the effect to which we looked, and moreover that it can be no longer maintained without risking an action with a squadron quite equal, if not superior, to that under your command, and under circumstances on our part of decided disadvantage. With regard to the probable objects of the enemy, and to what their squadron may be able to effect, I am of opinion that whatever may be their ultimate views, they will not undertake any offensive operations until their second large ship is ready, and even then I am very much disposed to concur with you that they will not venture in the face of your present squadron, and, with the knowledge of the powerful addition to it which is in rapid progress, to encumber theirs with troops and other means necessary for the invasion of any part of this province.

It follows, therefore, as my opinion, and I have no hesitation in giving it as such, that there exists at present no motive or object connected with the security of this province which can make it necessary for you to act otherwise than cautiously on the *defensive*, (but at the same time closely watching all their movements,) until the moment arrives when by the addition of the large ship now on the stocks you may bring the naval contest on this lake fairly to issue, or by a powerful combined expedition, (if the enemy, as is probable, should decline meeting you on the lake,) we may attack and destroy him in his stronghold.

In thus frankly giving you my ideas as to the line of conduct which it would be prudent and proper for you to pursue, it is scarcely necessary for me to observe that circumstances may arise which may render it expedient and necessary to adopt a widely different system, such, for instance, as the relief of the necessities of the advanced division, and expedition against Sackett's Harbor, &c., &c., &c.

But these circumstances as they may arise will be discussed by us with those feelings of perfect good understanding and cordiality which have, I think I may affirm, ever existed betwixt us, and which to me has been a source of great satisfaction and confidence.

Lieut.-General Drummond to Sir George Prevost.

SIR,—I have the honor to transmit herewith a letter (in copy) from Commodore Sir James Yeo, covering a statement of the enemy's naval force in addition to their old squadron at present preparing for service on Lake Ontario, and requiring of me, as the general officer with whom he is acting, my opinion with regard to the employment of the squadron as soon as the superiority of the enemy's fleet appears unequivocal.

Coinciding with the Commodore in the propriety of not risking an action until our ship on the stocks here shall have joined the squadron, I have communicated my opinion to Sir James Yeo accordingly, a copy of which I have the honor to enclose for Your Excellency's information, and I request to be favored with Your Excellency's ideas and instructions on this important subject.

The Commodore, in consideration of the enemy's new ship, Superior, being with the rest of their fleet afloat ready to take the lake, has not judged it prudent any longer to continue off Sackett's Harbor, and has therefore come over to the Upper Gap where the squadron is now at anchor, as well to protect supplies proceeding upwards to the Right Division as to receive the seamen on board who have lately arrived from England.

Lieut.-General Drummond to Sir George Prevost.

KINGSTON, June 7th, 1814.

SIR,—By a report I have received from the Right Division I find that the traitor Westbrook, who formerly lived near Deleware town, made his appearance with about 30 riflemen of the enemy at Port Talbot on the evening of the 30th ultimo, where they made prisoners Captain Wilson of the militia and the miller, as also Captain Patterson at the house of Colonel Talbot. The miller effected his escape, but the others were obliged to take an oath similar to that administered to the inhabitants of the new settlement under pain of their houses being immediately burnt, as well as all others in the neighborhood. The party came from the westward, did but little damage and returned after a very short stay, through apprehension of their retreat being cut off by the assembling of the militia on the information of the man who made his escape.

Capt. J. H. Holland. A. D. C., to Major Deane, Royal Scots.

FORT GEORGE, May 31, 1814.

SIR,—I am directed by Major-General Riall to transmit you the enclosed secret instructions for the officer commanding at Burlington, which you will be pleased to hand to Colonel Scott of the 103d regiment on his arrival to take command of the post.

An extract of the part No. 1 has been forwarded to Lieut.-Colonel Parry.

I am directed to request that you will be pleased to acknowledge the receipt of this.

Secret and Confidential.

FORT GEORGE, May 31, 1814.

SIR,—As the entire command which the enemy possess of Lake Erie and the means they have of moving from Detroit makes your position very assailable, either by a landing at Long Point or its vicinity, or a movement along the western road, and as my measures will very materially depend on the reports I may receive, and which I beg may be always instantly forwarded to me, of any attempts of the enemy in that quarter, I have put together a few observations upon the line of conduct I could wish you to adopt in the command of the post of Burlington and the advanced detachments.

1. From the recent events which have taken place, that part of the country is evidently exposed to marauding parties, whose sole object appears to be the destruction of private property. For the purpose of checking these depredations I shall keep a larger detachment there than I had otherwise intended, as small parties of

observation at Burford and Long Point I should have considered sufficient to watch the regular approaches of the enemy. You will therefore detach a field officer and 200 men to Long Point and instruct him accordingly. The officer selected for this command will find the greatest assistance and resources in communicating with Colonel Talbot, commanding the militia of the London District, and such is the spirit and determination lately shown by them that I not only consider this force as perfectly sufficient to protect the inhabitants against any further marauding attempts, but even, should the enemy appear in regular force, he will be enabled, with their co-operation, to annoy his landing and harass his advance with very considerable effect, retiring on the Grand River upon the troops which will have advanced to that position from Burlington. It will be advisable for him to detach small parties at such points in his neighborhood as he shall see best suited for observing the enemy's motions on the lake, and as I shall be much governed in my intentions by his reports of the number and description of the enemy's force, he cannot be too strictly cautioned on this subject; indeed it has been a principal object with me to have an officer of rank stationed there upon whose information I could place dependence.

2. On receiving intelligence of any attempt of the enemy you will, of course, send such support to your advanced detachment as you shall judge necessary from the report of the officer commanding. But should a landing in great force be effected I wish you immediately to despatch information to the officer commanding at York, in order that he may immediately advance to Burlington with the garrison of that place, which he has received instructions to do in this event without waiting till my orders could reach him, at the same time that yourself with the whole of the troops and Indians at Burlington (leaving a sufficient guard for the commissariat and other stores) make a forward movement to the Grand River, where your advanced detachment and militia will fall back, and which position I should hope you will, with the means you have, be enabled to maintain. But should you find it not possible, your retreat should be made at once upon Burlington, as should the enemy's force be so great as to force its passage you will find it impossible to keep the open country about Ancaster.

3. There is always at Burlington a superintendent of the Indian Department, with whom you may make arrangements for the necessary co-operation of the Indians in any movement, and with whom you will communicate on all subjects connected with them.

4. It will be necessary to station an officer and 20 men at

Burford to watch the road from Detroit, and also to give notice of any advance in that direction to the officer commanding at Long Point, that his retreat may not be cut off, the enemy reaching the Grand River before him.

There is a corps of very useful volunteers under Lieut. McGregor, which it would be advisable to keep in advance of Burford, at Campfield's.

Lieut.-Colonel John Harvey, D. A. G., to Colonel Hercules Scott, 103d Regt.

KINGSTON, June 28th, 1814.

SIR,—I am directed by Lieut.-General Drummond to desire that you will continue to afford every possible assistance to the sheriff, not only in guarding and escorting the prisoners for trial, but also such as are convicted and under sentence. Additional irons are to be made if necessary, and every means taken to ensure their safe custody.

The men employed on this duty are at all times to be commanded by steady officers.

Lieut.-Col. John Harvey to Colonel Hercules Scott.
(Secret.)

Deputy Adjutant-General's Office,
KINGSTON, July 5th, 1814.

SIR,—With reference to a former communication, I am directed to acquaint you that, in consequence of the reduced state of the garrison of York and other circumstances, Lieut.-General Drummond has thought proper to withdraw, for the present, the power which was granted you of calling upon the officer commanding at York for a reinforcement of half his force in the event of an attack being made by the enemy upon the post at Burlington.

The General desires me to request that you will yourself see the prisoners who are under sentence of death at Ancaster. As it is most desirable to ascertain their security, you will be pleased to make an immediate report on the subject, for the information of Lieut.-General Drummond, who also directs me to desire that additional irons, leg bolts, etc., may be made if necessary, and in fact that every possible precaution may be taken to obviate all danger of their escape or rescue, which will, of course, become greater as the time of their execution draws nearer. The Lieut.-General depends entirely on your vigilance and caution to prevent the ends of justice being defeated.

Lieut.-General Drummond to Lord Bathurst, Secretary of State for the Colonies.
(No. 17.)

KINGSTON, July 3, 1814.

MY LORD,—I was detained at York by the meeting of the Legislature till the 18th of March, when I returned to Kingston and gave up my whole time and consideration to concert measures for the safety of the province. I strained every nerve to place our fleet in a condition most confidently to meet the enemy, by furnishing Sir James Yeo every assistance that could possibly be derived from the troops. With this united exertion the two large ships, the *Prince Regent*, carrying 50 guns, and *Princess Charlotte*, 44, were completed ready for sea while the American fleet were still in port and by no means in a state to come out to meet ours under a considerable time.

I projected an attack on Sackett's Harbor, which I did not think in the least chimerical. On the 27th April I communicated my design to Sir George Prevost and stated the force I deemed necessary. When disappointed in this, I turned my thoughts to the destruction of the depot at Fort Oswego, by which the American fleet has been retarded beyond measure in acquiring that degree of strength which must be vastly superior to our own before the enemy could venture to take the lake, and it is only now I learn that in a few days their vessels will, for the first time this season, leave Sackett's Harbor.

The strict blockade kept up by Sir James Yeo on the harbor and line of coast until the affair of Sandy Creek did much to retard their naval preparations, as they were obliged to send all species of equipments by circuitous land routes on which they experienced extreme bad roads. But they are now so formidable that Sir James Yeo will be obliged to remain in port until his new ship is finished. To conciliate the people I have directed the magistrates of each district in full assembly to fix upon a fair price to be paid for every article. It is highly probable that a similar vote of censure will be passed on my conduct as on Major-General De Rottenburg last year, and I would like to know if my conduct is unconstitutional.

Sir Gordon Drummond to Sir George Prevost.

KINGSTON, July 5th, 1814.

SIR,—I have the honor to transmit herewith a copy of the letter addressed to the officer commanding at Presqu' Isle by Major-General Riall, on the subject of the conduct of the detachment of the enemy's troops which some time since landed at Turkey Point, together with Colonel Campbell's reply thereto.

This letter was received by Major-General Riall in the state I now forward it to Your Excellency, it appearing to have the seal of General Brown affixed to it, and as it enclosed a New York newspaper the supposition is that General Brown drew his pen across the insolent observation of the latter part of it.

Major-General Riall reports that the enemy broke up from Buffalo on the 27th ultimo and has proceeded to Eleven Mile Creek; from thence to the mouth of Tonnewanto it is only six miles of a good road, where it is thought they will collect their boats for the purpose of crossing over between Navy and Grand Islands.

The Major-General directed Lieut.-Colonel Pearson to make a reconnoissance from Niagara Fort, but nothing extraordinary was discovered within a circuit of six miles from the place. The Lake Erie squadron with troops on board sailed from Presqu' Isle the 20th ultimo, report said for Michilimakinac and Matchedash on Lake Huron. Nine gunboats carrying heavy metal were at Buffalo. The force of the enemy computed at nearly 5,000.

Captain Crowther of the 41st Regiment has arrived at Fort Niagara and is anxious to obtain a sanction from superior authority to return to his duty, as he conceives the parole exacted of him to be even more particular than that given to the other officers who came in before him.

On the relief of the King's Regiment Major-General Riall considered it advisable, in which I fully concur with him, to place the 100th Regiment at Chippawa and Fort Erie, the Incorporated Militia (now in an admirable state of discipline and efficiency under Captain Robinson of the King's Regiment,) with the Light Companies of the Royals and 100th under the command of Lieut.-Colonel Tucker, with the 41st Regiment at Fort Niagara, Lieut.-Colonel Pearson between those places, and Lieut.-Colonel Hamilton at Long Point.

Sir Gordon Drummond to Sir George Prevost.

KINGSTON, July 7th, 1814.

SIR,—I have the honor to acquaint Your Excellency that about 150 Western Indians, under Captains Caldwell and Elliott, were crossed over last week at Niagara for the purpose of ascertaining in which direction the enemy went when he broke up from Buffalo, and on this service they burnt the barracks at Hardscrabble, about five or six miles from Lewiston, capable of accommodating from 1,500 to 2,000 men. They returned without having committed the smallest act of personal violence to any individual. But having brought off some horses and cattle, private property, it was thought proper to induce them to leave them behind, which they did with very great reluctance and dissatisfaction, and in remuneration for this forbearance I have deemed it advisable to give directions that 30 dollars each shall be paid for the horses and 20 dollars each for the cattle.

I am concerned to inform Your Excellency that a gunboat and a Durham boat of the enemy landed a strong party at Presqu' Isle (Lake Ontario) on the night of the 1st inst., where they burnt the storehouse of a Mr. Gibson and a small schooner which was building there by him.

Major-General Peter B. Porter to Governor D. D. Tompkins.

BUFFALO, July 3, 1814.

SIR,—General Brown crossed the Niagara this morning in pursuance of an admirable plan which was admirably executed, and invested Fort Erie, which surrendered to him this afternoon with a garrison of 120 men. And all this without the loss of a man killed and scarcely a shot exchanged.

As to my corps, I need not tell you, because Your Excellency knows how egregiously my expectations have been disappointed in every respect. Instead of being provided with clothing, quartermaster's stores, &c., by the general government, it was not until long after the force was to have been assembled and organized that I was able to obtain from the Secretary of War any recognition or even any notice of the existence of such a corps. I have not yet received a rifle, sabre, bayonet, blanket, and but a partial supply of tents.

I have 500 Indians and 150 mounted men with me at the place where General Brown wished me to be at the time of his crossing. The infantry I left at Batavia with Colonel Swift, who was obliged to wait a few days for the arrival of some quartermaster's stores and for some companies not yet arrived. He is, however, now on his march to this place.

My whole force will be about 1,000 volunteers and 500 Indians. To this General Brown has agreed to add, as soon as Colonel Swift arrives, the regiment of Pennsylvania volunteers, which will increase the command to upwards of 2,000. With this respectable force and the fair support of General Brown, which I have no doubt he will give, I hope to gain some credit for the volunteers.

I find myself, however, commanded by two young brigadiers. Of my repugnance to the command of one of them (Scott ?), with whose character I am better acquainted than the world generally, you were apprised last winter.

Had I foreseen the situation in which I was to be thrown, nothing would have induced me to have undertaken the task I did. But I embarked, and if I have but ten men I will persevere. General Swift is with me and I feel anxious he should continue. The expense of two Generals in the corps need not be an objection. As to myself, in whatever situation, I want only enough to defray my current expenses. My object is not pay.

BURLINGTON, June (July ?) 4, 1814.

Having received information from Major-General Riall of the enemy having landed, and considering it probable that an attack may be soon made on this post, I have been led to look most attentively at the works which are now going on under the acting engineer, and from the wretched state they are in I am of opinion that they are not capable for a moment of being depended on, nor do I see any prospect of their being made so. Under these circumstances I have been led to consider what may be the best and most expeditious mode of rendering this position defensible, but well knowing the misrepresentations that may be made of my conduct and of the present state of the defences of this place, and consequently the censure that would follow were I at once to order the men to be employed on the works in a different mode to what they have hitherto been employed, I consider it necessary for the good of the service, and for my own justification, to call on the senior officers in garrison to inspect with me the present state of the works, and also to consider of the plan I have now to propose, so as with the means in our power to put the place in a state of defence. Officers present, viz.:

Major Maule, D. A. Q. M. General.
Major Smelt, 103d Regiment.
Captain Brown, 103d Regiment.
Lieut. Charlton, senior officer of R. A.
Lieut. Engouville, acting engineer.
Lieut. Reynolds, D. A. Commissary General.

I have now to propose that the ditch of the old works shall be immediately widened and picqueted with the piquets now on the beach, a small angle to be thrown up so as to flank the ditch, the rampart to be repaired and thickened, platforms placed for such guns as are disposable. Two guns to be mounted on the new blockhouse near the work, such as the officer of artillery may think proper, and placed on temporary platforms as he may direct. These

I consider the first and most important works. Should time and means permit, platforms to be laid in the new works lately thrown up so as to enable the fieldpieces (if judged expedient to be ran out) to be fired over those works and to retard the advance of an enemy. Abattis to be formed on the ravine near the Red House so as to retard an enemy advancing on the left, the whole of the timber on the right bank near the marsh and in advance of the old works to be felled so as to cover the right flank. Should further time permit an abattis to be formed so as to connect in some degree the new works and retard the advance of an enemy. These, gentlemen, are the proposals I have to make for the purpose of putting this place in some state of defence in two or three days. At present I have not a doubt that it will appear obvious to every one that it is in no state whatever, and from the works at present going on there is not the smallest prospect of its being in any state of defence for many days. I have now to request your opinions on the plan I have proposed, and shall be most happy to adopt any other which may be considered better. For the purpose of expediting the cutting of the timber, I propose that the militia shall be employed, to whom a reasonable allowance shall be made by three respectable persons, to be chosen. By this means I am confident the place will be in a state of defence in three days.

H. SCOTT,
Colonel, 103d.

We are of opinion that the proposal of Colonel Scott is extremely judicious and should be immediately carried into effect.

WM. SMELT, Major 103d.
J. MAULE, Major, D. A. Q. M. G.
J. BROWN, Capt., 103d Reg.
G. CHARLTON, Lieut., R. Arty.
ROBT. REYNOLDS, D. A. C. G.

Abstract of Weekly Distribution Return of the Right Division, Major-General Riall.

HEADQUARTERS, FORT GEORGE, June 22, 1814.

Fort Niagara, Lieut.-Col. Hamilton, 100th Regt.:

Staff—twenty-one officers.
Royal Artillery—one officer, twelve privates.
Royal Marine Artillery—two officers, three sergeants, thirty privates.
8th Regt.—one private.
100th Regt.—23 officers, 33 sergeants, 21 drummers, 535 rank and file—25 sick.

Total—47 officers, 36 sergeants, 21 drummers, 678 rank and file—25 sick.

Fort George and dependencies, Lieut.-Colonel Gordon, Royal Scots:
  19th Light Dragoons—two officers, two sergeants, one bugler, 28 rank and file—five sick.
  Provincial Light Dragoons—two officers, three sergeants, 16 rank and file.
  Royal Engineers—one officer.
  Royal Artillery—two officers, one sergeant, two buglers, 18 rank and file—five sick.
  Royal Marine Artillery—three officers, two sergeants, one bugler, thirty-two rank and file.
  Royal Artillery Drivers—three privates—four sick.
  Incorporated Militia Artillery—two sergeants, two privates.
  1st Royal Scots—twenty-three officers, 44 sergeants, 18 drummers, 677 rank and file—88 sick.
  103d—four officers, six sergeants, one drummer, 129 rank and fi
  Colored Corps—one officer, two sergeants, twenty rank and file—four sick.
  Total—38 officers, 62 sergeants, 23 drummers and buglers, 927 rank and file—106 sick.

Queenston and dependencies, Major Deane, Royal Scots:
  19th Light Dragoons—one sergeant, eight rank and file.
  Royal Artillery—40 rank and file.
  Royal Artillery Drivers—three sergeants, one bugler, 15 rank and file.
  1st Royal Scots—10 officers, 13 sergeants, four drummers, 195 rank and file—eight sick.
  Total—11 officers, 17 sergeants, five drummers and buglers, 258 rank and file—eight sick.

Chippawa and dependencies, Colonel Young, 8th Regt.:
  19th Light Dragoons—one sergeant, four rank and file.
  Royal Artillery—11 rank and file.
  Incorporated Militia Artillery—eight rank and file.
  Royal Artillery Drivers—seven rank and file.
  8th Regiment—25 officers, 28 sergeants, eight drummers, 398 rank and file—88 sick.
  Total—26 officers, 29 sergeants, 8 drummers, 428 rank and file—88 sick.

Fort Erie and dependencies, Major Buck, 8th Regt.:
  19th Light Dragoons—one officer, one sergeant, 23 rank and file.
  Royal Artillery—12 rank file.

8th Regiment—eight officers, seven sergeants, one drumm[er,] 111 rank and file.

Total—10 officers, 8 sergeants, one drummer, 146 rank and fi[le.]
Long Point and dependencies, Lieut.-Colonel Parry, 103d Regt.:

19th Light Dragoons—three officers, six sergeants, one bugl[er,] 53 rank and file—one sick.

Provincial Light Dragoons—one officer, one sergeant, 13 ra[nk] and file.

89th Regt.—one private sick.

103d Regt.—eleven officers, 13 sergeants, two drummers, 1[8] rank and file—four sick.

Kent Volunteers—three officers, three sergeants, 41 rank a[nd] file.

Total—18 officers, 23 sergeants, three drummers and bugle[r,] 249 rank and file—six sick.

Burlington, Colonel H. Scott, 103d Regt.:

Provincial Dragoons—three rank and file.

Royal Artillery—one officer, 18 rank and file—one sick.

Royal Artillery Drivers—one officer, one sergeant, 15 ran[k] and file.

1st Royal Scots—one sick.

89th Regt.—one sick.

103d Regt.—18 officers, 29 sergeants, 20 drummers, 350 ran[k] and file—20 sick.

Total—twenty officers, 30 sergeants, 20 drummers, 386 ran[k] and file—23 sick.

York, Colonel Stewart, Royal Scots:

Royal Artillery—one officer, 12 rank and file.

Royal Artillery Drivers—one officer, one sergeant, nine ran[k] and file.

Royal and Provincial Engineers—two officers, one sergeant, 1[7] rank and file.

1st Royal Scots—two officers, one sergeant, three rank and file—nine sick.

8th Regt.—one sergeant, three rank and file—four sick.

41st Regt.—29 officers, 33 sergeants, 17 drummers, 493 rank and file—twelve sick.

89th Regt.—one sergeant—one sick.

103d Regt.—one sergeant—one sick.

Royal Newfoundland Regt.—one officer, one private—one sick.

Incorporated Militia—29 officers, 27 sergeants, 11 drummers, 339 rank and file—25 sick.

Total—65 officers, 66 sergeants, 28 drummers, 877 rank and file—53 sick.

Major-General Riall to Sir Gordon Drummond.

CHIPPAWA, July 6th, 1814.

SIR,—I have the honor to inform you that the enemy effected a landing on the morning of the third inst., at the ferry opposite Black Rock, having driven in the picquet of the garrison of Fort Erie. I was made acquainted with this circumstance about eight in the morning and gave orders for an immediate advance to Chippawa of five companies of the Royal Scots to reinforce the garrison of that place. Lieut.-Colonel Pearson had moved forward from thence with the flank companies of the 100th, some militia and a few Indians, to reconnoitre their position and numbers. He found them posted on the ridge parallel to the river near the ferry and in strong force. I received information from Major Buck that they had also landed a considerable force above Fort Erie. In consequence of the King's Regiment, which I had reason to expect the day before from York, not having arrived, I was prevented from making an attack that night.

The following morning (the 4th) a body of their troops were reported to be advancing by the river. I moved to reconnoitre and found them to be in considerable force, with cavalry and artillery and a large body of riflemen. Lieut.-Colonel Pearson was in advance during the reconnoissance with the light company of the Royal Scots, the flank companies of the 100th, and a few of the 19th Dragoons, four of whom and eight horses were wounded in a skirmish with the enemy's riflemen.

Having been joined by the King's Regiment on the morning of the 5th I made my dispositions for attack at four o'clock in the afternoon. The light companies of the Royal Scots and the 100th Regiment, with the 2d Lincoln Militia, formed the advance, under Lieut.-Colonel Pearson. The Indian warriors were thrown out on our right flank in the woods. The troops moved in three columns, the third (the King's Regiment) being in advance. The enemy had taken up a position with his right resting on some buildings and orchards close to the river Niagara and strongly supported by artillery, his left towards the woods having a considerable body of riflemen and Indians in front of it.

Our Indians and militia were shortly engaged with the enemy's riflemen and Indians, who at first checked their advance, but the light troops being brought to their support they succeeded after a sharp contest in dislodging them in a very handsome style. I placed two light 24 pounders and a 5½ inch howitzer against the right of the enemy's position, and formed the Royal Scots and 100th Regiment with the intention of making a movement on his left, which deployed with the greatest regularity and opened a heavy fire. I immediately moved up the King's Regiment to the right while the 100th and Royal Scots were directed to charge the enemy in front, for which they advanced with the greatest gallantry under a most destructive fire. I am sorry to say, however, that in this attempt they suffered so severely that I was obliged to withdraw them, finding their further efforts against the superior numbers of the enemy would be unavailing.

From the report of some prisoners we have made, the enemy's force amounted to about six thousand men with a very numerous train of artillery, having been augmented by a very large body of troops which moved down from Fort Erie immediately before the commencement of the action.

Our own force of regular troops amounted to about fifteen hundred exclusive of the Indians and militia, of which description there were not above three hundred. Fort Erie, I understand, surrendered upon capitulation on the third instant.

Although this affair was not attended with the success which I had hoped for, it will be highly gratifying to you to learn that the officers and men behaved with the greatest gallantry. I am particularly indebted to Lieut.-Colonel Pearson for the very great assistance I have received from him and for the manner in which he led his troops into action. Lieut.-Colonel the Marquis of Tweeddale and Major Evans, commanding the King's Regiment. merit my warmest praise for the good example they showed at the head of their respective regiments. The artillery, under the command of Captain Mackonochie, was ably served and directed with good effects, and I am particularly obliged to Major Lisle of the 19th Light Dragoons for the manner in which he covered and protected one of the 24 pounders which had been disabled. I have reason to be highly gratified with the zeal, activity and intelligence of Captain Holland, my aide de camp, Captain Eliot, deputy-assistant-quartermaster-general, Staff Adjutant Greig and Lieutenant Fox of the Royal Scots, who acted as major of brigade during the absence of Major Glegg at Fort George. The conduct of Lieut.-Colonel Dickson of the 2d Lincoln Militia has been most exemplary, and I am very much indebted to him for it on this as well as on other occasions in which he has evinced the greatest zeal for His Majesty's service. The conduct of the officers and men of this regiment has also been highly praiseworthy.

Lieut.-Colonel Pearson has reported to me the excellent manner in which Lieut. Horton, with a party of the 19th Light Dragoons, observed the motions of the enemy while he occupied the position he took on his first landing and during his advance to this place.

Abstract of Return of Casualties in the Action Near Chippawa, 5th July, 1814.

General Staff—one captain wounded.
Royal Artillery—one killed, four wounded.
Royal Artillery Drivers—one subaltern wounded, two horses killed.
19th Light Dragoons—one sergeant, five rank and file wounded, one horse wounded.
1st Royal Scots—63 killed, 35 wounded, 30 missing.
8th Regiment—three killed, 24 wounded.
100th Regiment—69 killed, 134 wounded, 1 missing.
Lincoln Militia—12 killed, 16 wounded, 15 missing.
One twenty-four pounder limber blown up, two tumbrils damaged.

The men returned as missing are supposed to be killed or wounded.

Officers killed—Captain Bailey, Royal Scots: Lieut. Gibbon, Ensign Rea, 100th; Capts. Rowe and Turney and Lieut. McDonnell, Lincoln Militia.

Officers wounded—General Staff—Capt. Holland, A. D. C.; R. A. Drivers, Lieut. Jack; Royal Scots, Lieut.-Col. Gordon, Capts. Bird and Wilson (prisoner), Lieuts. W. Campbell, Fox, Jackson, Hendrick, McDonald, A. Campbell and Connell.

8th—Lieut. Boyle.

100th—Lieut.-Col. the Marquis of Tweeddale, Capts. Sherrard and Sleigh, Lieuts. Williams, Lyon, Valentine and Fortune (missing), Ensigns Clarke and Johnson, Adjutant Kingston.

Lincoln Militia—Lieut.-Col. Dickson, Lieuts. Clement and Bowman, Ensign Kirkpatrick.

Sir Gordon Drummond to Sir George Prevost.

KINGSTON, July 9th, 1814.

SIR,—I have the honor to acquaint Your Excellency that at a late hour last night I received a report from Major-General Riall, dated Chippawa, the 5th inst., in which he informed me that on the morning of the 3d the enemy landed opposite Black Rock in considerable force. The Major-General immediately moved forward with five companies of the Royal Regiment to Chippawa. On the 4th the enemy occupied a position along the banks of the creek which runs from the river by Mr. Street's house to the wood.

Being in hourly expectation that the King's Regiment would join him from York, (which it did on the 5th,) Major-General Riall did not move forward to the attack of the enemy until four o'clock on the afternoon of that day. I regret, however, to state that the Major-General found it necessary to retire on the position at Chippawa after having sustained a severe loss, not far short, I am apprehensive, of 500 in officers and men. The enemy's loss must have been considerable.

It is with great satisfaction that I have to report to Your Excellency the very high terms in which Major-General Riall expresses himself of the steadiness and good conduct of the troops, but the superior numbers to which his force was opposed, (for I imagine they could scarcely have exceeded one thousand men,) rendered their gallant efforts unavailing.

By information received from prisoners, it appears that the American army was estimated at 6,000 men, with a considerable train of artillery. They were commanded by Generals Brown, Scott, Ripley and Porter. From the same source the Major-General was made acquainted with the capture by capitulation of Fort Erie on Sunday last.

The 100th Regiment has suffered severely, having had 12 officers killed and wounded: the Royal Regiment has lost in the same proportion. I am concerned to add that amongst the wounded are Lieut.-Colonel Gordon, Lieut.-Colonel the Marquis of Tweeddale, and Capt. Holland, A. D. C. to Major-General Riall.

The Major-General has not correctly ascertained what are the intentions of the enemy as to the subsequent operations, but he was inclined to think their efforts would be directed to turning the right of his position at Chippawa.

Major-General Riall's official report has not yet been transmitted to me, but the moment it arrives it shall be forwarded to Your Excellency.

Major Clifford with three companies of the 89th arrived here on Tuesday: they proceed with the light company this evening to the Right Division. I expect Lieut.-Colonel Morrison to-morrow with the remainder, in the course of the day, when they shall be pushed forward also.

I request Your Excellency will be pleased to expedite the movement of the 6th and 82d Regiments to this place, as the garrison is extremely deficient in strength, consisting only of the 104th and De Watteville's Regiments, and that you will be pleased also to order such officers of the Royal Regiment and of the 100th as may be now in the Lower Province to join their regiments without delay.

Sir Gordon Drummond to Sir George Prevost.

KINGSTON, July 10th, 1814.

SIR,—I have the honor to transmit herewith a copy of Major-General Riall's official report on the subject of the landing of the enemy between Chippawa and Fort Erie on the 3d inst., and of the Major-General's attack upon their position on the 5th.

It is highly satisfactory to observe that the gallantry and steadiness of British soldiers throughout the conduct of every regiment engaged, and that the 2d Regiment of Lincoln Militia, under the command of Lieut.-Colonel Dickson, which composed part of the advance under Lieut.-Colonel Pearson, equally distinguished themselves, although their brave and vigorous efforts proved unavailing against the prodigious superiority in numbers which the enemy possessed, and which induced the Major-General to withdraw his small force to the position of Chippawa.

Sir Gordon Drummond to Sir George Prevost.
(Confidential.)

KINGSTON, July 10th, 1814.

DEAR SIR,—Your Excellency will receive by the same conveyance Major-General Riall's official report of his attack on the enemy in their position at Street's Creek.

The conduct of the troops and militia appears to have been highly creditable, and nothing but the exceedingly unequal numbers of the enemy could have prevented the attack from being covered with complete success.

Our artillery was well served, and a disabled brass twenty-four pounder, which had its limber blown up and the two shaft horses killed, was saved principally by the exertions of Major Lisle of the 19th Light Dragoons.

The enemy deployed into line, and withstood our attacks with the greatest steadiness.

They are now understood to be establishing batteries under cover of the wood in front of the position at Chippawa, from which Major-General Riall is apprehensive he will be under the necessity of retiring, as his force is so considerably diminished from the casualties of the action and from the fall of Fort Erie.

I regret extremely the loss of this place, which I had the strongest hopes would have made an excellent defence, or at all events held the enemy in check for several days. I felt the more confident in that expectation from Captain Marlowe's report of it on his return from that frontier.

Our Indian allies, as usual, proved of little service. There were but few on the ground—about 200 under Norton and about 100 of the western tribes, and these penetrated too far into the woods to afford the assistance required of them.

I perceive the Major-General has omitted, in the haste of transmission I presume, the numbers he had on the ground. The Royals took into the field about 500, half of whom have been killed or disabled for the present: the 100th, about 460, have suffered in even a greater proportion, and have not now more than four duty officers remaining. The King's, I imagine to have been from the embarkation returns from York, about 400, has not experienced much loss. These, with the artillery, the 19th Dragoons and the Lincoln Militia, would constitute a force of about 1,500.

I beg, therefore, again to request that every absent officer of these corps be ordered to join forthwith, as well as Lieut.-Colonel Ogilvie of the King's Regiment, Colonel Young being on his way from York to Montreal, and there being consequently but one field officer with the regiment.

I have been happy to learn of the arrival at Queenston of the Incorporated Militia, under Captain Robinson of the King's Regiment. This is the only disposeable corps I had left to send. But as soon as the 89th, which leaves this place to-day under Lieut.-Colonel Morrison, arrives at York, I propose pushing forward the Glengarry Light Infantry to Burlington to support Major-General Riall, or, with the 103d Regiment, to sustain that post, and I have placed the two flank companies of the 104th, completed to 60 each, under Lieut.-Colonel Drummond, for the purpose of acting with the Indians in that direction also, as circumstances may require.

I fear we shall suffer much difficulty in feeding all this force, Mr. Couche having received a letter from Mr. Turquand this day, expressing his apprehensions of a failure in the article of flour, which it is totally impossible to assist them in from Kingston from the want of means of transport from hence: I have even been under the necessity of taking twelve batteaux from the brigades which arrived yesterday to forward the 89th Regiment to York.

I am happy to observe that Major-General Riall states there is a sufficiency of provisions in each of the forts for the supply of their garrisons until our fleet can take the lake again.

Major-General Riall has heard that the enemy are collecting a force at Detroit.

The Marquis of Tweeddale's wound is in the leg and severe; Lieut.-Colonel Gordon's in the chin and neck; Captain Holland's in the head and through the left hand; Captains Sleigh and Sherrard in three places each, the former supposed to be mortal.

The General himself was struck on the hip, but without further injury than to tear his coat.

Sir James Yeo has received a letter from a very intelligent officer of the navy, captured at Sandy Creek. He states that the enemy's new ship *Superior* is very low between decks, and carries 32 pounders, her ports very close. The new ship *Mohawk* is less by a port on each side than the *Prince Regent*. This officer had a good opportunity of viewing the works of defence at Sackett's Harbor, which he states to have been considerably strengthened, so much so as to require at least 7,000 men to ensure success against them.

General Order.

Adjutant-General's Office, Left Division,
July 2, 1814.

Major-General Brown has the satisfaction to announce to the troops of his division that he is authorized by the orders of his government to put them in motion against the enemy. The first and second brigades, with the corps of artillery, will cross the Straights before them this night, or as early to-morrow as possible. The necessary instructions have been given to the brigadiers, and by them to the commanding officers of regiments and corps.

Upon entering Canada the laws of war will govern. Men found in arms, or otherwise engaged in the service of the enemy, will be treated as enemies: those behaving peaceably and following their private occupations will be treated as friends. Private property in all cases will be held sacred. Public property, wherever found, will be seized and disposed of by the commanding general. Our utmost protection will be given to all who actually join or evince a desire to join us.

Plundering is prohibited. The Major-General does not apprehend any difficulty on this with the regular army, or with honorable volunteers who press to the standard of their country to avenge her wrongs and to gain a name in arms. Profligate men who follow the army for plunder must not expect that they will escape the vengeance of the gallant spirits who are struggling to exalt the national character. Any plunderer shall be punished with death who shall be found violating this law.

By order of the Major-General.

C. K. GARDNER,
Adjutant-General.

(From Brannan's Official Letters, Washington, 1823.)

Major-General Brown to the Secretary of War.

CHIPPAWA PLAINS, July 6th, 1814.

SIR,—Excuse my silence. I have been much engaged. Fort Erie did not, as I assured you it should not, detain me a single day. At 11 o'clock on the night of the 4th I arrived at this place with the reserve, General Scott having taken the position about noon with the van. My arrangements for turning and taking in near the enemy's position east of Chippawa was made, when Major-General Riall, suspecting our intention, and adhering to the rule that it is better to give than receive an attack, came from behind his works about five o'clock in the afternoon of the 5th in order of battle. We did not baulk him. Before six o'clock his line was broken and his forces defeated, leaving on the field four hundred killed and wounded. He was closely pressed, and would have been utterly ruined but for the proximity of his works, whither he fled for shelter. The wounded of the enemy and those of our own army must be attended. They will be removed to Buffalo. This, with very limited means of transport, will take a day or two, after which I shall advance, not doubting but that the gallant and accomplished troops I have will break down all opposition between me and Lake Ontario, when, if met by the fleet, all is well—if not, under the favor of heaven, we shall behave in a way to avoid disgrace. My detailed report shall be made in a day or two.

Major-General Jacob Brown to the Secretary of War.

HEADQUARTERS, CHIPPAWA PLAINS, July 7th, 1814.

DEAR SIR,—On the second inst. I issued my orders for crossing the Niagara River and made arrangements deemed necessary for securing the garrison of Fort Erie. On the 3d inst. that post surrendered, at 5 p. m. Our loss in this affair was four wounded. I have enclosed a return of the prisoners of the ordnance, and the ordnance stores captured.

To secure my rear I have placed a garrison in this fort and requested Captain Kennedy to station his vessels near the post.

On the morning of the 4th, Brig.-General Scott with his brigade and a corps of artillery was ordered to advance towards Chippawa and be governed by circumstances, taking care to secure a good military position for the night. After some skirmishing with the enemy, he selected this plain with the eye of a soldier—his right resting on the river and a ravine being in front. At 11 at night I joined him with the reserve under General Ripley, our field and battering train, and corps of artillery under Major

indman. General Porter arrived next morning with a part of
the New York and Pennsylvania volunteers and some of the
arriors of the Six Nations.

Early in the morning of the 5th, the enemy commenced a petty
ar upon our pickets, and as he was indulged his presumption
creased; by noon he showed himself on the left of our exterior
ne, and attacked one of our pickets as it was returning to camp.
aptain Treat, who commanded it, retired disgracefully, leaving a
ounded man on the ground. Captain Biddle of the artillery, who
as near the scene, impelled by feelings highly honorable to him as
soldier and officer, promptly assumed command of this picket, led
back to the wounded man, and brought him off the field. I
dered Capt. Treat on the spot to retire from the army, and as I
n anxious that no officer shall remain under my command who
n be suspected of cowardice, I advise that Captain Treat and
ieut. (name illegible), who was also with the picket, be struck from
ne rolls of the army.

At 4 o'clock p. m., agreeably to a plan I had given General
orter, he advanced from the rear of our camp with the volunteers
nd Indians (taking the woods in order to keep out of view of the
nemy) with a hope of bringing his pickets and scouting parties
etween his (Porter's) line of march and our camp. As Porter
oved I ordered the parties advanced in front of our camp to fall
ack gradually under the enemy's fire, to draw them, if possible, up
o our line. About half-past four the advance of General Porter's
ommand met the light parties of the enemy in the woods upon our
xtreme left—the enemy was driven, and Porter advancing near
o Chippawa met their whole column in order of battle. From the
oud of dust rising and the heavy firing, I was led to conclude that
ne whole force of the enemy was in march and prepared for action.
immediately ordered General Scott to advance with his brigade
nd Towson's artillery and meet them upon the plain in front of
ur camp. The General did not expect to be gratified so soon with
field engagement. He advanced in the most prompt and officer-
ke style, and in a few minutes was in close action upon the plain
ith a superior force of British regular troops. By this time
eneral Porter's command had given way and fled in every
irection, notwithstanding his personal gallantry and great exertions
o stay their flight. The retreat of the volunteers and Indians
aused the left flank of General Scott's brigade to be greatly
xposed. Captain Harris, with his dragoons, was directed to stop
ne fugitives behind the ravine fronting our camp, and I sent
olonel Gardner to order General Ripley to advance with the 21st
tegiment, which formed a part of the reserve, pass to the left of

our camp, skirt the woods so as to keep out of view, and fall upon the rear of the enemy's right flank: this order was promptly obeyed and the greatest exertions were made by the 21st Regiment to gain their position, but in vain, for such was the zeal and gallantry of the line commanded by General Scott that its advance upon the enemy was not to be checked. Major Jessup, commanding the left flank battalion, finding himself pressed in front and in flank and his men falling fast around him, ordered his battalion to "support arms and advance." This order was promptly obeyed amidst the most deadly and destructive fire: he gained a more secure position and returned upon the enemy so galling a discharge as caused them to retire. By this time their whole line was falling back and our gallant soldiers pressing upon them as fast as possible. As soon as the enemy had gained the sloping ground descending towards Chippawa and distant a quarter of a mile, he broke and ran to gain his works: in this effort he was too successful, and the guns from his batteries opening immediately upon our line checked in some degree the pursuit. At this moment I resolved to bring up all my ordnance and force the place by a direct attack. Major Wood of the corps of engineers, and my aid, Captain Austin, rode to the bank of the creek towards the right of their line of works and examined them. I was induced by the lateness of their report the lateness of the hour, and the advice of General Scott and Major Wood, to order the forces to retire to camp.

My most difficult duty remains. I am depressed with the fear of not being able to do justice to my companions in arms, and apprehensive that some who had an opportunity of distinguishing themselves and promptly embraced it will escape my notice.

Brig.-General Scott is entitled to the highest praises our country can bestow: to him more than any other man am I indebted for the victory of the 5th of July. His brigade has covered itself with glory. Every officer and every man of the 9th, 22d, 11th, and 25th Regiments did his duty with a zeal and energy worthy of the American character. When every officer stands so preeminently high in the path of duty and honor, it is impossible to discriminate, but I cannot deprive myself of the pleasure of saying that Major Leavenworth commanded the 9th and 22d; Major Jessup the 25th, and Major McNeil the 11th. Colonel Campbell was wounded early in the action, gallantly leading on his regiment.

The family of General Scott was conspicuous in the field: Lieut. Smith of the 6th Infantry, Major of Brigade, and Lieutenants Worth and Watts, his aids.

From General Ripley and his brigade I received every assistance that I gave them an opportunity of rendering. I did not order any part of the reserve into action until General Porter's command had given way; and then General Scott's movements were so rapid and decisive that General Ripley could not get up in time with the 21st to the position as directed. The corps of artillery under Major Hindman were not generally in action: this was not their fault. Captain Towson's company was the only one that had a full opportunity of distinguishing itself; and it is believed that no company ever embraced an opportunity with more zeal or more success.

A detachment from the 2d Brigade, under the command of Lieut. McDonald, penetrated the woods with the Indians and volunteers, and for their support. The conduct of McDonald and his command reflects high honor upon the brigade to which they belong.

The conduct of General Porter has been conspicuously gallant. Every assistance in his power to afford with the description of force under his command has been rendered. We could not expect him to contend with the British column of regulars which appeared upon the plains of Chippawa. It was no cause of surprise to me to see his command retire before this column.

Justice forbids that I should omit to name my own family. They yield in honorable zeal, intelligence, and attention to duty. Colonel Gardner, Major Jones, and my aids, Captains Austin and Spencer, have been as active and as much devoted to the cause as any officers of the army. Their conduct merits my warmest acknowledgments. Of Gardner and Jones I shall have occasion again to speak to you. Major Camp, Deputy Quartermaster-General, deserves my particular notice and approbation. By his great exertions I was enabled to find the means of crossing. Captain Daliba, of the ordnance department, has rendered every service in his power.

The enclosed return will show you our loss and furnish you with the names of the dead and wounded officers. These gallant men must not be forgotten. Our country will remember them and do them justice.

In the above action the enemy had 208 killed, and 95 wounded —15 prisoners. Those reported under the head of wounded and prisoners were so severely injured that it would have been impracticable for them to have escaped. The enemy had the same facilities of carrying their wounded from the field at the commecement of the action as ourselves, and there can be no doubt from the information that I have received from unquestionable sources that they carried from the field as many of their wounded as is reported above in the total.

AZ. ORNE,
Asst. Ins.-Gen.

Inspector-General's Office, Headquarters, Left Division,
CAMP NEAR FORT ERIE, July 3d, 1814.

Return of the British prisoners of war who surrendered by capitulation with Fort Erie on the afternoon of the 3d July, 1814, to the left division of the United States army under the command of Major General Brown.

8th or King's Regiment—one major.

Royal Artillery—1 lieutenant, 1 corporal: 1 bombardier and 19 gunners.

100th Regiment—1 captain, 2 lieutenants, 1 ensign, 4 sergeants, 5 corporals, three musicians, 98 privates.

Aggregate, 137.

AZ. ORNE,
Asst. Inspector-General.

Inspector-General's Office, Headquarters, Left Division,
CHIPPAWA, July 9th, 1814.

Return of the killed, wounded, and prisoners of the enemy in the action fought on the plains within half a mile of Chippawa, between the left division of the United States army, commanded by Major-General Brown, and the English forces, under the command of Major-General Riall.

Killed—three captains, three subalterns, and 87 rank and file of the regular troops.

Wounded—two captains of the 1st Royal Scots, one lieutenant of the 100th Regiment, and 72 rank and file of the Royal Scots, 8th and 100th Regiments.

Prisoners—one captain of the Indians, and nine rank and file of the regulars.

Killed in the woods—of the Indians, 87; of the regulars and militia, 18.

Indian prisoners—one chief and four privates.

Total of the enemy placed *hors du combat*, that we have ascertained beyond doubt—6 captains, 4 subalterns, and 298 rank and file.

AZ. ORNE,
Asst. Inspector-General.

Report of the killed and wounded of the left division comanded by Major-General Brown, in the action of the 5th July, 1814, on the plains of Chippawa, Upper Canada:

Artillery—killed: 4 privates; wounded—severely: 3 corporals, privates; slightly: 8 privates.

General Scott's Brigade:

9th Infantry—killed: 2 musicians, 11 privates; wounded—everely: 1 captain, 2 subalterns, 2 corporals, 19 privates; slightly: sergeants, 18 privates.

22d Infantry, attached—killed: 8 privates; wounded—severey: 1 captain, 8 privates; slightly: 2 sergeants, 35 privates.

25th Infantry—killed: 1 sergeant, 4 privates; wounded—everely: 1 captain, 2 subalterns, 5 sergeants, 2 corporals, 37 privates; slightly: 2 sergeants, 2 corporals, 1 musician, 19 privates.

11th Infantry—killed: 1 sergeant, 4 corporals, 10 privates; rounded—severely: 1 colonel, 1 subaltern, 3 sergeants, 5 corporals, !8 privates; slightly: 3 sergeants, 19 privates.

General Ripley's Brigade:

21st Regiment—none.

19th Infantry, attached—killed: 3 privates; wounded severey: 2 privates; missing: 2 privates.

23d Infantry—wounded severely—1 private.

General P. B. Porter's Command:

Fenton's Regiment of Pennsylvania Militia—killed: 3 privates; wounded—severely: 1 private; slightly: 1 private; missing: 3 officers, 4 non-commissioned officers and privates.

Corps of Indians—killed: 9 privates; wounded—severely: 4; missing: 10.

Grand total—2 sergeants, 4 corporals, 2 musicians, 52 privates, killed; 1 colonel, 3 captains, 5 subalterns, 8 sergeants, 12 corporals, 105 privates, severely wounded; 9 sergeants, 2 corporals, 1 musician, 103 privates, slightly wounded; 3 officers, 16 non-commissioned officers and privates, missing. Aggregate, 328.

Names and rank of officers wounded—Colonel Campbell, 11th Infantry, severely; Captain King, 22d Infantry, dangerously; Captain Read, 25th Infantry, badly; Captain Harrison, 42d, doing duty in 9th Infantry, severely; Lieut. Barron, 11th Infantry, severely; Lieut. DeWitt, 25th Infantry, severely; Lieut. Patchin, 25th Infantry, badly; Lieut. Brimhall, 9th Infantry, slightly.

Note—The slightly wounded are fast recovering.

C. K. GARDNER,
Adjt.-General.

Major Hindman to the Adjutant-General.

Agreeably to general orders, I transmit the following report:

At the commencement of the action of the 5th July, Capt. Towson's company of artillery with the first brigade was solely engaged with the enemy; he maintained his position on the right and kept up a spirited and destructive fire during the charge of the enemy. Amidst the fire and charge of the enemy the captain and his subalterns, Lieuts. Campbell and Schmuck, and Lieut. Randolph of the infantry, commanding the reserve of the artillery, behaved with the greatest gallantry, and I am proud to say tended greatly to check the impetuosity of the enemy.

At an early part of the battle the captain's piece was thrown out of action by a 24-pound shot of the enemy, yet his zeal and exertions were given with his characteristic spirit to the remaining pieces, and he reports handsomely of the conduct and services of his officers, non-commissioned officers and men.

About the time the enemy commenced their charge, and at the moment they broke, Captain Ritchie's company of artillery and one piece, (a 12-pounder,) of Captain Biddle's company of artillery, under Lieut. Hall, participated in the action. The captains, officers, non-commissioned officers and men, conducted themselves as brave and faithful soldiers, and the whole artillery then on the field pursued under the fire of the enemy's batteries with rapidity, and saw them precipitate themselves within their works. At this period of the action two 18-pounders under Captain Williams, and the remainder of Captain Biddle's artillery, were brought upon the ground without being permitted to open a battery upon the enemy's works.

To particularize, if all had been engaged from first to last, would have been invidious, but in this case Captain Towson and company deserve particular mention. The captain, being so fortunate as to be ordered in advance with his company of artillery, only, had an opportunity of showing his gallantry and distinguishing himself, officers and soldiers, above all others.

With due respect, yours, etc.,

J. HINDMAN,
Major Commanding Battalion of Artillery.

Brig.-General Winfield Scott to the Adjutant-General.

QUEENSTON, U. C., July 15, 1814.

SIR,—By the general order of the 13th inst., a methodical and detailed report is called for, designating the names of such persons, hether commissioned or not, who in the action of the 5th contibuted in a particular manner to the successful result of that day.

I am not asked for an account of the disposition made of the oops under my command during the action. I shall, therefore onfine myself strictly to the general order.

A severe action has been fought and a signal victory gained. he general order of the 6th inst. attributes that victory to the 1st igade of infantry and Captain Towson's company of artillery, nder my command. It was believed at the time, and has since een clearly ascertained, that, of the forces engaged, the enemy ere greatly superior in numbers. Under such circumstances ictory could not have been obtained without a very general rticipation of all ranks and grades in the event.

The truth of this observation was most conspicuous in the ery crisis of the action. Conduct universally good leaves but ttle room for discrimination. Accordingly, but few names are ported to me by the several commandants of battalions as entitled) select mention (in respect to their gallant comrades) and those ses are noticed principally from accidental circumstances of good r bad fortune, as in the instance of Captain Ketchum of the 25th fantry, whose good fortune it was to be detached with his comny, by order of Major Jessup, to attack a much superior force hilst the battalion was engaged with another body of the enemy. aptain Ketchum gallantly sustained himself in the execution of is orders till the battalion had cleared its own front in order to arch to his support.

The good conduct of Captain Harrison, commanded by Major eavenworth and observed by myself, was of another kind. A nnon ball shattered and carried away part of his leg. The ptain preserved a perfect serenity under the tortures of his ound, and utterly refused any assistance till the enemy should be eaten. So glorious a display of fortitude had the happiest effect.

Of the three battalions of infantry composing the First rigade, the first consisted of the 9th and a detachment of the 22d, nder command of Major Leavenworth. The 2d Battalion, or the 1th Regiment, was gallantly conducted towards its place in order f battle by Colonel Campbell, who, being early wounded, was ucceeded by Major McNeil. Major Jessup commanded the 25th egiment, or the remaining battalion of the brigade. Of these hree excellent officers it would be difficult to say which was the ost meritorious or most conspicuously engaged. The 25th egiment, having been detached to my left to turn the enemy's ight wing, was rested in a wood. Major Jessup was less under my ersonal observation than the other two commanders, but I have every evidence of the able disposition he made of his corps, as well b[y] the report of my aids as by the effect he produced on that part of th[e] enemy's line immediately opposed to him and which contribute[d] much to the general result of the day. Major Jessup had his hor[se] shot under him.

The other two battalions, with an enlarged interval betwee[n] them, received the enemy in open plain, that under Major Leaver[n]worth parallel to the attack, that under Major McNeil with its le[ft] wing thrown forward to take the enemy in front and flank at th[e] same time. Captain Towson, who commenced the fire before th[e] troops were in order of battle, immediately afterwards advanced t[o] the front of the extreme right with three pieces of artillery, an[d] took post on the river. Majors Leavenworth and McNeil mad[e] prompt dispositions to receive the charge. The fire of these corp[s] (including the artillery) produced a prodigious effect on the enemy['s] ranks. That of Major McNeil's was most effective from the obliqu[e] position which his corps judiciously occupied. The enemy['s] batteries were also admirably served, to the fire of which all th[e] corps were exposed, that of Major Leavenworth in particula[r.] This cannonade, however, did not prevent the latter from preservin[g] his corps in the most excellent order, at all times prepared t[o] advance or to fire, to give or to receive the charge.

Captain Towson finally silenced the enemy's most effective bat[-]tery by blowing up an ammunition wagon, which produced grea[t] confusion. Turning next a heavy discharge of canister on th[e] enemy's infantry, now nearly in contact with our line advancing t[o] the charge, the enemy could not long withstand this accumul[a]tion of fire; he broke and fled to his strong works behind Chi[p]pawa. All the corps pursued with promptitude.

To mention them in order of their rank, (I know of no othe[r] in this case,) Majors Jessup, Leavenworth and McNeil, and Captai[n] Towson, deserve, in my humble opinion, every thing which co[n]spicuous skill and gallantry can wish from a grateful country.

I cannot close this account of meritorious conduct witho[u]t mentioning the great services rendered me by those two galla[nt] young soldiers, Lieuts. Worth and Watts, my aids.

There was no danger they did not cheerfully encounter i[n] communicating my orders, and by their zeal and intrepidity wo[n] the admiration of the whole brigade. They both rendered essen[-]tial service at critical moments by assisting the commandants o[f] corps in forming the troops under circumstances which prevent[ed] the voice from being heard.

This conduct has been handsomely acknowledged by th[e]

officers of the line, who have joined in requesting that it might be particularly noticed.

My brigade-major, Lieut. Smith, rendered me every assistance that his accidental situation on foot permitted. He is entitled to my thanks.

During the action Major Wood of the engineers, and Captain Harris of the dragoons, whose troop could not act, came up and very handsomely tendered their services. The latter had his horse shot under him.

It is proper I should take this opportunity to mention the case of Captain Crooker of the 9th Regiment of Infantry, in the affair of the 4th of July, on the same ground on which the action of the 5th was fought. I have already had the honor to mention this case verbally to the Commanding-General.

It is due to the gallant individual particularly concerned that his conduct should be formally noticed.

My brigade constituted the advance of the army. In descending the left bank of the Niagara from Fort Erie we met an advanced corps of the enemy at Black Creek, strongly posted behind that stream. Capt. Towson, who was with the advance, obliged the enemy to fall back, who, on retreating, took up the bridge over the creek. Captain Crooker, who flanked out to the left of our march, crossed the stream some distance above the bridge, and was pursuing the enemy just as the head of the brigade column arrived at the bridge, which could not be passed until the pioneers had replaced the boards, which the enemy had hastily removed.

While this operation was going on Captain Crooker immediately, within my view, was suddenly enveloped by a troop of the 19th Light Dragoons, composing a part of the enemy's rear guard. He fought his way to a house then near him, turned upon the dragoons, and put them to flight.

Captains Hull and Harrison and Lieut. Randolph with a small party were at the same time marching to the support of Captain Crooker, and arrived just as the enemy took to flight. I have witnessed nothing more gallant in partizan war than was the conduct of Captain Crooker and his company.

From Niles' Register, Vol. 6, Page 306.

(From the Ontario Messenger.)

We have received the following account and plan of attack of the battle of Chippawa from a valued and obliging correspondent at the west, who was an eye witness to the engagement.

On the 3d of July, General Scott, by orders from Major-

General Brown, broke up his encampment and advanced upon Chippawa, and with Capt. Towson's division of artillery, drove the enemy's pickets across the bridge. In the afternoon General Ripley, with the field and park artillery under Major Hindman, took the same route and encamped on the ground with General's Scott's advance.

On the morning of the 4th of July the British Indians, who had filled the woods contiguous to the American encampment, commenced firing at our pickets. Reconnoitering parties from Chippawa were frequently observed during the day along the river road, and information was received that reinforcements had arrived.

On the 5th the same course was pursued. The Indians were discovered almost in rear of our camp. At this moment General Porter arrived with his volunteers and Indians. General Brown immediately ordered them to enter the woods and effectually scour them. Generals Brown, Scott and Ripley were at the White House (marked O) reconnoitering. General Porter's corps seemed sweeping like a torrent everything before them, until they almost debouched from the woods opposite Chippawa. In a moment a volley of musketry convinced General Brown that the whole British force had crossed the Chippawa bridge and that the action must become general. He gave immediate orders to General Scott to advance and feel the enemy, and to General Ripley to be in readiness to support. In a few minutes the British line was discovered formed and rapidly advancing—their right (the Royal Scots) upon the woods and the left (the Prince Regent's) near the river, with the King's Own in reserve. Their object was to gain the bridge across the creek in front of our encampment, which if done would have compelled us to retire. General Brown feared a flank movement through the woods on the left of our camp with a view to seize our reserve of artillery, and directed General Ripley not to advance until he gave him orders. At the same time he rode to the first line with his staff and an escort of about 30 dragoons, in order to direct the whole movements of the field and animate the troops by his presence. Meanwhile General Scott, under a most tremendous fire of the enemy's artillery, crossed the bridge, which the enemy had endeavored to gain, and formed his line. The enemy's orders were to give one volley at a distance and immediately charge. But such was the warmth of our musketry that they could not stand it. At this moment General Brown sent orders to General Ripley to make a movement through the woods upon the enemy's right flank. With the 21st Regiment he passed a ravine in his front, where the men had to wade up to their chins, and advanced as rapidly as possible. But before he commenced filing from the woods into the open land under the enemy's batteries they had been completely broken by the cool bravery and discipline of General Scott's brigade.

(From Boston Sentinel, 1814.)

Extract from a letter from a captain in Fenton's Regiment of Pennsylvanian Volunteers, dated at Chippawa, July 7, 1814:

"On the afternoon of the 4th inst., Fenton's detachment was ordered to cross the river, which we did with eight companies, leaving two companies at Buffalo. We arrived at Chippawa and had one hour's rest, when General Porter called for 100 men to go scouting with the Indians to drive the British Indians out of the woods, where they were harassing our outposts. We turned out 150, and, accompanied by 336 Indians, advanced half a mile, when we were fired on by their Indians, but we drove them three-quarters of a mile, when we were compelled to retreat by the British regulars and Indians. We rallied and drove them back when they came out of their hiding place, but we were outflanked and again forced to retreat. I had two men missing from my company. We went out yesterday afternoon to bring in the dead who had not been found by the regulars in the morning, and found one of my men dead. We found a great number. Every company among us lost two or three."

Extract from a letter from Captain Mackonochie, R. A., to Major-General Glasgow, dated Montreal, August 19, 1814:

"Two artillerymen, deserters from the enemy, stated to Major Glegg that they had lost at one gun alone (in the battle of Chippawa) seventeen men, and they were no sooner replaced than they were swept away by our shot and grape. The two 24 pounders and the $5\frac{1}{2}$ inch. howitzer were never further than 400 yards from the enemy, and at times much nearer: the 6 pounder never further than 500 yards."

(From the Baltimore Federal Gazette, July 25, 1814.)

Extract from a letter written by an officer in the United States army to a friend in this city, dated Chippawa, July 7:

"We pursued them three miles, and drove them into Fort Chippawa. Just as we arrived in sight of this place my piece, a twelve pounder, being the largest on the ground, was dismounted, Towson's men being exhausted by a constant fire of six or seven hours. He had fired 120 rounds from two sixes, besides shells and canister from his howitzer. I did not get into action until the

British line was formed. The numbers engaged were about equal. The British artillery fired very well, but were exceeded by Towson who bore the brunt of the battle.

General Order.

Adjutant-General's Office, Headquarters,
MONTREAL, 13th July, 1814.

His Excellency the Governor-in-Chief and Commander of the Forces has received from Lieutenant-General Drummond the official report of Major-General Riall of the sortie which took place on the 5th inst. from the lines of Chippawa.

His Excellency derives a proud consolation in the undaunted gallantry and exemplary discipline displayed in this unequal contest, in which Major-General Riall represents Lieut.-Col. Pearson in command of a detachment of light troops, Lieut.-Col. the Marquis Tweeddale, 100th Regiment: Major Evans, 8th or King's Regiment; Major Lisle, 19th Light Dragoons, and Capt. Mackonochie, Royal Artillery, to have afforded the most able support in zealous and judicious command of their respective corps, and that the zeal and intelligence evinced by his aide-de-camp, Capt. Holland, Capt. Elliot, Deputy-Assistant-Quartermaster-General, Lieut. Fox, Royal Scots, Acting-Brigade-Major, and Staff-Adjutant Greig, merited his approbation, and that the conduct of Lieut.-Colonel Dickson, Lincoln Militia, was most exemplary.

His Excellency laments the loss of so many valuable officers and men, but this sentiment is greatly aggravated by the disappointment and mortification he has experienced in learning that Fort Erie, entrusted to the charge of Major Buck, was surrendered on the evening of the third instant, by capitulation, without having made an adequate defence.

Return of killed, wounded and missing :—

Royal Artillery—1 gunner killed, 4 gunners wounded.

Royal Artillery Drivers—1 subaltern wounded.

1st or Royal Scots—1 captain, 4 sergeants, 43 rank and file killed ; 1 field officer, 2 captains, 7 subalterns, 4 sergeants, 121 rank and file wounded : 30 rank and file missing.

8th or King's Regiment—3 rank and file killed ; 1 subaltern, 1 sergeant, and 22 rank and file wounded.

100th Regiment—2 subalterns, 3 sergeants, 64 rank and file killed ; 1 field officer, 2 captains, 6 subalterns, 11 sergeants, 114 rank and file wounded ; 1 subaltern missing.

Militia—2 captains, 1 subaltern, 9 rank and file killed ; 1 field officer, 3 subalterns, 1 sergeant, 11 rank and file wounded; 1 sergeant and 14 rank and file missing.

19th Light Dragoons—1 sergeant and 5 rank and file wounded.

Weekly Distribution Return of the Right Division, Major-General Riall.

HEADQUARTERS, FORT GEORGE, July 8th, 1814.

Fort Niagara, Lieut.-Colonel Tucker, 41st Regt.:

Staff—21 officers.

Royal Marine Artillery—four officers, five sergeants, one drummer, 62 rank and file.

41st Regiment—25 officers, 29 sergeants, 18 drummers, 466 rank and file.

100th Regiment—one sergeant, twelve rank and file.

Fort George, Lieut.-Colonel Gordon, Royal Scots:

Fort Mississauga, Major Evans, 8th Regiment:

19th Light Dragoons—three officers, six sergeants, one bugler, 64 rank and file—four sick.

Provincial Light Dragoons—two officers, three sergeants, 15 rank and file.

Royal Engineers—two officers.

Sappers and Miners—six rank and file.

Royal Artillery—eight officers, three sergeants, three buglers, 162 rank and file—two sick.

Incorporated Militia Artillery—one officer, two sergeants, ten rank and file.

Royal Artillery Drivers—one officer, three sergeants, one bugler, 28 rank and file—one sick.

1st Royal Scots—29 officers, 53 sergeants, 22 drummers, 726 rank and file—153 sick and wounded.

8th Regiment—27 officers, 35 sergeants, 10 drummers, 515 rank and file—11 sick and wounded.

100th Regiment—5 officers, 15 sergeants, 17 drummers, 261 rank and file—121 sick and wounded.

Incorporated Militia—33 officers, 27 sergeants, 10 drummers, 309 rank and file.

Colored Corps—one officer, two sergeants, one drummer, 22 rank and file—four sick.

Long Point and Dependencies, Lieut.-Colonel Parry, 103d Regt.:

19th Dragoons—three officers, four sergeants, one bugler, 56 rank and file—one sick.

Provincial Dragoons—one officer, 13 rank and file.

103d Regiment—12 officers, 11 sergeants, two drummers, 173 rank and file—five sick.

Burlington, Colonel H. Scott, 103d Regiment:
Provincial Dragoons—three rank and file.
Royal Artillery—one officer, three rank and file.
Royal Artillery Drivers—one officer, one sergeant, 15 rank and file.
103d Regiment—24 officers, 37 sergeants, 23 drummers, 598 rank and file—27 sick.

York, Lieut.-Colonel Battersby, Glengarry Light Infantry:
Royal Artillery—one officer, one sergeant, ten rank and file.
Royal Artillery Drivers—one officer, one sergeant, nine rank and file.
Royal and Provincial Engineers—one officer, one sergeant, 15 rank and file.
1st Royal Scots—one officer, one sergeant, two rank and file—seven sick.
8th Regiment—two officers, six sergeants, two drummers, 70 rank and file—49 sick.
41st Regiment—two officers, two sergeants, four rank and file—14 sick.
89th Regiment—one sergeant, two rank and file—one sick.
103d Regiment—two rank and file.
Royal Newfoundland Regiment—one officer, one private—one sick.
Glengarry Light Infantry—18 officers, 30 sergeants, 15 drummers, 346 rank and file—35 sick.
Incorporated Militia—one officer, one sergeant, 17 rank and file—12 sick.
Embodied Militia—seven officers, six sergeants, one drummer, five rank and file—six sick.

Sir Gordon Drummond to Lord Bathurst.
(Extract.)

KINGSTON, July 10th, 1814.

A considerable party of this description (disaffected residents) had been formed and organized in the District of London, who, it appears, had placed themselves under a notorious partizan leader of the enemy, who had frequently before made incursions into the unprotected parts of the country, committing depredations on private property and carrying off the loyal inhabitants. Nor was this party less active in these respects than him under whose directions they proposed to act. Their principal object, it appears, was to disorganize the militia by making prisoners of, and delivering up to the enemy, every militia officer upon whom they could lay hands, and which they to some extent effected. They acted chiefly in the District of London, of which the greater part of them were inhabitants.

Alarmed at their depredations, a small band of the loyal and well disposed of the militia volunteered under one of their officers to march and attack them at their place of rendezvous, with a determination to capture or destroy them, in which they fortunately succeeded, after a sharp resistance from a number far exceeding their own.

A special commission was formed for their trial but did not open till the 23d day of May, and continued its sitting until the 21st of June, when it adjourned till the 10th of August. Seventeen were brought to trial out of upwards of seventy in those three districts, (Western, London, and Niagara,) the greater part being in the London district; fifteen were convicted and sentenced to be executed on the 20th of July. Three judges of the King's Bench formed the commission and presided in turns, two being always present. I have selected seven of the condemned men as the least guilty, whom I have reprieved until His Majesty's pleasure is known.

Opinion of the Acting-Attorney-General, Mr. Robinson, enclosed, dated 18th June, 1814:

Aaron Stevens, Dayton Lindsay, Benjamin Simmonds, George Peacock, Jr., Adam Crysler, Isaiah Brink and John Durham are the most guilty. John Johnson is an ignorant man. He behaved with great humanity towards prisoners, and expresses his regret. Samuel and Stephen Hartwell returned to their native country at once when war was commenced and avowed their hostility. They were taken prisoners by General Brock and paroled at Detroit. He advises that in natural justice they should be reprieved and banished.

Remarks of Chief Justice Scott:

Fourteen were convicted, one pleaded guilty. The two Hartwells should be pardoned. Cornelius Hovey, who pleaded guilty, is so sick that he may not live to abide the sentence of the law—this probably was the cause of the plea.

Reprieved—Samuel and Stephen Hartwell, Isaac Petit, Jacob Overholser, Garret Neil, John Johnson, Cornelius Hovey.

To be Executed—Aaron Stevens, Benjamin Simmonds, Noah Hopkins, Dayton Lindsay, George Peacock, Isaiah Brink, Adam Crysler, John Durham.

General Riall to General Drummond.

FORT GEORGE, July 8th, 1814.

SIR,—I much regret to have to report to you that I have been obliged to retire this afternoon from Chippawa to this place, the enemy having cut a road through the wood from Street's house to where Lyon's Creek falls into the Chippawa and brought along it 7 guns covered by the whole of their riflemen and Indians, under the fire of which they bridged the river. This operation was attempted to be opposed by the flankers of the Royal Scots and three field pieces, under Lieut.-Colonel Pearson, but it was found impossible.

The right of my position being thus turned, it was no longer tenable, and as at this moment a report was brought that another division of the enemy were passing the river four miles higher up, which would enable them to get into my rear by Lundy's Lane, I felt the necessity of retiring from it.

My force, having been considerably diminished by the loss it sustained on the 5th, and by the total defection of the militia and Indians, I thought it more advisable to fall back at once on Forts George and Missassauga than to hazard another action with so superior a force without the support of light troops.

General Riall to General Drummond.

FORT GEORGE, July 9th, 1814.

SIR,—I wrote you last night by express to inform you that the enemy had passed the Chippawa about a mile and a-half above the village, and obliged me to retire from that position. I understand his advance is this morning at St. Davids: an officer of the Provincial Dragoons, who was there to watch them, having been fired at by some dragoons. Our wounded have just gone off to York in the schooners. My whole force is retired here, without having left anything to fall into the hands of the enemy.

General Drummond to Sir George Prevost.

KINGSTON, July 11th, 1814.

SIR,—I have just received a communication from Major-General Riall of the 7th instant, in the afternoon, observing upon the omission, in his public despatch of the same day, of the number of men engaged under his command at Street's Creek, which he should have inserted (as I imagined) at fifteen hundred.

The Major-General also states that previous to his attack upon the enemy's position he had, with Lieut.-Colonel Pearson, reconnoitred them at an early hour in the day with much precision, when, from the extent of ground their encampment occupied, and other observations, and from the information of militia men of good character and intelligence, and from Indians who got close to them and climbed trees to overlook their position, he was induced to believe that their force did not exceed 2,000 men, and as the Major-General had not heard at that time of the fall of Fort Erie, he concluded that there must have been a strong force occupied in its investment. These observations proved perfectly just, for the enemy was joined but a few hours afterwards by that strong force from above.

Colonel Scott, commanding at Burlington, has directed Lieut.-Colonel Parry to fall back to the Grand River from Long Point. By this means the communication between these two officers may be preserved, or Lieut.-Colonel Parry can retire still further upon Burlington if occasion should require.

I have received likewise a letter from Major-General Riall, of the 8th instant. Nothing of moment has occurred since the attack on the 5th. The enemy still occupied the same position, and on the 7th received a reinforcement of 400 men. Their loss in the action of the 5th appears to have been, from good authority, very severe. They suffered much from the fire of our artillery. Brigadier-General Scott is among the wounded, being shot through the foot. Not a single Indian remained with the Major-General at Chippawa.

I have the honor to transmit the copy of information received from a person sent from hence to Sackett's Harbour on the morning of the 8th inst.

P. S.—Since writing the foregoing I have received information from a source to be depended on that the plan of the enemy is to wait the result of their army's proceedings on the Niagara, in the expectation that General Riall will be driven back by degrees, when their fleet is to leave Sackett's Harbor with a strong force on board, which is to be landed at the Forty or Fifty Mile Creek in General Riall's rear and thus get possession of the provisions and stores at Burlington. This information left Sackett's Harbor on the 2d inst.

General Drummond to Sir George Prevost.

KINGSTON, July 11th, 1814.
Half past 6 o'clock p. m.

SIR,—I have the honor to transmit herewith a despatch this minute received from Major-General Riall, stating that the enemy had crossed the Chippawa about a mile and a half from its mouth, whereby the Major-General was under the necessity of retiring from that position.

I trust Your Excellency will see the pressing necessity of expediting the intended reinforcements for this place, which I cannot avoid expressing my anxiety about, from its present very defenceless state in consequence of the reduced numbers of the garrison, as it is impossible to say what may be the intentions of the enemy on leaving Sackett's Harbor, when they will probably be accompanied by a considerable land force. It is natural to suppose that they obtain as good information of our force here as we do of theirs at Sackett's Harbor.

General Drummond to Sir George Prevost.

KINGSTON, July 13th, 1814.

SIR,—Major-General Riall's official despatch of the 8th inst. has just now reached me. By the enclosed copy Your Excellency will perceive that the enemy having crossed the Chippawa in two places above the village the Major-General thought proper to retire upon Fort George and Missassauga.

The flank companies of the Royal Scots, with three field pieces, attempted to oppose them in their passage to the river, but, covered as their advance was by seven guns, it was found impossible to prevent them.

The enemy have established themselves at Queenston, where they have placed guns on Mr. Hamilton's house and commenced fortifying the heights, as appears by a further communication from the Major-General of the 10th inst., wherein he also represents that every exertion is making to resist any attack which may be made upon Fort George or Missassauga, although he considers the former in so defective a state of defence as to be incapable of holding out for any length of time should it be seriously bombarded.

With the superior force of the enemy, covered as it is by numerous light troops and Indians, the Major-General feels it at present impossible, especially as he is now deprived of both these means, to give much effective interruption in their operations without reinforcements.

Lieut.-Colonel Pearson had just returned before Major-General Riall's letter was sent, from reconnoitering the enemy's position at Queenston. They had not any advanced party at a distance of a mile from that place.

Arrangements for Collecting a Force at Burlington.
(Secret.)

The Glengarry Light Infantry to be pushed on to Burlington without waiting for the arrival of the 89th Regiment, leaving all non-effectives at York.

The 89th to push on in like manner, leaving the two boy-companies and all non-effectives and incumbrances at York, Lieut.-Colonel Morrison to take with him two brass field-pieces under Lieut. Armstrong from York.

One wing of the Regiment DeWatteville to be pushed on to Burlington immediately, the other to be in readiness to follow on the arrival at or near Kingston of the head of the 6th or 82d Regiment.

Five companies of the Canadian Regiment to proceed to Kingston without waiting for the 104th going down.

The latter regiment (104th) to remain at Kingston until further orders.

If found necessary, Commodore Sir James Yeo must be applied to to land 200 of the Marine Battalion for the garrison of Point Frederick until the arrival of the 82d.

Lieut.-General Drummond intends proceeding to the head of the lake in a few days to assume command of the troops assembling there.

The following officers of the staff will accompany him, viz:

The officers of his personal staff, including the adjutant-general of militia, and his assistant, deputy-quartermaster-general and one assistant, Capt. Powell, Major Philott, commanding artillery, the quartermaster-general of militia.

J. HARVEY, D. A. G.

Sir Gordon Drummond to Sir George Prevost.
(Private.)

KINGSTON, July 13th, 1814.

DEAR SIR,—The official despatch of Major-General Riall sent by this express was forwarded to York by water, which in consequence of tempestuous weather caused the delay in the receipt of it here.

The Major-General is strongly inclined to think that the intentions of the enemy are shortly to invest the forts upon which he has retired. Fort George is not capable of much resistance, yet he assures me that every possible exertion shall be made to place it in the best state of defence that time and means will permit.

The Indians, he says, have behaved most shamefully, literally speaking, not one remaining of the hundreds that were with him prior to the retreat.

Such of the militia as are disposed to keep the field, the Major-General has ordered to rendezvous at Burlington.

Several officers and 120 wounded men have arrived at York in the schooners.

From the report of a deserter, it appears that the enemy lost about 500 men in the action of the 5th; this number they could well afford, but to us it was the loss of one-third of our men.

The Royals and 100th Regiments are in the greatest want for officers. The latter has but one captain and three subalterns doing duty and about 250 effective men.

Major-General Riall calls upon me strongly for, and indeed expects, reinforcements, but Your Excellency must be aware that I have not a man to send him, and that those expected from the Lower Province cannot be calculated at arriving higher than Cornwall before the latter end of this week. I have, however, ordered the Glengarry Light Infantry to proceed to Burlington, and the 89th on its arrival at York, leaving there its boy companies, to follow on the same route. I have likewise made some further arrangements, which shall be communicated to Colonel Baynes by the deputy-adjutant-general for Your Excellency's information, and as the troops cannot be forwarded without provisions, I have requested Sir James Yeo to send his two brigs immediately, with as much flour and pork as they can carry, to York and Burlington.

As soon as the five companies of Canadian Fencibles arrive here I propose proceeding to Burlington myself, and with the force I shall collect there to form a junction with Major-General Riall.

York, in the meantime, will be protected by such of the 89th and Glengarry Light Infantry as are unfit for more active service, by a body of militia, and perhaps by the crew of the *Star* brig.

Mr. Turquand to Major David Secord.

You are hereby authorized to take under your charge a party of militia for the purpose of collecting all the cattle you can procure in the country, for which you will receive a fair price, according to estimation on their being delivered over to the person employed in the Commissariat Department appointed to receive the cattle, at Fort George or its vicinity.

Chippawa, 8th July, 1814.

PETER TURQUAND,
Dy. Comm'y Gen'l.

Sir Gordon Drummond to Sir George Prevost.

KINGSTON, July 15th, 1814.

SIR,—Since my letter to Your Excellency of the 13th inst., I have not received any communication from Major-General Riall.

I have received letters from Colonel Scott at Burlington stating his intention of moving to the Forty Mile Creek, his force at present being the 103d Regiment, a detachment of the 19th Dragoons, about 1,000 militia and some Indians, but whose number I could scarcely ascertain. I have disapproved of this movement and directed him to return and retain his post at Burlington, as well as to dismiss all the too young, elderly, and inactive men of the militia, as I consider he is much better without such description of men, and to keep only those of healthy and serviceable appearance, as well from this reason as that it would be impossible to provision such numbers.

Major-General Conran shall be pushed on to Burlington without delay on his arrival here.

The 89th Regiment is, I trust, well on its way to York from the Carrying Place, from whence it proceeds by land.

This day has been so boisterous from the westward as to prevent the right wing of De Watteville's Regiment from leaving this by water. It will proceed by land to-morrow morning; the left wing on the arrival of the 82d Regiment.

Three companies of the Canadian Regiment arrived here this morning.

Although I should have wished it, I am apprehensive that I shall not have it in my power to forward any further reinforcements to the right division, from the inability of the commissariat to supply provisions, and in fact dread their failing in due supplies to those already ordered there.

I acquainted Your Excellency in my private letter of the 13th inst. that I had been under the necessity of calling on Commodore Sir James Yeo to send up his two brigs, the *Star* and *Charwell*, with flour and pork. One sailed yesterday, the other is now taking in her cargo and will be ready to proceed this night if the wind, at present foul, permits, and if the enemy's fleet does not prove to have taken the lake.

Four of their vessels were telegraphed as being off Pidgeon Islands.

I propose leaving this place on Sunday morning for Burlington.

Sir Gordon Drummond to Sir George Prevost.

KINGSTON, July 16th, 1814.

SIR,—I have the honor to transmit a despatch from Major General Riall of the 12th inst., covering a copy of the opinion of the officers of the Royal Artillery and Royal Engineers upon the state of the defences and means of resistance of the three forts at the mouth of the River Niagara.

I approve of the Major-General's retiring to Burlington. But I am of opinion that he cannot make any serious impression upon the enemy with the force he at present has, as little reliance can be placed on the numbers of the militia, and still less on the Indians I trust, however, that when the reinforcement of the De Watteville's Regiment shall have got up to his succour that something may be done worthy of observation.

I wish it were in my power still further to increase the numbers of the right division, either by forwarding the 6th or 82d Regiment to the frontier, but I feel afraid the commissariat could not supply them. So much alarmed am I even with the present numbers that I have directed all the women and children of the troops to be sent down from Niagara, Burlington and York, and the families of the Indians to be placed on half allowance.

The *Charwell* brig sailed from here yesterday evening for the head of the lake with provisions and some ammunition. I am in very strong hopes she will arrive safe at her destination, for Mr McKenzie, an intelligent master of the squadron, has returned this morning from reconnoitering the enemy in Sackett's Harbor, where their whole squadron was lying with all their sails bent and apparently ready for sea, but the *Mohawk*, on board of which from her foremast forward no guns could be perceived, and as she appeared to be very much by the stern it is imagined she cannot be completely armed yet.

I have urged Dy.-Commissary-General Couche to forward supplies to the head of the lake so much that it will be necessary to push on the next brigades of batteaux which arrive from below. This may answer for the present, but with the decided naval superiority of the enemy it will be a most extraordinary circumstance if they will permit our communication by water to proceed unmolested.

I am concerned to observe that none of the engineer officers (so much wanted in this province) have as yet made their appearance.

I hope to be at Burlington in the course of a few days.

Major-General Riall to General Drummond.

FORT GEORGE, July 12, 1814.

SIR,—The enemy still occupy the same position and I imagine are waiting for the arrival of their fleet to furnish them with heavy ordnance for their operations against our forts. I have required the opinion of the officers of artillery and engineers upon the state of their defence. If their opinion be correct the fall of these places is inevitable if vigorously attacked, unless the besiegers are interrupted in their operations or a diversion made to draw their attention elsewhere. Having left in Forts George, Mississauga and Niagara such garrisons as the officers of engineers shall consider necessary, I shall move from this towards Burlington with between 800 and 900 men. I have directed Colonel Scott to meet me with the 103d, the militia collected at Burlington, of whom I understand there are a considerable body, and the whole of the Indians that can be assembled and will get into the enemy's rear by the Short Hills and Lundy's Lane. I have also directed Lieut.-Colonel Battersby to move from York with the Glengarry Light Infantry, as I conceive the protection of that place a secondary consideration and that it is not likely to be attacked. If you are forwarding reinforcements to this place, part of them may be left at York, but I am decidedly of the opinion that every man should be taken to create such a force here as will make the discomfiture and annihilation of the enemy beyond doubt.

Answers to questions submitted to officers of engineers:

Fort George is in a very bad state of defence and can make little or no resistance against an army computed at between 5,000 and 6,000 men, with a due proportion of heavy artillery, and the only thing to prevent its being taken by assault is a bad row of pickets. If Fort George falls into the enemy's hands, he will be enabled to carry on a regular attack against Fort Niagara on his own side of the river, which he would otherwise find difficult to do. Forts George and Niagara having fallen, Fort Mississauga will be very much weakened, as all the supplies without that fort will be cut off entirely. There is no secure cover for the garrison of Fort Mississauga and it would soon fall if attacked by land, Fort Niagara being the protection of our supplies outside it. Fort Mississauga would not be easily taken by assault, but is incapable of holding out against a bombardment.

Major Thomas Evans to Major-General Riall.

FORT GEORGE, 13th July, 1814.

SIR,—I have the honor to report to you that, conformable your instructions, I last night proceeded with the company of th[e] King's Regiment, consisting of two sergeants and 32 rank and fil[e] to execute the orders with which you had been pleased to entru[st] me. The vicinity of the road leading to Colonel Hamilton's hou[se] was well examined, and every means used to ascertain if an[y] enemy was in the neighborhood. The field at Hamilton's bearin[g] suspicious marks that an enemy had been there, a non-commissione[d] officer and four rank and file were left to watch that positio[n.] Soon after our approach to Cope's and adjacent houses, a single sho[t] was fired in the rear, but not being followed by others was disre[-]garded, except by the company being kept in a most profound stat[e] of defence. Whilst examining the inhabitants on the point referred to me by you, the company was vigorously attacked fro[m] the rear by the road by which it had advanced. The enemy, how ever, notwithstanding his prodigious numbers, was foiled in hi[s] attempting to intercept its return, and his loss occasioned by th[e] fire of my small party must have been great, from the fact of hi[s] so early desisting to act offensively against us. As the preservatio[n] of the company naturally became the first object, and being in th[e] neighborhood of the enemy, I trust it will be thought enough wa[s] done to entitle the officers and men to the claim of their usua[l] steadiness and gallantry. Every credit is due to Captain Sadleir his subalterns, Lieuts. Barstow and Young—the former for his vigilance and caution : the latter for their animated example under very trying circumstances.

I enclose a list of casualities, and have the honor to be,

THOS. EVANS,

Maj. Comd'g King's Regt.

P. S.—Since writing the above, information has been received that the party by which the light company was attacked amounted to 200 men, under General Swift, who was killed in the affair with 17 of his men.

Major-General Riall to Lieut.-General Drummond.

20 MILE CREEK, 14th July, 1814.

SIR,—I have the honor to enclose you a report of Major Evans of the King's Regiment, whom I had sent out with a small party on the evening of the 12th inst. I have every reason to be satisfied with the conduct of the Major and of the officers and men of that regiment on this occasion. The report of the death of Brigadier-General Swift is fully confirmed.

Brigade Orders.

QUEENSTON, July 13, 1814.

It is with the most painful sensations that Brigadier-General Porter announces the death of his friend and companion in arms, Brigadier-General John Swift. He yesterday generously volunteered his services to the Commanding General to reconnoitre the enemy's position and works at Fort George, accompanied by a party of 120 volunteers, and having by the most judicious arrangement succeeded in capturing, without the discharge of a gun, an outpost, a picquet with a corporal and five men, from whom he expected to obtain important information, he was assassinated by one of the prisoners, who after begging for and receiving quarter shot him through the breast.

The alarm occasioned by the discharge of the gun immediately brought towards the ground a patroling party of the enemy about 50 or 60 strong, when General Swift formed his men, advanced at their head upon the patrol and commenced a successful attack, when he fell exhausted by his wounds. The other officers of his command, of whom notice will hereafter be taken, animated by the example of heroism and fortitude which had been set them, fought, beat and drove the enemy into Fort George, from which they were not more than half a mile distant, and then retired, bearing their wounded and expiring General with them.

It is impossible for General Porter to express the poignancy of his own grief, or to appreciate the loss which the corps has sustained in the fall of this excellent officer. After serving his country for seven years in the war of the Revolution, he again stepped forward as a volunteer to give the aid of his experience in support of the violated rights of this country, and never was that country called on to lament the loss of a firmer patriot or a braver man.

He will be interred at 6 o'clock this afternoon with military honors. The brigade will parade at 5 p. m.

By order of Brig.-Gen. P. B. Porter.

JACOB DOX, A. D. C.

Extract from Niles' Register.

BALTIMORE, Md., July 30, 1814.

"There have been several small affairs between the piquets. On Tuesday night last a party from our army, commanded by General John Swift (late of Palmyra, Ontario County,) of the volunteers, encountered a party of the enemy, a part of whom surrendered, and while our party were advancing to receive those of the enemy who had surrendered a fellow shot General Swi[ft] through the body, which wound proved mortal next morning.

"We understand the man escaped, but those who surrendere[d] were brought in.

"On Friday last several wagons in the employ of the Unite[d] States were taken by the enemy near St. David's, four miles fro[m] Queenston. Seth Cotton of Buffalo and his team were among th[e] captured.

"On Saturday night last a party of the enemy, said to b[e] Indians, surprised our picket at Fort Erie, consisting of eight mer[,] two of whom were killed and the rest taken."

General Brown to Commodore Chauncey.

HEADQUARTERS, QUEENSTON, July 13, 1814.

MY DEAR SIR.—I arrived at this place on the 10th, as I assured you that with the blessing of God I would. All accounts agree that the force of the enemy in Kingston is very light. Meet me on the lake shore north of Fort George with your fleet, and we will be able, I have no doubt, to settle a plan of operations that will break the power of the enemy in Upper Canada, and that in the course of a short time. At all events, let me hear from you. I have looked for your fleet with the greatest anxiety since the 10th. I do not doubt my ability to meet the enemy in the field, and to march in any direction over his country—your fleet carrying for me the necessary supplies. We can threaten Forts George and Niagara, carry Burlington Heights and York, and proceed direct to Kingston and carry that place. For God's sake let me see you. Sir James will not fight: two of his vessels are now in the Niagara.

If you conclude to meet me at the head of the lake and that immediately, have the goodness to bring the guns and troops that I have ordered from the harbor: at all events have the politeness to let me know what aid I am to expect from the fleet of Lake Ontario.

There is not a doubt resting in my mind but we have between us the command of sufficient means to conquer Upper Canada within two months if there is prompt and zealous co-operation, and a vigorous application of these means; now is our time, before the enemy can be greatly reinforced.

Major-General Riall to Lieut.-General Drummond.

20 MILE CREEK, 15th July, 1814.

SIR,—I have the honor to report to you that, agreeable to the [in]tentions conveyed to you by my letter of the 12th, I caused the [de]tachment of troops, as per margin, to move from Fort George on [th]e morning of the 13th: and Colonel Scott having at the same [ti]me moved forward with the 103d Regiment from Burlington, a [ju]nction was formed at this place, where I have for the present [pl]aced the troops in position on the height above the creek.

I had ordered the Glengarry Regiment from York: three com[pa]nies are, I understand, near at hand, and the remainder, I presume, [fr]om the Deputy-Adjutant General's letter, will soon arrive.

I have great satisfaction in stating to you the loyal and patri[ot]ic spirit of the militia of the London District, who have marched [hi]ther in numbers. The Lincoln Regiments are assembling, and in [th]e course of to-morrow I expect the militia will muster in strength, [an]d I have some hopes of the more spirited co-operation of the [In]dians.

With these favorable circumstances I meditated another attack [up]on the enemy, and conceiving that the sanction you gave for my [w]ithdrawing the garrison of York in the event of the enemy [ap]pearing in force from the westward would equally apply in other [ca]ses of great emergency, I yesterday despatched an order to Lieut.-[C]olonel Morrison to join me with the 89th without delay. With [th]is regiment I had hoped that the capture or destruction of the [gr]eatest part of the enemy's force at Queenston would have been [w]ithin my power.

From Lieut.-Colonel Morrison's instructions, a copy of which [I] received from the Deputy-Adjutant-General this day, I doubt [w]hether that officer will feel himself authorized in obeying my [or]ders, which I must greatly regret, because, from the information [I] along received of the enemy's means, it is to be pre[su]med, speaking with reference to the force he has brought, that [hi]s private intentions are directed solely against the forts. York [is] therefore safe for the moment and I wished the attack immediate [w]hile in possession of the co-operation of the militia and Indians, [w]hich delay must deprive me of.

```
Artillery—Three 6-pounders, one 5½-inch howitzer.
Royals          .   .   .   .   .   .   320
King's          .   .   .   .   .   .   200
Incorporated Militia    .   .   .   316
                                        ——— 836
Colonel Scott.
    Artillery—Four 6-pounders.
    103d    .   .   .   .   .   .   .   600
```

General Riall to General Drummond.

20-MILE CREEK, 16th July, 1814.

SIR,—I have the honor to enclose you a report from Lieut Colonel Tucker, left in the command of the forts on the frontie and I hope the activity shown by that officer and the spirit evince by the troops will meet with your approbation.

I propose to-morrow to take up a more advanced position a the 12 Mile Creek, for the purpose of favoring some parties c militia and Indians, who will be pushed forward with a view t gain information of the enemy's movements and prevent his r ceiving supplies from the country.

From the report of deserters and some prisoners who hav been made, I learn that the enemy has been reinforced by 700 me who were crossed over at Lewiston. A return of the troops an militia is forwarded by this express to the Deputy-Adjutan General.

Lieut.-Colonel Tucker to Major-General Riall.

MISSISSAGA FORT, 15th July, ½ past 10 p. m.

SIR,—When I had the honor of addressing you this afternoo the enemy's columns were advancing in great force in every dire tion, with a view of driving in my picquets and establishing thei position, as I apprehend to open and carry on their operatior against the fortresses which you did me the honor to entrust to m surveillance. I lost no opportunity of directing my picquets t contest the advance of the enemy with vigor and resolution, an happy am I to report that this arduous duty was executed wit vigor and skill, which enabled me to complete every arrangemer which I thought expedient (under circumstances of peculiar intere and anxiety) to adopt. The prisoners and other individuals wh had been in the enemy's camp afforded me an assurance that t American army destined for the reduction of these three fortress amounted to 8, 9 or 10,000, and the very formidable columns whi they brought forward and the extent of ground which they occu pied, extending from the left to the right of these fortresses, suff ciently proved that their numbers were considerable, and not les than three thousand men.

I wish to do justice to a brave enemy on every occasion, an must therefore confess that they pushed forward in a spirited mai ner, our picquets retiring before them. You are aware of the ver extraordinary and peculiar mode of warfare, advantageous an only applicable to American troops in this country, and I trust yc will approve my having allowed my advanced posts to retire wit view of drawing them into an open country to enable me to take dvantage of the superior skill of British troops.

I had every reason to believe, from many concurrent accounts, hat the American army intended and expected to carry everything efore it from its vast superiority of numerical force, but I am roud to assure you that a very different opinion was entertained y every individual under my command, all equally determined to o their duty to their country.

Skirmishing with the advanced posts continued from the nemy until three o'clock, when I deemed it prudent to move out f this fortress two six-pounders under Lieut. Tomkyns, Royal rtillery, (the enemy having formed a very solid column, supported ith a six-pounder and howitzer, on the road leading to Colonel [amilton's,) which were so well served and judiciously directed nat I had the pleasure of seeing them retire after having made a eeble resistance. The six-pounders were supported and protected y a detachment of the King's Regiment under Captain Campbell. he Royal Regiment also moved out of Fort George, agreeable to 1y orders, to be in readiness to move on any point which circumtances might require. The zeal and exertions of Major Deane of he Royals, and Captain McLauchlan, Royal Artillery, both in command of important forts, afforded me the highest satisfaction, and ispired me with a perfect confidence in their co-operation should he enemy make a vigorous effort to possess himself of my guns, r to turn the flanks of my small parties. After a very brisk canonade of near an hour, I had the satisfaction of seeing the enemy 1ove off one of his field-pieces, having, I imagine, suffered from he fire of our artillery. The enthusiasm and zeal of the troops nder my command, viz.: Royal Artillery, Royals, King's and 41st legiment, will ever deserve my esteem, and I hope will afford you confidential reliance on a gallant defence of the three forts hould the threatened siege ever take place.

Every individual seemed to be actuated by one sentiment of istinguishing himself on the field of battle, and every encouragenent was given to the enemy to come forward to try the temper f our troops. To all I feel deeply indebted for various services, ut I beg to call to your particular notice Lieut. Hill, King's Regi1ent, Staff Adjutant: Lieut. Le Breton, Deputy-Assistant-QuarterIaster-General, and Lieut. O'Reilly, acting as my aide-de-camp. 'hese officers afforded me the greatest satisfaction—their conduct as conspicuous to all. Lieut. Philpot, Royal Engineers, has a just laim to my regard and perfect approbation;—animated in the field nd judicious in his opinions, I derived great assistance from him.

The Canadian Militia harassed the enemy in a very manly and spirited style. They merit my most favorable opinion.

I congratulate you, sir, on the complete failure of a dashing enterprize of the enemy to establish his superiority over us, which he vainly imagined might lead to the reduction of these fortresses without much resistance. We have driven him back without having suffered on our part, although we were sensible that his loss alone induced him to retire. From my own observation and every account from other officers I am persuaded that three thousand troops occupied our front at the time of my advance. Thus, sir, you may perceive the just degree of credit due to Lieut. Tomkyns and his artillery for that execution which induced so large a force to retire.

I write at a very late hour to despatch a message to you, in the hope that your advance may enable me to act offensively, and as I am much tired, which must plead my excuse for this very hasty letter.

JOHN G. P. TUCKER, Lt.-Col.

General Peter B. Porter to General Jacob Brown.

QUEENSTON HEIGHTS, July 16, 1814.

SIR,—In pursuance of your instructions to me to move round Fort George, interrupt the enemy's communication with the country and reconnoitre his works, I marched yesterday morning at reveille, accompanied by that excellent officer, Major Wood of the engineers, with the whole of my brigade and two pieces of artillery under Captain Ritchie of the regular army, by the way of St. Davids and the Cross Roads to Lake Ontario, where we had an opportunity to examine the northern face of Forts Riall and Niagara, about two miles distant. From the lake I returned to the Cross Roads, moved in upon Fort George, drove the enemy's pickets and formed the brigade in full view and within a mile of the fort. Lieut.-Colonel Wilcocks with his command, Captains Hull, Harding and Freeman with their companies of New York Volunteers, and Captain Fleming with part of our Indian warriors, advanced under cover of a tuft of woods within musket shot of the fort, and afforded Major Wood a fair opportunity to examine the works.

After remaining an hour and a half, and having accomplished the object of the expedition, I returned slowly around the south side of Fort George and joined General Ripley on the Niagara, and with his brigade retired to camp at nine in the evening.

The enemy fired but a few shots from his batteries, and, with the exception of two or three small parties that were sent out and immediately driven back by our light troops, kept close within his works until we were retiring, when several pieces of artillery were sent out and a brisk fire commenced on our rear.

We lost not a man killed, and but two (both of Colonel Swift's regiment) wounded. Lieut. Fontaine of the artillery and one of Colonel Boughton's officers had their horses killed under them by cannon shot.

But I have to report the loss of five men of Capt. Boughton's fine company of New York Cavalry made prisoners. They are the victims of your own generous policy of suffering the inhabitants, who profess neutrality, to remain unmolested. The safety of my brigade required me to place videttes at the several roads leading from Fort George and crossing my line of march at right angles. Five of them were surprised and taken by a party of 15 or 20 militia who live on the road, but who had secreted themselves in the woods on our approach, and were advised of all our movements and positions by the women who were thronging around us on our march. Some of these men, I am informed, have been in our camp professing friendship.

The conduct of every part of my command was such as not only to meet my approbation, but considering the descripton of force to excite my highest admiration. They performed a march of thirty miles, drove in the enemy's pickets, lay for some hours under his batteries, retired in good order, and in every movement of the day exhibited examples of order, fortitude and gallantry, which would have been honorable to the oldest corps.

General Riall to General Drummond.

20 MILE CREEK, 17th July, 1814.

SIR,—Since I wrote you yesterday transmitting a report of Lieut.-Colonel Tucker of the enemy's appearance before Fort George and of his having retired to Queenston, nothing extraordinary has occurred. I had the honor to receive your letter of the 13th, informing me of your intention to come up here and of the reinforcements we may shortly expect, at both of which circumstances I am very highly pleased. Under the circumstances that have taken place it is very much to be regretted that Fort Niagara should have been so weakened as it is to our side. The officers of engineers did intend to do something to protect and strengthen it when I left Fort George, and I make no doubt are working there. I shall write to Lieut.-Colonel Tucker on the subject immediately. Fort George has not, as you imagine, a 24-pounder mounted in it. There are three 18-pounders, two garrison 12-pounders and two field 12-pounders that were brought from Queenston Hill, one 9, and one 8-inch mortar and howitzer, but I do not think the twelves that are mounted on the land or western face are sufficiently heavy in case the enemy shall erect batteries against it, which of course he will do; the only 24-pounders that were sent up, four in number, are mounted in Mississauga, as are the two brass guns of that calibre: the 24-pounder belonging to the *Magnet* is mounted in the southwest angle of Fort Niagara, which is a very important situation, as it overlooks the plain and Fort George better than any other position it affords. I gave direction that the rampart of the north face of Fort George is to be levelled in order to open the plain as much as possible to the fire of Niagara. The Commissary of Ordnance, Mr. Gordon, deserves to be displaced from his situation for the most gross neglect. I have more than once remarked to him on seeing his returns that the quantity of powder was not sufficient, but being assured by him that it was equal to 200 rounds for every piece of ordnance we had, which was all we are allowed by the Board of Ordnance, I did not myself make a calculation to see whether it was or not. When Sir James Yeo arrived at Niagara, I sent for Mr. Gordon and further asked if he wanted powder, as if he did I should make an application to the Commodore for it. He told me he did not want any, that he had an ample supply. In the course of two or three days after he reported to me that there was not sufficient powder and that it would be necessary to get up some both from York and Burlington, which has been effected with a good deal of trouble, to the amount of, I believe, 40 barrels. There wants a great reformation in that department of the ordnance here. I have much reason to be dissatisfied with the conduct of Captain Norton in a circumstance which has occurred within a day or two, and which possibly may be attended with very serious consequences, and which I am sorry to say places him, I think, in a very suspicious point of view. Two American Indians arrived at Burlington, bringing with them an old Cayuga chief, who had been taken in the action at Chippawa. Captain Norton was not only acquainted with this circumstance, but permitted them to attend a council of the Six Nations in order to deliver a message from those in the interest of America. It is true, I believe, that the officer who was left in command at Burlington was informed of the circumstance, but he was ignorant of the customs of those people and uncertain how he should act and did not apprehend them. Whatever those fellows have said has caused much dissatisfaction among the Indians, and the western people have reason to suspect the Six Nations of treachery. Colonel Caldwell had told Norton that he should not only have prevented the American Indians from intercourse with his, but that he should have apprehended them immediately, which he would not do, and when I asked him why he had not done so, he replied that he had neither guard nor place to put them in, and that it was the business of the officer commanding the post. There is something extraordinary, I do think, in Mr. Norton's conduct altogether in this business. Very few of the Cayugas and Onondagas have come forward with the other Indians.

There is a considerable body of militia collected here, and it will be a great pity if the reinforcements you have ordered up should not arrive to take advantage of it. Their hay being now receiving injury and their corn ripening fast, they will not be induced, I fear, to remain long. They are all fine, serviceable men, few or none coming under the description you wish should be sent home. The whole of our wounded men have arrived at York. Lieut.-Colonel Tucker has been instructed to hold out to the last extremity all the forts. The garrisons that have been left in them are fully sufficient for their defence. In Fort George are nearly 400 of the Royals, 200 of the 100th, and upwards of 60 artillery. In Missassauga 290 odd of the King's, the Colored Corps, Military Artificers, and others, making, with artillery, not far from 400 men. In Fort Niagara the 41st and the whole of the marine artillery. I have not heard from Lieut.-Colonel Tucker since I received the report which has been transmitted to you.

P. S.—I have only this moment, just as I was closing this letter, received yours of the 14th, brought, I am told, by an officer, whom I have not seen. I am glad I anticipated your supposition that I had fallen back on the 14th. I know nothing of the circumstances attending the fall of Fort Erie. The garrison consisted of 100 men of the 100th Regiment, and 20 artillery. The reinforcement you directed me to send there was on its way, and was very near falling into the hands of the enemy. All the wounded officers are doing well; most of them are gone to York. Capt. Holland never would confine himself for a moment, though shot through the left hand and wounded in the head. Capt. Bridge and Lieut. Armstrong have arrived at York some time since. We have not made many prisoners, in all not more than 10 or 12. Several deserters have come to us—six in one day—they have been sent to York. I am happy to say we have not lost any. One, I understand, attempted to desert, but was apprehended by some of the militia. There are now several parties out, who prevent the enemy from coming beyond their picquets. One party surprised some dragoons in St. Davids, took three dragoons and four horses. Willcocks was in the village at the time, but unfortunately escaped. Mallory was very near being taken by another party, near the Beaver Dams. A party of militia, Indians, and a few soldiers were sent to Chippawa the other night to endeavor to surprise a guard they were said to have there, but there was neither man nor boat to be found. They get everything across from Lewiston, to which place they have brought their boats. It is impossible now to send over any Indians to the other side of the Niagara, indeed, if they were at Fort George I do not think they would go. My reason for preventing them from bringing the horses and cows across the water, you must, I hope, be aware, was because I was at the moment claiming restitution from American officers for private property taken or destroyed by their soldiers at Dover. If the same latitude is to be given to our Indians, have we any right to complain?

General Riall to General Drummond.
12 MILE CREEK, July 19th, 1814.

SIR,—Since I had the honor of writing to you on the 17th nothing of an important nature has occurred. The troops at present occupy the position of the Twelve Mile Creek, having in advance at the 10 to the right, extending to DeCoo's and Street's Mills, the 1st, 2nd, 4th, and 5th Regiments of Lincoln Militia and a body of Indians, the main body of whom is with the advance of the troops at the Twelve. There was a good deal of skirmishing yesterday with the advance of the militia and the enemy's outposts near St. David's, and they have in consequence burnt that village and several of the neighboring houses. They have also, I understand, burnt the whole of the houses between Queenston and the Falls. The 2d Brigade of militia, under Lieut.-Colonel Hamilton, is at the 40 Mile Creek. I am happy to be able to inform you that almost the whole body of militia is in arms, and seem actuated by the most determined spirit of hostility to the enemy. The Indians also are in great numbers, not less, I believe, than 900, and evince the same spirit. It is very much to be regretted that it cannot be taken advantage of at the moment. Everything goes well at Fort George.

Extract from the Memorial of Major David Secord to the Assembly of Canada.

While the American army was at Queenston, in the District of Niagara, under the immediate command of General Brown, a detachment of his troops under the direction of a Colonel Stone entered the village of St. Davids and said it was their avowed intention to burn, plunder, and destroy that Tory village, as they had been well informed that it had been headquarters for the British troops, and they were fully determined that they should not find shelter in that place if they should ever return.

Accordingly they went to work and burnt, plundered, and destroyed of his real and personal property as follows:

One frame house, three stories, 22 by 80 feet, with three stacks of brick fire chimneys, seven fire-places, built and furnished for a house of entertainment, with sheds and stables thereto belonging.

One stone dwelling house, two stories, 24 by 30 feet.

One stone ditto, two stories, 24 by 60 feet.

One grist mill, stone and timber, 22 by 40 feet, with bolts and machinery.

One blacksmith shop and all the tools.

One new frame barn, 34 by 44 feet, with two fanning mills and other property.

Two log buildings, 22 by 20 feet.

One thousand weight of candles contracted for with the British troops at 2 per pound.

Seven horses and four cows, 20 fat hogs supposed to weigh from 150 to 250 each.

One new wagon with a large yoke of oxen, laden with furniture.

One store of merchant goods, priced at £500.

All his household furniture and family clothing.

Nearly all the above property burnt and destroyed on the 19th July, 1814.

Major MacFarland, 23d U. S. Infantry, to his wife.
(Extract.)

The (American) militia and Indians plundered and burnt everything. The whole population is against us: not a foraging party but is fired on, and not unfrequently returns with missing numbers. This state was to be anticipated. The militia have burnt several private dwelling houses, and on the 19th inst. burnt the village of St. Davids, consisting of 30 or 40 houses. This was done within three miles of our camp, and my battalion was sent to cover the retreat, as they had been sent to scour the country and it was presumed they might be pursued. My God, what a service! I never witnessed such a scene, and had not the commanding officer of the party, Lieut.-Colonel Stone, been disgraced and sent out of the army, I would have resigned.

Colonel Isaac W. Stone to Governor D. D. Tompkins.

VILLAGE OF ROCHESTER,
GENESEE FALLS, July 25th, 1814.

SIR,—On the 18th inst. I was, with a small detachment of volunteers, by order of General Peter B. Porter, ordered to go and dislodge a party of the enemy's troops at a small village called St. Davids, about three miles from Queenston, who were annoying our reconnoitering parties and picquets. Accordingly, I went, and in a short time after followed a few regulars under the command of a lieutenant, as I understood. We drove the enemy from the said village. When on my return, about one mile and a-half from the said village, with most of the men under my command, (I have since been satisfied that none of them were in the village at the time,) I discovered the village of St. Davids to be on fire. By whom it was set, or by whose order, I am yet to learn. On the morning of the following day, without notice, without inquiry, or any investigation to my knowledge, I was served by the Brigade-Inspector with the following order:

"*General Order.*

"Asst.-Adj.-General's Office,
"QUEENSTON, 19th July, 1814.

"The accountability for burning the houses at St. Davids yesterday must rest with the senior officer. It was directly contrary to the orders of the Government and those of the Commanding General published to the army.

"Lieut.-Colonel Stone will retire from the army.

"By order of Major-General Brown.
"C. K. GARDNER,
"Adjt.-Gen."

In consequence of which order two captains and one adjutant of the volunteers have resigned their commissions, not knowing how soon they might share the same fate. I feel injured, inasmuch as I am not guilty of the charge alleged against me. My reputation is somewhat impeached before the public. All I ask for is a fair investigation of my conduct, whether I am guilty or not guilty. As I am at a loss how to get this investigation, I pray Your Excellency to advise with me in what manner I shall proceed.

Extract from Niles' Register.

BALTIMORE, August 6, 1814.

"It is untrue that Fort Erie had been retaken as stated in our last; 300 troops had arrived there from Erie, Pa., in three of our schooners. The *Buffalo Gazette* of the 25th ult. says, 'Since the American army arrived at Queenston there were several teams in the United States' employment attacked by armed inhabitants of a place called St. Davids, about four miles from Queenston. A few teams were captured and some of the drivers and men attached to to the wagons wounded, and several other instances of this kind of petty skirmishing took place in the vicinity of that place. In order to put a stop to these proceedings, a party of General Porter's volunteers, commanded by Colonel Stone, marched to St. Davids; a skirmish began, in which several of the inhabitants and a few of the volunteers were killed, a part of the village was then burnt. The act, we learn, was perfectly unauthorized. General Brown has dismissed the officer who commanded the expedition.'

"On the 20th ult., 100 men of the 22d Regiment embarked at Erie in the U. S. schooner *Porcupine* for Buffalo, and the next day 220 men of the 1st Regiment, under Lieut.-Colonel Nicholas, left the same place with the like destination, in the schooners *Ohio* and *Tygress*. Two fine companies of the 19th Regiment passed through Zanesville, Ohio, (to embark at Cleveland) on the 15th ulto."

General Riall to General Drummond.

12 MILE CREEK, 20th July, 1814.

SIR,—I received a report from Lieut.-Colonel Tucker this day informing me that about 7 o'clock this morning the officer commanding the picquet at Wilson's house, on the road from Fort George to Queenston, had been obliged to withdraw from thence in consequence of the advance of the enemy in that direction with a body of cavalry and infantry and four pieces of artillery. It appears to be the intention of the enemy to take up that position, in order to prevent which Lieut.-Colonel Tucker directed a fire to be commenced upon them from the batteries of Fort George, but with what effect he could not ascertain on account of the quantity of brushwood that interposed. When Lieut.-Colonel Tucker wrote to me the communication with this place was still open, and the enemy at that time occupied McFarlane's and Wilson's, and had a picquet of cavalry near to the ruins of Dickson's house. As I have not heard the report of any guns since 9 o'clock, although the Lieut.-Colonel mentioned that he would occasionally throw some shot and shells to annoy them, I imagine they have retired again to their position at Queenston. Three deserters were brought in here about 3 o'clock. One of them appears to be a very intelligent young man, and has given the enclosed report of the amount of their force according to the best of his judgment. I anxiously wait your arrival here, and I beg leave to express my hope that you will by all means push forward the 89th Regiment, the first division of which I understood from Colonel Morrison was to arrive at York this day. There is a very fine body of militia under Lieut.-Colonel Hamilton at the 40 Mile Creek, which it may be necessary to bring forward also.

Substance of information given by three deserters of the 23d Regiment, United States Army, who came to our advanced posts 20th July, 1814.

They left Queenston at 10 a. m., and having been separately examined report as follows :—

The American army, believed to amount to nearly 6,000 men exclusive of nearly 1,400 volunteers and Indians. Strength of the artillery not known, tho' the following pieces have been seen by the parties :

Five iron 18 pounders,
One brass 18 do.,
and several pieces of smaller calibre.

Two regiments of cavalry, about 100 men ; mounted volunteers, (licensed plunderers engaged for six months at 25 dollars per month,) 180 men.

The following regiments are at Queenston :

	Supposed strength.
23d	600
21st	900
9th	not known.
11th	
13th	
22nd	
25th	
	= 6,000 men.

One company bombardiers.

Informants further mention that a general parade was ordered last night at Queenston, when it was publicly declared that Colonel Stone of the volunteers was cashiered the service *(Credat Judæus Appella !)*

Informants add that the army was put in motion at 7 this morning, with the avowed intention of proceeding against Fort George. A strong division was at the same time sent across the river. The brigade to which the deserters belonged did not leave Queenston. It was Scott's brigade that was sent towards Fort George.

Major-General Riall to Lieut.-General Drummond.

12 MILE CREEK, 20th July, ½ past 10 p. m.

SIR,—Since I wrote you this evening I have received a letter from Lt.-Col. Tucker, informing me that he has been enabled to ascertain the position of the enemy between McFarlane's and Wilson's, where he is in very great force. Lt.-Col. Tucker apprehended a very serious attack will be made upon him, probably this night. He believes the enemy is throwing up a work on the rising ground in front of Wilson's, as his advanced sentries think they hear people at work and the noise of plank being thrown upon the ground from wagons. I am really in a very unpleasant predicament. It will be expected that I should do something to relieve Fort George, which I certainly have every inclination to do, but if I advanced from this I leave the country in my rear perfectly exposed to the enemy's advance from Queenston, or if I move in that direction and from thence to Fort George, the enemy may, if he pleases, detach a part of his force by the cross roads to effect the object of getting into my rear and to Burlington. If, besides, I should advance and any reverse happen, I look upon it as fraught with the greatest danger to the province. I am most anxious for your arrival, and I entreat you will direct the 89th to be pushed forward with all despatch, and also the flank companies of the 104th, whom Lt.-Col. Morrison detained at York. If Fort George should be seriously attacked I fear, from the report of officers of engineers and artillery that I send you, that it will not be capable of much resistance. Lt.-Col. Tucker had four men wounded in a skirmish with one of the enemy's piquets, one of whom lost his leg.

———— ———————— **to the Secretary of War.**

SACKETT'S HARBOR, July 20, 1814.

SIR,—Taking a warm interest in the success of the campaign, and suspecting that the government has not been as reguarly informed of things at this post as might be proper, I have ventured to give you the following statement of facts which have recently taken place, which for clearness and brevity I give the form of a journal:

8th July.—Saw the Commodore, who said he was now nearly ready, and would leave the harbor in a few days and take a station off the Ducks to watch Yeo, who was in Kingston.

12th.—Fleet yet in port. General Gaines had a free conversation with the Commodore, who said he should not go to the head of the lake unless called by Yeo's movements.

14th.—No change in the situation of the fleet nor in the intentions of the Commodore. When he does sail will go to the Ducks.

15th.—The Commodore sick with a fever, expected to be able to go out in three or four days.

17th.—Morgan's rifle battalion, conveying a battering train sent for by General Brown, sailed yesterday in boats supplied by the quartermaster. Their fate doubtful, our fleet being yet in the harbor, detained by something wanted for the *Mohawk*. Yeo and his fleet at the Ducks. The Commodore expects to be out by the 20th, but will not go to the head of the lake unless Yeo leads him there.

20th.—Morgan, with the riflemen and cannon, prevented from sailing by Yeo's blockade of the harbor. Expected the fleet (now ready) would break the blockade to-day. Prevented by the continued illness of the Commodore. Captain Jones would have gone out and settled the matter with Yeo, but had not authority to do so. Strange, that when the chief of a squadron is *non compos* the officer next in rank is not entitled to the command. If this be a rule in the navy it should be altered. There was a fine opportunity of fighting and winning the long wished for battle, but lost because the only man in the fleet who was not ready was the commanding officer.

(*From General John Armstrong's Notices of the War of 1812, Vol. II., pp. 237-8.*)

Gen. Riall to Gen. Drummond.

12 MILE CREEK, 21st July, 1814.

SIR,—I have received no report from Lt.-Col. Tucker since last night. The enemy has concentrated his whole force, with the exception of about 300 men who have crossed the river to Lewiston, between De Puisaye's and McFarlane's. He is certainly erecting batteries against Fort George, a little in advance of Wilson's house. A deserter brought in this day says he thinks they will be completed to-morrow. The ordnance which he has with him consists of four 18-pounders, an eleven inch mortar, two heavy howitzers, and several smaller pieces. The deserter who gave this information belonged to the artillery, and I believe it to be correct. All the deserters who come in agree pretty well in the computation of their numbers. A man, who came over here on some business with one of the American officers, was made prisoner this evening by a party of our militia. He says they are in hourly expectation of the arrival of the fleet with a large reinforcement of troops. It is very much to be lamented that we have not sufficient force to attack them before its arrival. Our militia occupy Queenston and St. Davids this evening. In the former place they made three prisoners. I have just got a report from the officer commanding at Burlington to say that he has received information that a party of the enemy, consisting of about 200 infantry and 80 horsemen, have been at Port Talbot, where they have done a great deal of injury to the crops in that settlement, and that they threaten to advance into the country for a similar purpose. Lt.-Col. Hamilton has sent the Oxford Regt. of militia and some Indians in that direction from the 40 Mile Creek. I have the honor herewith to enclose you a return of the officers and troops composing the garrisons of the several forts as called for in the deputy-adjutant-general's letter of the 16th inst., received this day. Capt. Jervois arrived here this evening.

Gen. Riall to Gen. Drummond.

12 MILE CREEK, 22 July, 1814.

SIR,—I have just received the enclosed letter from Lt.-Col. Tucker, which I lose not a moment in forwarding to you. I also enclose to you the information received from some deserters that came into Fort George last evening. The troops shall be ready to move at a moment's warning, but I shall wait for your orders before I put them in motion. The number I have here amount, with the Incorporated Militia, to about 1,700 men, the militia that may be collected probably amount to between 7 and 800, the Indians to about a similar number. Capt. Jervois takes this letter and goes by the Beach. I send a duplicate by Burlington. If you send your orders by express they shall be instantly obeyed. I have resolved to wait for your directions, as the attempt may involve the safety of the whole of the troops as well in the field as in the garrisons. Fort George may fall, but I cannot think there can be much danger for Missassauga and Niagara for some days. The enemy have a considerable body of troops on their own side of the river, which have been lately marched down from Buffalo. They are constructing a battery at the old Salt Battery near Youngstown, for which they have got, by the reports of deserters, two 32-pounders and two 12 inch mortars.

P. S.—I have ordered the Lincoln Militia to concentrate at the 10 Mile Creek, and Lt.-Col. Hamilton's brigade to move from the 40 to this place.

Information of Deserters to Fort George.

Stanley Rose, private, 8th Co., 9th Regt., Maj. Leavenworth, deserted because he was afraid of hard fighting:

1st Brigade, commanded by Gen. Scott, consists of 3,000 men, the whole force consists of 6,000 or 7,000 men on this side the river, and 2,000 on the other side, with two long 32-pdrs. and two 12 inch mortars for a battery at Youngstown: four 5 or 6 inch howitzers on this side, four long 18-pdrs., three 6 or 9-pdrs.

It will not be long before they attack, most likely next day.

They expect the schooners up the river and have a battery near McFarlane's to prevent their advancing.

Gen. Brown is on this side; the first brigade is commanded by Gen. Scott, the second by Gen. Ripley, the 3rd by Gen. Porter, total 5,000 or 6,000 men: 2,000 regulars at Youngstown; 1,000 militia and 500 Indians in 3rd Brigade: 4,000 regulars in 1st and 2nd Brigades. When they crossed the river there were 500 Indians and 1,500 volunteers and militia.

Originally the army was 8,000 men, reduced to about 5,000 fighting men. When at Chippawa 85 were buried and 150 wounded. A shell burst yesterday and killed Gen. Scott's horse under him near McFarlane's. Lieut. Childs and about a dozen wounded and one killed yesterday.

Orders were issued that all tents should be struck before daybreak in order to surround us and cut off all communication with Burlington.

Some long 18-pdrs. with the howitzers to come to-morrow to attack the fort, while the army will go to the 4 Mile Creek to surround us. This information from the officers of his regiment, who heard it on parade in the orders. He thinks the men much more determined than the officers.

They have about 150 or 200 horse.

Benj. Barnard, 9th Regt., deserted because his time was out and they would not give him his discharge:

On this side are four 18-pdrs., four 12-pdrs., four 6-pdrs., two howitzers; on other side: two 32-pdrs., two 12 inch mortars; on this side about 5,000 regulars, 1,000 volunteers; 2,000 regulars on other side. Their intention to strike their tents at daybreak and attack Fort George tomorrow by surrounding it. They expect we have about 1,000 men towards St. Davids. Originally the army was 7,000 on this side, and only 2,000 and some horse re-crossed. About 44 killed and not 100 wounded. Gens. Brown, Scott and Porter are on this side. Plenty of provisions. The first shot fired yesterday struck Gen. Scott's horse in the neck. The artillery belonging to the 18-pdrs. said they have prepared ladders for scaling Fort George. The enemy will come by day, not before 8 or 9 a. m.

The enemy are building a battery on the other side against Fort George, and one beyond McFarlane's against our vessels. No battery nearer to Fort George than Wilson's. The enemy intends to attack Fort George and Niagara at once.

General Riall to General Drummond.

12 MILE CREEK, 22 July, 1814.

SIR,—I had the honor to write to you this morning by Capt. Jervois and enclosed you a letter I had received from Lt.-Col. Tucker, stating his apprehensions for the safety of Fort George from the vast preparations the enemy seemed to be employed in making for its reduction, and urging me to advance immediately for its relief. About 3 o'clock p. m. I received a report from Capt. Fitzgibbon of the Glengarry Regt., whom I had sent out with a party for the purpose of reconnoitering and gaining information of the enemy's intentions, that he had withdrawn from his position before Fort George and was again falling back upon Queenston. From the top of the hill, over that place where Capt. Fitzgibbon was enabled to see his whole force, which was in column, extending from near the village to De Puisaye's house. The wagons and baggage seemed to be halted at Brown's. When Capt. Fitzgibbon left the hill, which he was obliged to do by the advance of a body of cavalry and riflemen, the column was moving towards St. Davids, and when about 1,000 men, &c., entered into that direction it was halted. Capt. Fitzgibbon was obliged to retire with his party through St. Davids, and was pursued about a mile upon the road leading from thence to this place. I understand some riflemen have advanced to within a mile of the 10 Mile Creek, which is the rendezvous of Lt.-Col. Parry's brigade of militia. That officer has been indefatigable in his exertions and has acquired great influence with the militia. I have directed Lt.-Col. Pearson to detach two companies of the Glengarry Regt. to his support and he has besides a considerable number of Indians with him.

I make no doubt the enemy has either retired or been driven back before this, or I would have received further information. I have not been able to learn what the enemy has intended by this movement, which he evidently wished to mask by the numbers of riflemen and dragoons which he had thrown out in his front. I have received a report also from Lt.-Col. Tucker that their army had abandoned his position before Fort George and that his picquets were again established at Wilson's and McFarlane's. The communication with this place is perfectly open.

Col. Harvey to Gen. Riall.

YORK, 23[...]

SIR,—I am directed by Lt.-Gen. Drummond [to acknowledge]
the receipt of your letter by Capt. Jervois, with t[...]
Lt.-Col. Tucker, and to acquaint you that the L[ieut.-General]
is by no means inclined to balk the ardor of the [...]
his intention immediately to employ in offensive o[perations;]
the arrival, however, of some part of the reinfor[cements]
on their march to this point, the Lieut.-General d[eems it]
prudent, highly as he thinks of the bravery of th[e...]
an attack on a force so powerful as that which [the]
enemy to have on this side of the river: the conse[quence]
might be the immediate fall of the forts and the [loss of]
that part of the province. Conceiving, however, [...]
that the disposition the enemy is making for a[n attack on]
George affords a favorable opportunity for o[perations on the]
Niagara side, Lt.-Col. Morrison, with 400 of the [...]
moment embarking on board the *Star* and *Cha[rwell*, to reinforce]
the garrison of Fort Niagara, and to enable L[t.-Col. ... to]
make a sortie from the fort for the purpose of g[etting possession]
of the guns the enemy may have in the Salt [...]
batteries, and which, if suffered to remain, wo[uld render Fort]
George untenable in a few hours. Lt.-Col. Dru[mmond, with the]
flank companies of the 104th Regt., is also ins[tructed to throw]
himself into Fort Niagara to assist in this oper[ation. It has]
been suggested to Lt.-Col. Tucker to draw a coupl[e of companies]
from Forts George and Missassauga, (in such prop[ortion as you may]
think proper,) to leave in Fort Niagara in the abs[ence of the other]
troops. Lieut.-Gen. Drummond proposes that t[his operation shall]
take place on Monday at daylight, and from the [quality of the]
officers and troops to be employed he feels very s[anguine as to]
its success. In order to favor this operation, howe[ver, and to divert]
the attention of the enemy from that side of t[he river, it is the]
Lieut.-General's wish that you should march to St[amford and con-]
centrate the whole of the regular force under your [command at that]
place, throwing the militia and Indians into the w[oods between the]
enemy's position and the lake. The Lieut.-Gene[ral conceives that]
this movement may be made with perfect safety o[n your part; in the]
event of the enemy's pushing promptly forward t[o interpose or to inter-]
pose betwixt you and Burlington, you can always [(as you would]
move on so much shorter a line) reach Shipma[n's corner (or the]
junction of the roads) before him, that is, provi[ded you take pre-]
cautions to cause his movements to be properly [watched and re-]
ported, and even in this case the diversion in [...]

Tucker would be effected. It is not probable, however, in the Lieut.-General's opinion, that the enemy would move with that degree of promptness expecting an attack from you; he would, it is conceived, rather wait in his position than anticipate it. In this event (of his making no immediate movement towards you) the Lieut.-General conceives that by showing your force towards the Queenston Road, at the moment of Lieut.-Col. Tucker's attack, at the same time driving in the enemy's picquets by means of your Indians and militia, he would be deterred from passing over reinforcements to support the batteries at Youngstown, which movement might further be prevented by the fire of our schooners, which, with the gunboat, must take a position for that purpose two hours previous to moving out to the attack. Lt.-Col. Tucker is directed to throw up two rockets, and not to excite alarm or suspicion they will be thrown up from Fort George or Missassauga. To annul this signal, should unexpected intelligence or other circumstances occur to render it expedient, one rocket will be fired.) From the moment of your putting the troops in motion from their present position, the whole of your militia and Indian force should be thrown forward, and from their numbers and description must be superior to any body of light troops which the enemy can have. The importance of placing the militia under the direction of intelligent officers is very obvious. In addition to those at present acting with that force he recommends Lt.-Col. Pearson being so employed. Should the enemy by pressing suddenly and boldly on you make an action unavoidable, you must, by means of the Glengarry Light Infantry and Incorporated Militia, endeavor to check his light troops until you reach an open space in which, keeping your guns in your centre and your force concentrated, your flanks secured by light troops, militia and Indians, you must depend upon the superior discipline of the troops under your command for success over an undisciplined though confident and numerous enemy. It is Lieut.-Gen. Drummond's intention to pass over to Fort Niagara in the course of to-morrow, in order to ascertain the accuracy of the intelligence respecting the state of the enemy's force and of his preparations on the right bank of the river. He will then proceed to your headquarters, probably by way of the 10 Mile Creek. In event of the operation above alluded to taking place on Monday morning, and of its success, he may be induced to take advantage of the impression produced to risque an attack with the whole of the force on the frontier (including the garrisons of the forts) without waiting for the junction of the DeWatteville Regt., which, however, is expected to arrive here on Monday, and is ordered to push on with all possible expedition. In the present state of the wind the American fleet, even were it out, could not reach Niagara in less than 7 or 8 days from the time of its sailing. It had not sailed on the 20th.

Lt.-Col. Drummond is ordered to deposit the musket ball cartridges he has in charge, 50,000 rounds, at Burlington. Captain Dobbs will take over a further supply, but the Lieut.-General is in ignorance as to the quantity you have with you, never having received returns of ordnance stores and ammunition with the right division.

I have the honor to be, &c.,
J. HARVEY,
Lt.-Col. D. A. G.

Lt.-Col. Harvey to Lt.-Col. Tucker.
(Secret.)

YORK, 23rd July, 1814.

SIR,—Lt.-Gen. Drummond directs me to acquaint you that Lt. Col. Morrison, with 400 rank and file of the 89th Regt., who are sent to Fort Niagara, as well as Lt.-Col. Drummond, with the flank companies of the 104th Regt., for the purpose of enabling you to gain the guns, with which the Lieut.-General understands the enemy is arming the batteries at Youngstown, by an attack upon the troops stationed for their protection, which, it is the Lieut.-General's wish should take place on Monday morning at daylight. In order to enable you to employ the whole of the 41st Regt., in addition to the troops above mentioned, in this sortie, Lieut.-General Drummond will approve of you drawing a couple of hundred men from the garrisons of Forts George and Missassauga, in such proportions as you may think proper, to be sent back immediately after the performance of the service. Maj.-General Riall has received instructions to draw the enemy's attention from your side of the river and operate a diversion in favor of your sortie by advancing the whole of his force to St. Davids, pushing forward his militia and Indians towards the enemy's position. It is not Lieut.-General Drummond's wish to risque an action on the left bank of the river until the arrival of part of the reinforcements, which are marching on this place and expected to arrive on Monday. Should the attack on the right be *successful*, the impression which it may occasion on the force of the enemy on this side, particularly if his *boats* are *gained by us* may afford a favorable opportunity, which Maj.-General Riall is directed to improve, and in that case, or in the event of the failure of your attack and the enemy forcing Maj.-General Riall to action you are to move out every man who can be spared from the three forts, and favor the Maj.-General's operations by threatening or

e enemy's rear. It is conceived that with the 89th,
companies and *two thirds* of your garrisons, you would
amounting to nearly 1500 for this purpose. The more
prevent the enemy from passing over troops to the
those to be attacked by you at Youngstown, should
Riall's movements fail in deterring him from doing it,
has been requested to station one or more of the
ar in such a manner as to command the passage, and if
roy the enemy's boats. The destruction of their boats,
aware, is an object of the greatest possible importance.
your gaining the guns and being enabled to make use
artillery officers must be instructed to keep this object
pt. Dobbs will land a party of 30 or 40 marines to
attack. As Lieut.-Gen. Drummond is going over to
, you will receive from him verbally such further
as he may consider necessary, but should anything
reaching Niagara to-morrow, the attack is not on that
e deferred, should the 89th and 104th flank companies
d, and should no circumstances (connected with the
e, position, or state of preparation,) with which Lieut.-
immond is unacquainted render it expedient in your
postpone it until you can have further communication
with Maj.-General Riall. Two rockets thrown up two
you mean to attack will be seen and understood by
l Riall, one rocket fired subsequently will annul the
al. To avoid creating suspicion it is desirable these
ld be made from Fort George or Mississauga.

  I have the honor to be, &c.,
     J. HARVEY,
     Lt.-Col., D. A. G.

Gen. Drummond to Sir George Prevost.

     YORK, 23rd July, 1814.

n my arrival late last evening at this post, I was
h Your Excellency's despatch of the 15th inst., acquaint-
the *Leopard*, with the left wing of the 4th Batt. of the
been wrecked on the island of Anticosti. It is at the
iost consoling that the troops and crew are saved.
recommended Sir James Yeo, in consequence of the
is under of invaliding a number of his seamen, to apply
of the *Leopard*. The two brigs, the *Star* and *Charwell*,
fety to this place with their cargoes, which has, in a
re, assisted us in our straitened circumstances as regards

provisions, tho' even this additional supply is by no means adequat[e]
to the necessary consumption. Two brigades of batteaux are o[n]
their way up loaded with provisions, which, if they arrive in safet[y]
will still further relieve us, tho' even then our supply will be ver[y]
far from sufficient; I have, therefore, been under the necessity [of]
ordering all the women belonging to the Right Division (beyon[d]
3a company) to go down to the Lower Province, with a view [of]
decreasing as much as possible the issues. The Sedentary Militi[a]
have been for some time called for service to this post, but I find [it]
absolutely impracticable to keep them any longer, as the whole pr[o]
duce of the neighboring country is in the greatest danger of bein[g]
lost. I enclose an application made to me on this head, which wi[ll]
clearly show Your Excellency the urgency of the case.

I am very glad to find that Maj.-General Conran and sever[al]
officers of the Royal Scots are on their way up, as their services a[re]
particularly required.

The effective part of the 89th Regt., Your Excellency will pe[r]
ceive by the enclosed copies of letters to Maj.-Gen. Riall and Lieut[.]
Col. Tucker, will, in consequence of arrangements I have found
necessary to make, be sent across this evening to Fort Niagara i[n]
the brigs *Star* and *Charwell*, and to-morrow I shall likewise cros[s]
in one of the schooners which are expected in to-night for t[he]
purpose. As soon as the troops moving on Kingston arrive at th[at]
place I propose ordering up the 82nd Regt., which, I beg leave [to]
observe to Your Excellency, will leave that important post in [a]
state to be still further strengthened.

I am fully persuaded that Your Excellency will afford me ever[y]
assistance in the very great difficulties I have to encounter, and
cannot but remark that it will require every exertion to overcom[e]
them.

P. S.—Since closing the above, Lieut. Radcliffe of the *Magn[et]*
has come over from Niagara, which he left early this morning. H[e]
brings information that the enemy have retired from their positi[on]
at McFarlane's and re-occupied Queenston Heights.

Major-General Brown to the Secretary of War.

H. Q., QUEENSTON, July 22nd, 1814.

DEAR SIR,—On the 20th the army moved and encamped in th[e]
rear of Fort George. General Scott with the van had some skir[
mishing before the main body came up, but as the enemy kept clos[e]
to their works nothing important occurred. No force was left i[n]
our rear, the heights were abandoned to the enemy, and we di[d]
hope that the movement would have induced him to re-occupy the[m]

r close in nearer to us, so as to bring on an engagement out of his works; in this we were disappointed. The army returned to-day and found a body of militia and a few regulars in and about the heights. Porter pursued them with his command and a few regulars, and was so fortunate as to come up with and capture seven officers and ten privates—they will be sent to Greenbush.

Major-General Brown to the Secretary of War.

H. Q., CHIPPAWA, July 25, 1814.

DEAR SIR,—On the 23d inst. I received a letter by express from General Gaines, advising me that on the 20th the heavy guns that I had ordered from the harbor to enable me to operate against Forts George and Niagara were blockaded in that port, together with the rifle regiment I had ordered up with them. I had ordered these guns and troops in boats, provided the Commodore should not deem it proper or prudent to convey them in his fleet, not doubting but that he would have been upon the lakes for their protection and that the enemy would have been driven into port or captured. As General Gaines informed me that the Commodore was confined to his bed with a fever, and as he did not know when the fleet would sail or when the guns and forces which I had been expecting would even leave Sackett's Harbor, I have thought proper to change my position with a view to other objects. You know how greatly I am disappointed, and therefore I will not dwell on that painful subject, and you can best perceive how much has been lost by delay and the command of Lake Ontario being with the enemy, reliances being placed upon a different state of things. The Indians all left me some time since: it is said they will return, but this you will perceive depends upon circumstances. The reinforcements ordered from the west have not arrived.

Sir Gordon Drummond to Sir Geo. Prevost.

HEADQUARTERS, NIAGARA FALLS, 27th July, 1814.

SIR,—I embarked on board His Majesty's schooner *Netley* at York on Sunday evening, the 24th instant, and reached Niagara at daybreak the following morning. Finding from Lieutenant-Colonel Tucker that Major-General Riall was supposed to be moving towards the Falls of Niagara to support the advance of his division, which he had pushed on to that place on the preceding evening, I ordered Lieut.-Colonel Morrison, with the 89th Regiment and a detachment of the Royals and Kings, drawn from Forts George and Missassauga, to proceed to the same point, in order that with the united force I might act against the enemy (posted at

Street's Creek, with his advance at Chippawa,) on my arrival, if it should be found expedient. I ordered Lieut.-Colonel Tucker at the same time to proceed on the right bank of the river with three hundred of the 41st, and about two hundred of the Royal Scots, and a body of Indian warriors, supported (on the river) by a party of armed seamen under Captain Dobbs, Royal Navy. The object of this movement was to disperse or capture a body of the enemy which was encamped at Lewiston. Some unavoidable delay having occurred in the march of the troops up the right bank, the enemy had moved off previous to Lieutenant-Colonel Tucker's arrival. I have to express myself satisfied with the exertions of that officer.

Having refreshed the troops at Queenston, and having brought across the 41st, Royals, and Indians, I sent back the 41st and 100th Regiments to form the garrisons of the Forts George, Mississaga and Niagara, under Lieutenant-Colonel Tucker, and moved with the 89th and detachments of the Royals and King's and Light Company of the 41st, in all about 800 men, to join Major-General Riall's division at the Falls.

When arrived within a few miles of that position, I met a report from Major-General Riall that the enemy was advancing in great force. I immediately pushed on and joined the head of Lieutenant-Colonel Morrison's column just as it reached the road leading towards the Beaver Dam, over the summit of the hill at Lundy's Lane. Instead of the whole of Major-General Riall's division, which I expected to have found occupying this position, I found it almost in the occupation of the enemy, whose columns were within 600 yards of the top of the hill and the surrounding woods filled with his light troops. The advance of Major-General Riall's division, consisting of the Glengarry Light Infantry and Incorporated Militia, having commenced their retreat, I countermanded these corps and formed the 89th Regiment and Royal Scots detachments and 41st Light Company in the rear of the hill, their left resting on the great road: my two twenty-four pounder brass field guns a little advanced in front of the centre on the summit of the hill; the Glengarry Light Infantry on the right; the battalion of Incorporated Militia and the detachment of the King's Regiment on the left of the great road: the squadron of the 19th Light Dragoons in rear of the left on the road. I had scarcely completed this formation when the whole front was warmly and closely engaged. The enemy's principal efforts were directed against our left and centre. After repeated attacks the troops on the left were partially forced back, and the enemy gained a momentary possession of the road. This gave him, however, no material advantage, as the troops which had been forced back formed in the rear of the

9th Regiment, fronting the road and securing the flank. It was during this short interval that Major-General Riall, having received a severe wound, was intercepted as he was passing to the rear by a party of the enemy's cavalry and made prisoner. In the centre the repeated and determined attacks of the enemy were met by the 9th Regiment, the detachments of the Royals and King's and the light company of the 41st, with the most perfect steadiness and intrepid gallantry, and the enemy was constantly repulsed with very heavy loss. In so determined a manner were these attacks directed against our guns that our artillerymen were bayoneted by the enemy in the act of loading, and the muzzles of the enemy's guns were advanced within a few yards of ours. The darkness of the night during this extraordinary conflict occasioned several uncommon incidents. Our troops having for a moment been pushed back, some of our guns remained for a few minutes in the enemy's hands: they were, however, not only quickly recovered, but the two pieces, a six-pounder and a five and a half-inch howitzer, which the enemy had brought up, were captured by us, together with several tumbrils, and in limbering up our guns at one period one of the enemy's six-pounders was put by a mistake upon a limber of ours, and one of our six-pounders limbered on his, by which means the pieces were exchanged, and thus, though we captured two of his guns, yet as he obtained one of ours we have gained only one gun.

About nine o'clock (the action having commenced at six) there was a short intermission of firing, during which the enemy was employed in bringing up the whole of his remaining force, and he shortly after renewed his attack, but was everywhere repulsed with equal gallantry and success. About this period the remainder of Major-General Riall's division, which had been ordered to retire on the advance of the enemy, consisting of the 103d Regiment, under Colonel Scott, the headquarter division of the 8th (or King's,) flank companies, 104th, and some detachments of militia, under Lieut.-Colonel Hamilton, inspecting field officer, joined the troops engaged: and I placed them in a second line, with the exception of the Royal Scots and flank companies, 104th, with which I prolonged my front line on the right, where I was apprehensive of the enemy's outflanking me. The enemy's efforts to carry the hill were continued until about midnight, when he had suffered so severely from the superior steadiness and discipline of His Majesty's troops that he gave up the contest and retreated with great precipitation to his camp beyond the Chippawa. On the following day he abandoned his camp, threw the greatest part of his baggage, camp equipage, and provisions into the rapids, and having set fire to Street's Mills and destroyed the bridge at Chippawa, continued his retreat in great disorder towards Fort Erie. My light troops, cavalry, and Indians are detached in pursuit and to harass his retreat, which, I doubt not, he will continue until he reaches his own shore.

The loss sustained by the enemy in this severe action cannot be estimated at less than fifteen hundred men, including several hundreds of prisoners left in our hands. His two commanding generals, Brown and Scott, are said to be wounded; his whole force, which has never been rated at less than five thousand, having been engaged. Enclosed I have the honor to transmit a return of our loss, which has been very considerable. The number of troops under my command did not, for the first three hours, exceed sixteen hundred men; the addition of the troops under Colonel Scott did not increase it to more than two thousand eight hundred, of every description.

A very difficult but at the same time a most gratifying duty remains, that of endeavoring to do justice to the merits of the officers and soldiers by whose valor and discipline this important success has been obtained. I was very early in the action deprived of the services of Major-General Riall, who, I regret to learn, has suffered the amputation of his arm in the enemy's possession; his bravery, zeal, and activity have always been conspicuous.

To Lieut.-Colonel Harvey, Deputy-Adjutant-General, I am so deeply indebted for his valuable assistance previous to as well as his able and energetic exertions during this severe contest, that I feel myself called upon to point Your Excellency's attention to the distinguished merits of this highly deserving officer, whose services have been particularly conspicuous in every affair that has taken place since his arrival in this province. The zeal and intelligence displayed by Major Clegg, Assistant-Adjutant-General, deserve my warmest approbation. I much regret the loss of a very intelligent and promising young officer, Lieutenant Moorsom, 104th Regiment, Deputy-Assistant-Adjutant-General, who was killed towards the close of the action. The active exertions of Captain Elliot, Deputy-Assistant-Quartermaster-General, of whose gallantry and conduct I had occasion on two former instances to remark, were conspicuous. Major Maule and Lieutenant Le Breton, of Quartermaster-General's department, were extremely useful to me; the latter was severely wounded.

Amongst the officers from whose active exertions I derived the greatest assistance, I cannot omit to mention my aides-de-camp, Captains Jervois and Loring, and Captain Holland, aide-de-camp to Major-General Riall; Captain Loring was unfortunately taken prisoner by some of the enemy's dragoons, whilst in the execution of an order.

In reviewing the action from its commencement, the first object which presents itself is the steadiness and good countenance of the squadron of 19th Light Dragoons, under Major Lisle, and the very creditable and excellent defence made by the Incorporated Militia battalion, under Lieutenant Colonel Robinson, who was dangerously wounded, and a detachment of the 8th (King's) Regiment, under Captain Campbell. Major Kerby succeeded Lieutenant-Colonel Robinson in the command of the Incorporated Militia battalion and continued very gallantly to direct its efforts; this battalion has only been organized a few months, and much to the credit of Captain Robinson of the King's Regiment (Provincial Lieutenant-Colonel) has attained a highly respectable degree of discipline.

In the reiterated and determined attacks which the enemy made upon our centre for the purpose of gaining at once the crest of the position and our guns, the steadiness and intrepidity displayed by the troops allotted for the defence of that post were never surpassed: they consisted of the 89th Regiment, commanded by Lieutenant-Colonel Morrison, and, after the Lieutenant-Colonel had been obliged to retire from the field by a severe wound, by Major Clifford: a detachment of the Royal Scots under Lieut. Hemphill, and after he was killed Lieut. Fraser: a detachment of the 8th (or King's) under Captain Campbell: light company, 41st Regiment, under Captain Glew, with some detachments of militia under Lieutenant-Colonel Parry, 103rd Regiment. These troops repeatedly, when hard pressed, formed round the colours of the 89th Regiment, and invariably repulsed the attacks made against them. On the right the steadiness and good countenance of the 1st Battalion, Royal Scots, under Lieutenant-Colonel Gordon, in some very trying moments excited my admiration. The King's Regiment, (1st Battalion,) under Major Evans, behaved with great gallantry and firmness, as did the light company of the Royals, detached under Captain Stewart; the Grenadiers of the 103rd, detached under Captain Browne; and the flank companies of the 104th under Captain Leonard. The Glengarry Light Infantry, under Lieutenant-Colonel Battersby, displayed most valuable qualities as light troops. Colonel Scott, Major Smelt, and the officers of the 103rd deserve credit for their exertions in rallying that regiment after it had been thrown into momentary disorder. Lieutenant-Colonel Pearson, Inspecting Field Officer, directed the advance with great intelligence, and Lieutenant-Colonel Drummond, having gone forward with my permission early in the day, made himself actively useful in different parts of the field under my direction. These officers are entitled to my best thanks, as is Lieutenant-Colonel Hamilton, Inspecting Field Officer, for his exertions after his arrival with the troops under Colonel Scott.

The field artillery so long as there was light was well served. The credit of its efficient state is due to Captain Mackonachie, who has charge of it since his arrival with this division. Captain McLauchlan, has charge of the batteries at Fort Missassaga, volunteered his services in the field on this occasion; he was severely wounded. Lieutenant Tomkins deserves much credit for the way in which the two brass 24-pounders, of which he had charge, were served, as does Sergeant Austin of the rocket company, who directed the Congreve rockets, which did much execution. The zeal, loyalty and bravery, with which the militia of this part of the province have come forward to co-operate with His Majesty's troops in the expulsion of the enemy, and their conspicuous gallantry in this and the action of the 4th, claim my warmest thanks.

I cannot conclude this despatch without recommending in the strongest terms the following officers, whose conduct during the late operations has called for marked approbation, and I am induced to hope Your Excellency will be pleased to submit their names for promotion to the most favorable consideration of His Royal Highness the Prince Regent, viz: Captain Jervois, my aide-de-camp; Captain Robinson, 8th (King's) Regiment, (Provincial Lieutenant-Colonel) commanding the Incorporated Militia; Captain Elliot, Deputy-Assistant-Quartermaster-General; Captain Holland, aide-de-camp to Major-General Riall, and Captain Glew, 41st Regiment.

This despatch will be delivered to you by Captain Jervois, my aide-de-camp, who is fully competent to give Your Excellency any further information you may require.

District General Order.

HEADQUARTERS, FALLS OF NIAGARA, 26th July, 1814.

Lieutenant-General Drummond offers his sincerest and warmest thanks to the troops and militia engaged yesterday, for their exemplary steadiness, gallantry and discipline in repulsing all the efforts of a numerous and determined enemy to carry the position of Lundy's Lane, near the Falls of Niagara. Their exertions have been crowned with complete success by the defeat of the enemy, and his retreat to the position of Chippawa with the loss of two of his guns and an immense number of killed and wounded, and several hundred prisoners. When all have behaved nobly it is unnecessary to hold up particular instances of merit in corps or individuals. The Lieut.-General cannot, however, refrain from expressing in the strongest manner his admiration of the gallantry and steadiness of the 89th Regiment, under Lieut.-Colonel Morrison and Major Clifford, who ably and gallantly supplied the Lieut.-Colonel's place after he was wounded; 41st Light Company under Captain Glew, and detachment of the 8th or King's Regiment under Captain Campbell, and Royals acting with them: also a party of Incorporated Militia, by whom the brunt of the action was for a considerable time sustained, and whose loss has been severe. To the advance under Lieutenant-Colonel Pearson, consisting of the Glengarry Light Infantry under Lieut.-Colonel Battersby, a small party of the 104th under Lieut.-Colonel Drummond, the Incorporated Militia under Lieut.-Colonel Robinson, and detachments from the 1st, 2d, 4th and 5th Lincoln Militia and 2d York under Lieut.-Colonel Parry, the Lieut.-General offers his warmest thanks. They are also due to the troops which arrived under Colonel Scott during the action, viz.: The 1st or Royal Scots under Lieut.-Colonel Gordon, 8th or King's under Major Evans, 103d Regiment under Colonel Scott, flank companies, 104th, with the Norfolk, Oxford, Kent and Essex Rangers and Middlesex Militia, under Lieut.-Colonel Hamilton.

The admirable steadiness and good conduct of the 19th Light Dragoons, under Major Lisle, and of the detachment of Royal Artillery, under Captain MacLauchlan, are entitled to particular praise: the latter officer having been badly wounded, the command of the artillery devolved to Captain Mackonochie, with whose gallantry and exertions Lieut.-General Drummond was highly pleased. Sergeant Austin, who directed the firing of the Congreve Rockets, deserves very great credit. To the officers of the general and of his own personal staff, and to Captain Holland, aide-de-camp to Major-General Riall, Lieut.-General Drummond feels himself greatly indebted for the assistance they afforded him.

He has to lament being deprived (by a wound early in the action) of the services of Major-General Riall, who was most unfortunately made prisoner, whilst returning from the field, by a party of the enemy's cavalry, who had a momentary possession of the road. Lieut.-General Drummond has also to regret the wounds which have deprived the corps of the services of Lieut.-Colonel Morrison, 89th Regiment, and Lieut.-Colonel Robinson of the Incorporated Militia. In the fall of Lieut. Moorsom, serving as Deputy-Asst.-Adjutant-General, the service has lost a gallant, intelligent and meritorious young officer.

The Lieut.-General and President has great pleasure in dismissing to their homes the whole of the Sedentary Militia, who have so handsomely come forward on the occasion, confident that on any future emergency their loyalty will be again equally conspicuous. He will perform a grateful duty in representing to His Majesty's government the zeal, bravery, and alacrity with which the militia have co-operated with His Majesty's troops.

J. HARVEY, Lt.-Col.,
Deputy-Adjt.-General.

Return of Killed, Wounded and Missing in the Action at Lundy's Lane, on the 25th July, 1814.

Staff—one officer killed, four officers wounded, one officer missing.

19th Dragoons—two rank and file wounded, one private missing.

Royal Engineers—one subaltern missing.

Royal Artillery—four rank and file killed, one captain, twelve rank and file wounded; seven privates missing.

Royal Marine Artillery—three rank and file wounded, two rank and file missing.

1st Royal Scots—one subaltern, 15 privates, killed; three officers, 112 non-commissioned officers and men, wounded; two officers and 39 non-commissioned officers and men missing.

8th, or King's—twelve non-commissioned officers and men killed, three officers and 57 non-commissioned officers and men wounded, one officer and twelve non-commissioned officers and men missing.

41st Regt.—three privates killed, 34 non-commissioned officers and men wounded.

89th Regt.—two officers, 27 non-commissioned officers and men, killed; eleven officers and 177 non-commissioned officers and men wounded, 37 non-commissioned officers and men missing.

103d Regt.—six privates killed, one officer and 46 non-commissioned officers and men wounded, three officers and four non-commissioned officers and men missing.

104th Regt.—one private killed, five privates missing.

Glengarry Light Infantry—four privates killed, one officer, 30 non-commissioned officers and men, wounded; one officer and 21 non-commissioned officers and men missing.

Incorporated Militia—one officer and six men killed, four officers and 39 non-commissioned officers and men wounded; 75 non-commissioned officers and men missing; three officers and 14 men prisoners.

Provincial Light Dragoons—two rank and file wounded, one captain missing.

1st Lincoln Militia—one private killed.
2d do do —one private wounded.
4th do do —two officers, three men wounded; two officers missing.
5th Lincoln Militia—one officer and three men wounded.
2d York Militia—three officers and six men wounded.

Officers Killed.

General Staff—Lieut. Moorsom, 104th Regt., Deputy-Assist.-Adjt.-General.
1st, or Royal Scots—Lieut. Hemphill.
89th Regt., 2d Battn.—Captain Spunner, Lieut. Latham.
Incorporated Militia—Ensign Campbell.

Officers Wounded.

General Staff—Lieut.-General Drummond, severely, not dangerously; Major-General Riall, do., and prisoner; Lieut.-Colonel Pearson, slightly; Lieut. Le Breton, severely.
Royal Artillery—Capt. McLauchlan, dangerously.
1st, or Royal Scots—Capt. Brereton, slightly; Lieut. Haswell, severely, not dangerously; Lieut. D. Fraser, do., do., and missing.
1st Battn., 8th or King's—Lieut. Noel and Ensign Swayne, slightly; Ensign MacDonald, severely.
89th Regt.—Lieut.-Colonel Morrison, Lieuts. Sanderson, Street, Pierce, Taylor, Lloyd and Miles, severely, not dangerously; Lieut. Ledmond and Adjutant Hopper, slightly; Lieut. Gray and Ensign Saunders, dangerously.
103d Regt.—Lieut. Langhorne, slightly.
Glengarry Light Infantry—Lieut. R. Kerr, slightly.
Incorporated Militia—Lieut.-Col. Robinson, dangerously; Captain Fraser, severely; Capt. Washburn, slightly; Captain McDonald, severely, left arm amputated; Lieut.-MacDougall, mortally; Lieut. Cuttan and Ensign McDonald, severely; Lieut. Hamilton, slightly.
2d Lincoln Militia—Adjutant Thompson, slightly.
4th Lincoln Militia—Captain H. Nelles and Ensign Kennedy, slightly.
5th Lincoln Militia—Major Hatt, severely.
2d York Militia—Major Simons, severely; Captain Rockman, Lieuts. Orrfield and Smith, severely.

Officers Missing.

Royal Engineers—Lieut. Yule.
1st, or Royal Scots—Lieuts. Clyne and Lamont, supposed to be prisoners.
8th, or King's Regt.—Quartermaster Kirnan.
4th Lincoln Militia—Capt. H. Nelles and Quartermaster Ball.

Officers Prisoners.

General Staff—Captain Loring, A. D. C. to Lieut.-General Drummond.
89th Regt.—Capt. Gore.
103d Regt.—Capt. Brown, Lieut. Montgomery (wounded,) and Ensign Lyner.
Glengarry Light Infantry—Ensign Robins.
Incorporated Militia—Captain McLean, Ensign Wharf and Quartermaster Thompson.
Provincial Light Dragoons—Capt. Merritt.
Total, including officers—killed, 84; wounded, 559; missing 193; prisoners, 42.

In consequence of the great use made by the enemy of buckshot, many of the wounds have proved slight.

Captain L. Austin, A. D. C. to Major-General Brown, to the Secretary of War.

H. Q., BUFFALO, 29th July, 1814.

SIR,—I have the honor of addressing you by desire of Gen Brown, who is now confined by wounds received in a severe and desperate engagement with the enemy on the afternoon and night of the 25th inst.

Our army had fallen back to Chippawa. The enemy collecting every regiment from Burlington and York, and meeting with no opposition on Lake Ontario, transported by water troops to Fort George from Kingston and even Prescott, which enabled them to bring against us a force vastly superior, under command of Lieut.-Gen. Drummond and Maj.-Gen. Riall. They were met by us near the Falls of Niagara, where a most severe conflict ensued: the enemy disputed the ground with resolution, yet were driven from every position they attempted to hold. We stormed his batteries directly in front and took possession of all his artillery; notwithstanding his immense superiority both in numbers and position, he was completely defeated, and our troops remained on the battle ground without any interruption. As, however, both Generals Brown and Scott had received severe wounds—almost every chief of battalion disabled, and our men quite exhausted, it was thought prudent to retire to our encampment, which was done in good order without any molestation from the enemy—our wounded having been first removed.

Maj.-Gen. Riall, with the aide-de-camp of Gen. Drummond and about twenty other officers, are taken prisoners.

The loss on both sides is immense, but no account has been yet returned. The aide and brigade major of Gen. Scott are both severely wounded, and Capt. Spencer, an aide of Gen. Brown, most probably dead, having received two balls through his body. Both Generals Brown and Scott are on this side confined by their wounds. Gen. Ripley commands on the other. General Brown received his wounds at the same instant during a late part of the action, but still continued to keep his horse until exhausted by loss of blood—this, probably, has rendered his wounds more painful than they would otherwise have been.

Major-General Brown to the Secretary of War.

BUFFALO, 7th August, 1814.

SIR,—Confined as I was and have been since the last engagement with the enemy, I fear that the account I am about to give may be less full and satisfactory than under other circumstances it might have been made. I particularly fear that the conduct of the gallant men it was my fortune to lead will not be noticed in a way due to their fame and the honor of our country.

You are already apprised that the army had, on the 25th ult., taken a position at Chippawa. About noon of that day Col. Swift, who was posted at Lewiston, apprised me by express that the enemy had appeared in considerable force in Queenston and on its heights; that four of the enemy's fleet had arrived during the preceding night and were then lying near Fort Niagara, and that a number of the enemy's boats were in view moving up the Straight. Within a few moments after this intelligence had been received, I was further informed by Captain Denman of the Quartermaster's Department that the enemy was landing at Lewiston, and that our baggage and stores at Schlosser and on their way thither were in danger of immediate capture. It is proper here to mention that having received advices as late as the 20th from Gen. Gaines that our fleet was then in port and the Commodore sick, we ceased to look for co-operation from that quarter, and determined to disencumber ourselves of baggage and march directly for Burlington Heights. To mask this intention and to draw from Schlosser a small supply of provisions, I fell back upon Chippawa. As this arrangement, under the increased force of the enemy, left much at hazard on our side of the Niagara, and as it appeared by the before mentioned information that the enemy was about to avail himself of it, I conceived the most effectual method of recalling him from this object was to put myself in motion towards Queenston. Gen. Scott with the 1st Brigade, Towson's Artillery, and all the dragoons and mounted men, were accordingly put in march on the road leading thither, with orders to report if the enemy appeared—then to call for assistance if necessary.

On the General's arrival at the Falls he learned that the enemy was in force directly in his front, narrow pieces of woods along intercepting his view of them. Waiting only to give this information, he advanced upon them; by the time Assistant-Adj. Jones had delivered his message, the action began; and before the remaining part of the division had crossed the Chippawa, it had become close and general between the advanced corps. Though Gen. Ripley with the second brigade, Major Hindman with the corps of artillery and Gen. Porter at the head of his command, had respectively pressed forward with ardor, it was not less than an hour before they were brought to sustain Gen. Scott, during which time his command most skilfully and gallantly maintained the conflict. Upon my arrival, I found that the General had passed the wood and engaged the enemy on the Queenston road and on the ground to the left of it with the 9th, 11th and 22d Regiments, with Towson's Artillery—the 25th had been thrown to the right to be governed by circumstances. Apprehending that these corps were much exhausted, and knowing that they had suffered severely, I determined to interpose a new line with the advancing troops, and thus disengage Gen. Scott and hold his brigade in reserve; orders were accordingly given to General Ripley. The enemy's artillery at this moment occupied a hill which gave him great advantages and was the key to the whole position; it was supported by a line of infantry. To secure the victory it was necessary to carry this artillery and seize the height. This duty was assigned to Col. Miller, while to favor its execution the 1st Regiment, under the command of Col. Nicholas, was directed to menace and amuse the infantry. To my great mortification this regiment, after a discharge or two, gave way and retreated some distance before it could be rallied, though it is believed the officers of the regiment exerted themselves to shorten this distance. In the meantime Col. Miller, without regard to this occurrence, advanced steadily and gallantly to his object, and carried the height and the cannon. Gen. Ripley brought up the 23d (which had also faltered) to his support, and the enemy disappeared from before them. The 1st Regiment was now brought into line on the left of the 21st and the detachments of the 17th and 19th, Gen. Porter occupying with his command the extreme left—about the time Col. Miller carried the enemy's cannon.

The 25th Regiment, under Major Jessup, was engaged in a more obstinate contest with all that remained to dispute with us the field of battle. The Major, as has been already stated, had been ordered by General Scott at the commencement of the action to take ground to the right : he had succeeded in turning the enemy's left flank—had captured (by a detachment under Captain Ketchum) Gen. Riall and sundry other officers—and showed himself again in a blaze of fire, which defeated or destroyed a very superior force of the enemy. He was ordered to form on the right of 22d Regiment. The enemy rallying his forces and, as is believed, having received reinforcements, now attempted to drive us from our position and regain his artillery ; our line was unshaken and the enemy repulsed. Two other attempts having the same object had the same issue. Gen. Scott was again engaged in repelling the former of these, and the last I saw of him on the field of battle he was near the head of his column, and giving to its march a direction that would have placed him on the enemy's right. It was with great pleasure I saw the good order and intrepidity of Gen. Porter's volunteers from the moment of arrival: but during the last charge of the enemy those qualities were conspicuous—stimulated by the example set them by their gallant leader, by Major Wood of the Pennsylvania corps, by Col. Dobbin of New York, and by their officers generally—they precipitated themselves upon the enemy's line and made all the prisoners which were taken at this point of the action.

Having been for some time wounded, and being a good deal exhausted by loss of blood, it became my wish to devolve the command on Gen. Scott and retire from the field, but on inquiry I had the misfortune to learn that he was disabled by wounds. I therefore kept my post, and had the satisfaction of seeing the enemy's last effort repulsed. I now consigned the command to General Ripley.

While retiring from the field I saw and felt that the victory was complete on our part if proper measures were promptly adopted to secure it. The exhaustion of the men was, however, such as made some refreshment necessary ; they particularly required water—I was myself extremely sensible of the want of this necessary article. I therefore believed it proper that Gen. Ripley and the troops should return to camp after bringing off the dead, the wounded and the artillery ; and in this I saw no difficulty, as the enemy had entirely ceased to act. Within an hour after my arrival in camp I was informed that Gen. Ripley had returned without annoyance and in good order. I now sent for him, and after giving him my reasons for the measure I was about to adopt, ordered him to put the troops in the very best possible condition ; to give to them the necessary refreshment ; to take with him the picquets and camp guards and every other description of force ; to put himself on the field of battle as the day dawned, and there to meet and beat the enemy if he appeared. To this order he made no objection and I relied upon its execution; it was not executed. I feel most sensibly how inadequate are my powers in speaking of the troops to do justice either to their merits or to my own sense of them—under able direction they might have done more and better.

From the preceding detail you have new evidence of the distinguished gallantry of Generals Scott and Porter, of Col. Miller and Major Jessup.

Of the 1st Brigade, the chief with his aide-de-camp, Worth, his major of brigade, Smith, and every commander of battalion, were wounded. The 2d Brigade suffered less, but as a brigade their conduct entitled them to the applause of their country. After the enemy's strong position had been carried by the 21st and detachments of the 17th and 19th, the 1st and 23d assumed a new character—they could not again be shaken or dismayed. Major McFarland of the latter fell nobly at the head of his battalion. Under the command of Gen. Porter the Militia Volunteers of Pennsylvania and New York stood undismayed amidst the hottest fire, and repulsed the veterans opposed to them. The Canadian Volunteers, commanded by Col. Wilcocks, are reported by General Porter as having merited and received his approbation. The corps of artillery commanded by Major Hindman behaved with its usual gallantry. Capt. Towson's battery attached to the 1st Brigade was the first and the last engaged, and during the whole conflict maintained that high character which they had previously won by their skill and valor. Captains Biddle and Ritchie were both wounded early in the action, but refused to quit the field; the latter declared that he would never leave his piece, and true to his engagement fell by its side covered with wounds.

The staff of the army had its peculiar merit and distinction. Col. Gardner, Adj.-Gen., though ill, was on horseback and did all in his power; his assistant, Major Jones, was very active and useful; my gallant aids-de-camp, Austin and Spencer, had many and critical duties to perform, in the discharge of which the latter fell. I shall ever think of this young man with pride and regret—regret that his career has been so short; pride that it has been so distinguished. The engineers, McRea and Wood, were greatly distinguished on this day, and their high military talents exerted with great effect; they were much under my eye and near my person, and to their assistance a great deal is fairly to be ascribed. I most earnestly recommend them as worthy of the highest trust and confidence.

The staff of Generals Ripley and Porter discovered great zeal and attention to duty. Lieut. E. B. Randolph of the 20th is entitled to notice; his courage was conspicuous.

I enclose a return of our loss. Those noted as missing may generally be numbered with the dead. The enemy had but little opportunity of making prisoners.

Return of prisoners taken from the enemy in the above action, viz.: 1 Major-General (Riall,) 1 aid (to Lt.-Gen. Drummond,) 6 captains, 11 subalterns, 150 rank and file—total, 169.

Az. ORNE,
Assist. Insp. Gen.

Major-Gen. Peter B. Porter to Governor D. D. Tompkins.

FORT ERIE, U. C., July 29, 1814.

SIR,—Our Canadian campaign seems drawing to a close, or must, at any rate, be suspended for want of reinforcements. After a month spent in marching and countermarching we have got back to the point from which we set out, much impaired in strength but I hope not disheartened.

Besides almost daily skirmishing we have had two severe general engagements. In the first of these we were *lucky*, (I use this term because so far as depended on any previous arrangements or knowledge of the commanding officer, both engagements were wholly accidental and unexpected,) and obtained a splendid victory, if not with a trifling yet a very disproportionate loss. In the last we were most unlucky both as to time and place, the action having been commenced three miles from camp about sundown, with one-third of our army against a greatly superior force occupying a commanding position. But no disadvantage of time, place or circumstance, could resist the desperate bravery of the American soldiery.

The enemy's battery of seven pieces of artillery was carried by a charge, his commanding position occupied and four desperate and deliberate attempts to regain it by desperate charges successfully repelled. Our victory was complete, but, alas, this victory gained by exhibitions of bravery never surpassed in this country, was converted into a defeat by a precipitate retreat, leaving the dead, the wounded and captured artillery, and our hard earned honor to the enemy. I entered my remonstrance against this measure, and I confess at the time I almost wished that fate had swept another General from the combat. But it is certain that no Militia General is to gain any military fame while united to a regular force and commanded by their officers.

The purpose of this letter is to request that I may be permitted to retire from the service, for in truth the volunteer force is is now so small as not to warrant a Brigadier's command. You well know how greatly my expectations have been disappointed in relation to this command. I expected that the force would amount to something near what was authorized, that it would be supplied with the means enabling it to live, march and fight, that in point of numbers it would be respectable and form so large a part of the army as to enable it to assert its equal rights and privileges with the regular troops, and not be what an inferior militia force always will be, the tools and drudges of the regular troops. As regarded myself I did expect, too, that I would not be lower than second in command, and that if the fortune of war should dispose of the first, I might take my chance to fill his place. But all hopes of such an event have vanished, for altho' I am now second in command, another Brigadier has been sent for to Sackett's Harbor. In short, I have been brigadiered till I am quite satisfied.

Nothing but the shame of abandoning a measure, which under mistaken auspices I had engaged and made some progress in, would have induced me to take the field with a ragged, unprovided and undisciplined force. I have done with them all I could, and altho' I may not retire with much credit, I hope I shall not go home wholly disgraced.

I have just seen General Brown's report of the battle of Chippawa. Altho' he has been very civil to me personally by giving me credit for a quality which in the sense in which it is commonly used I am sure I do not possess, he has done great injustice to the Pennsylvania Volunteers and Indians, who fought as bravely and in proportion to their numbers did double the execution of any other troops that day. I participated in all their disgrace, and the only unpleasant feeling I have on the business of that day is that I rallied and led a scattered line, (formed to scour the woods and not to fight a regular force,) exhausted by the fatigue of pursuit a *second* time, against a compact line of British regular troops perfectly fresh, and this when we were more than half a mile in advance and unsupported by our regular troops, by which I lost several valuable officers. General Brown does not hesitate to acknowledge that on the night of the 25th the volunteers fought *at least* as well as the regulars.

Do not understand me as intending to cast a heavy censure on General Ripley for the retreat from Lundy's Lane. He is a very clever fellow, and besides having been in opinion opposed to General Brown's plan of operations, he on that night, I am told by him, received a positive order from General Brown at Chippawa to retire. Had I, however, been in his situation I should, without a moment's hesitation, have disobeyed the order, for he commanded the battle and was answerable for its issue, and ought not to have been dictated to by a wounded man four miles from the scene of action.

Second Sheet.

In the report of the battle of the 25th, the volunteers will probably be put down as one of the three brigades which were engaged, and as our number of killed, wounded and missing will, of course, be considerably less than that of other brigades, it will seem that we were cowardly and did not do our duty, when, in fact, the reverse is the case. Our brigade, as I stated before, is the servant of the army. 250 men were detached and acting under Colonel Swift across the river, one company was at Buffalo, part of company at Erie (Fort Erie,) and two companies during the battle were ordered to remain at Chippawa to protect the camp, so that in fact we carried less than 300 men into the field, and detachments were made again to send off prisoners. But in proportion to the numbers engaged we lost more than any other corps, and I believe, small as we were, we actually lost more officers killed than either of the other brigades. Our whole loss was 65. I mention this not to boast, but to show how unequally the policy observed towards volunteers bears upon them.

Major-General Brown to Governor D. D. Tompkins.

BUFFALO, 1st August, 1814.

SIR,—Will it not be possible for you to increase General Porter's command, and that promptly. I have found General Porter a brave and efficient officer. In the midst of the greatest danger I have found his mind cool and collected, and his judgment to be relied upon. These are rare qualifications, and therefore it is that I desire all the militia force may be continued under his command.

It does appear to me to be an object of great material importance to *this State* that the enemy should be driven out of the Peninsula, and a line drawn between him and his savage allies to extend from near York or Burlington if it cannot be pressed farther down. If you could by any means bring out a force of from three to four thousand militia to operate with my gallant little army, I do not doubt but that the object could be effected.

It is in vain for the people of this country to attempt to shrink from the war in which they are engaged: if they do not arm and exert themselves at a distance from their farms they will soon find the war brought to their firesides.

This State has suffered in reputation this war; its militia have done nothing, or but little, and that, too, after the State had been for a long time invaded.

Being resolved not to order my army out of Canada under existing circumstances without further instructions from the War Department, I have deemed it proper to call upon Major-General Hall for a thousand militia for the defence of the frontier. I hope you will approve the measure, but if you do I am not sure the force will be found unless stronger and more military measures are adopted than have hitherto been, as I find the inhabitants of this frontier more disposed to skulk from the danger which threatens them than to arm in defence of their country and her rights.

My wounds are very troublesome but not dangerous. I send you the enclosed statement of Dr. Bull for your information, but not for publication. The battle of the 25th, it is believed, will find but few parallels. More desperate fighting has rarely been known. I hope the nation will be satisfied by our conduct—we have endeavored to do our duty.

The official returns are not yet in, but I am informed that I have lost above sixty officers, killed and wounded, among which first, I fear, is my aid-de-camp, Captain Spencer.

Dr. Bull to ———

BUFFALO, 31st July, 1814.

In conversation with Major-General Brown, after dressing his wounds on the evening of the 25th, I understood from him that General Ripley was ordered to move early in morning of the following day to the scene of action of the day preceding for the purpose of burying the dead, securing all the trophies captured, and driving back the enemy should they appear. I did not doubt from the observations of other officers but such a movement would take place agreeably to the order. In consequence I rode to the battle ground about daylight without witnessing the presence of a single British officer or soldier. The dead had not been removed during the night, and such a scene of carnage I never beheld, particularly at Lundy's Lane, red coats and blue and grey were promiscuously intermingled, in many places three deep, and around the hill where the enemy's artillery was carried by Colonel Miller, the carcasses of 60 or 70 horses disfigured the scene. I went forward more than a mile beyond this point and saw no enemy.

E. W. BULL,
Hospital Surgeon, Army, U. S.

Col. James Miller to ———

(From the Adjutant-General's Report for New Hampshire, for 1868.)

FORT ERIE, July 28, 1814.

On the evening of the 25th instant, at the Falls of the Niagara, we met the enemy and had, I believe, one of the most desperately fought actions ever experienced in America. It continued for more than three hours stubbornly contested on both sides, when about ten o'clock at night we succeeded in driving them from their strong position. Our loss was severe in killed and wounded. I have lost from our regiment in killed, wounded and missing, one hundred and twenty-six. The enemy had got their artillery posted on a height in a very commanding position, where they could rake our columns in any part of the plain, and prevented their advancing. Maj. McRae, the chief engineer, told Gen. Brown he could do no good until that height was carried and those cannon taken or driven from their position. It was then evening, but moonlight. Gen. Brown turned to me and said: "Col. Miller, take your regiment and storm that work and take it." I had short of three hundred men with me, as my regiment had been much weakened by the numerous details made from it during the day. I, however, immediately obeyed the order. We could see all their slow matches and port-fires burning and ready. I did not know what side of the work was the most favorable of approach, but happened to hit upon a very favorable place notwithstanding. We advanced upon the mouths of their pieces of cannon. It happened there was an old rail fence on the side where we approached undiscovered by the enemy, with a small growth of shrubbery by the fence and within less than two rods of the cannon's mouth. I then very cautiously ordered my men to rest across the fence, take good aim, fire, and rush, which was done in style. Not one man at the cannons was left to put fire to them. We got into the centre of their park before they had time to oppose us. A British line was formed and lying in a strong position to protect their artillery. The moment we got to the centre they opened a most destructive fire on us, killed a great many and attempted to charge with their bayonets. We returned the fire so warmly they were compelled to stand. We fought hand to hand for some time, so close that the blaze of our guns crossed each other, but we compelled them to abandon their whole artillery, ammunition, wagons, and all, amounting to seven pieces of elegant brass cannon, one of which was a twenty-four pounder, with eight horses and harnesses, though some of the horses were killed. The British made two more attempts to charge us at close quarters, both of which we repulsed before I was reinforced, after which the First and Twenty-third Regiments came to my relief; and even after the British charged with their whole line three several times, and after getting within half pistol shot of us, were compelled to give way. I took with my regiment between thirty and forty prisoners while taking and defending the artillery. Lieut. Aaron Bigelow of my regiment was killed; Capt. Burbank and Lieut. Cilley badly wounded, a number of others slightly; Gen. Brown and his aide both dangerously wounded; Gen. Scott and his Brigade-Major, Lieut. Smith, both badly wounded; Gen. Ripley and his aide both shot through the hat; Maj. McFarland killed; Col. Brady badly wounded; Maj. McNeil badly wounded, so he must it is said lose his leg. It is unnecessary for me to enumerate a quarter of our loss, but we have very few officers left for duty. I now command a brigade; Gen. Ripley is Commander-in-chief. I am the only full Colonel, and we have but one Lieutenant-Colonel left to all the regular troops here. We expect reinforcements soon. But I forgot to tell you we were unfortunate about our artillery at last. After Generals Brown, Scott and others were wounded, we were ordered to return back to our camp about three miles, and preparations had not been made for taking off the cannon. It was impossible for me to defend it and make preparations for that too, and it was all left upon the ground except one beautiful brass six-pounder, which is made a present to my regiment in testimony of their distinguished gallantry.... We wounded Maj.-Gen. Drummond, took Maj.-Gen. Riall prisoner, with between thirty and forty other officers; how many non-commissioned officers and privates I have not yet learned, as they were sent hastily across the river, but a very considerable number."

From the Pittsfield (Mass.) Sun.
(Reprinted in Niles Register, Vol. 6, p. 413.)

Extract of a letter from Dr. E. L. Allen of the 21st Regiment to his brother in this town, dated Buffalo, 26th July, 1814:

"Last night was fought the most sanguinary action the annals of this country record. General Ripley by the blessing of heaven is safe; a musket shot perforated his hat just by the crown of his head without injury. The 20th, we invested Fort George, their shells and shot did little execution. 22nd, fell back to Queenston Heights, probably on account of the powerful reinforcements arriving from Kingston. 24th, fell back to Chippewa, which is two miles above the Falls. 25th, at noon the enemy sent 500 across the river to Lewiston and destroyed some baggage our sick had just left.

"In the afternoon the enemy advanced towards Chippewa with a powerful force. At six o'clock General Scott was ordered to advance with his brigade and beat them. He was soon reinforced by General Ripley's brigade; they met the enemy in great force below the Falls. They had selected their ground for the night, intending to attack our camp before daylight. The action began just before seven, and an uninterrupted stream of musketry continued till half-past eight, when there was some cessation, the British falling back. It soon began again with some artillery, which, with slight interruption, continued till half-past ten, when there was a charge, and a tremendous stream of fire closed the conflict. Both armies fought with a desperation bordering on madness; neither would yield the palm, but each retired a short distance wearied with fatigue. Such a constant and destructive fire was never before sustained by American troops without falling back.

"The enemy had collected their whole force in the peninsula and were reinforced by the troops from Lord Wellington's army, just landed from Kingston. For two hours the two hostile lines were within twenty yards of each other, and so frequently intermingled that often an officer would order an enemy's platoon. The moon shone bright, but part of our men being dressed like their Glengarian Regiment, caused the deception. They frequently charged, and as often were driven back. Our regiment, under Colonel Miller, was ordered to storm the British battery. We charged and took every piece of the enemy's cannon. We kept possession of the ground and cannon until twelve o'clock at night, when we fell back to camp, distant more than two miles. This was done to secure our camp, which might otherwise have been attacked in the rear. Our horses being most of them killed, and there being no ropes to the pieces, we got off but two or three. The men were so extremely fatigued they could not drag them. We lost one howitzer, the horses being on full gallop towards the enemy to attack them the riders were shot off and the horses ran through the enemy's line. We lost one piece of cannon, which was too much advanced, every man being shot that had charge of it but two. Several of our caissons were blown up by their rockets, which did some injury and deprived our cannon of ammunition. The lines were so near that cannon could not be used with advantage. This morning General Ripley marched out our whole force to the battle ground to bury our dead and secure what wounded were left. The enemy had gotten many who were badly wounded and left on the ground. He marched near their army, but neither were disposed to engage.

We took about 200 non-commissioned officers and privates

prisoners, and 21 officers, including Major-General Riall, who was wounded in the shoulder. They acknowledge Colonel Gordon of the 100th and many other British officers killed, their rank yet unknown. The enemy must have suffered very severely. Our loss is immense, but was not known when I left the army this morning.

Copy of a Letter from an Officer in the Army to his friend in Alexandria, dated Fort Erie, U. C., July 28.

(Niles' Register, Vol. 6, p. 414.)

On the 23rd I found myself so far recovered as to join the army at Queenston Heights, although that part of my foot which was fractured will never be of much service. On the 24th we retired to Chippewa, and on the 25th, at half-past 4 p. m., our first Brigade, commanded by General Scott, engaged the enemy's advance about 2½ miles from Chippewa. The main body of both armies soon supported the advances, and a tremendous battle was fought, lasting 5 hours and 23 minutes, mostly within half musket shot and sometimes within pistol shot, which ended in the enemy's total defeat, leaving 2 brass 24-pounders and 1 brass six-pounder in our possession. We kept the battle ground until midnight, when, having removed our wounded and part of our dead, we retired to Chippewa, taking with us his brass 6-pounder. We were unable to bring off his two 24-pounders from a want of horses, almost all ours being killed, and our pieces were generally taken off with bricoles. The enemy's loss in killed, wounded and prisoners, must be about 12 or 1300. Of prisoners we have taken Major-General Riall, Gen. Drummond's aide-de-camp, 19 officers and 350 or 400 men. His force engaged was, by their own account, about 4,500 regulars, besides his Indians, &c., commanded by Lieut.-Gen. Drummond and Maj.-Gen. Riall. We had not an Indian engaged, and our force did not exceed twenty-eight hundred men. Our loss is severe. Generals Brown and Scott, and an aide of each, with several field officers, are wounded. Several other officers are killed, among whom was my captain, (Ritchie.) He was wounded in the body, but refused to quit his piece, when a cannon shot took most of his head off. All the men at his piece were killed or wounded. He was brother to the editor of the *Richmond Enquirer*, and formerly lived in Alexandria.

Extract of a Letter from an Officer to the Editor of the Buffalo Gazette, July 31, 1814.

(Niles' Register, Vol. 6, p. 414.)

I have this moment seen your extra of July 28, giving an account of the battle at Bridgewater, in which Captain Towson's company of artillery is the only one mentioned.

It is due to Major Hindman's battalion to state that he advanced with the First Brigade. When the action commenced he returned to camp and brought up Captains Biddle's and Ritchie's companies to its support. It is to be regretted that the enemy's position did not permit our artillery to be as destructive as his, but any credit it may deserve should be shared by the companies mentioned.

Captain Ritchie was killed and Captain Biddle was twice wounded.

The (Phila.) Democratic Press has the Following Letter from Buffalo, dated July 29.

"Our killed were interred in one grave, and a sermon preached over them by the Rev. David Jones, formerly chaplain to General Wayne's army. The artillery which was taken from the enemy was left behind in consequence of the horses being mostly killed. Lieut. Gen. Drummond, as well as Maj.-Gen. Riall, had surrendered, but it being 9 o'clock, and the enemy having possession of our watchword, the Lieut.-Gen. escaped.

Another from Fort Erie, dated August 1, Informs:

"Our army still remains at this place, and are busily employed in entrenching. The enemy's advanced parties are daily skirmishing with our pickets and foraging parties. Nothing of material consequence has as yet occurred. We have just received a reinforcement of about two hundred riflemen from Sackett's harbor. I am happy to find that our loss on the 25th ult. was not so great as at first apprehended. The battle being fought at night, many of men scattered and secreted themselves in the woods, and have not until within a day or two all been collected.

Extract of a Letter Dated Buffalo, August 3, 11 a. m.

"The whole of the enemy's forces have moved up within about one mile of our army. This morning at daylight he crossed over about 500 men just below Black Rock: his object was, no doubt, to attack Buffalo and destroy our stores, etc. He was gallantly met by 200 riflemen and a party of volunteers under Major Morgan.

After contending nearly five hours, he recrossed the Niagara. The loss or gain by either party was not great. We lost two or three men killed and several wounded. Capt. Hamilton is supposed to be mortally wounded.

"We took several prisoners. The enemy's loss is much greater than ours. The armies are still skirmishing."

From Niles' Register, Baltimore, Aug. 13. Vol. 6, p. 415.

Gen. Brown has made a demand on Maj.-Gen. Hall for 1,000 militia. Gen. Hall has issued his orders for an immediate draft of that number.

☞ Brown's army was hourly receiving reinforcements. Brig.-Gen. Gaines from Sackett's Harbor, an officer highly spoken of, arrived at Buffalo about the 4th inst., and is supposed to have taken the command at Fort Erie, which by great exertion has been made a strong place. The corps of volunteers under Colonel Swift, late at Lewiston, had crossed and joined the army, as well as considerable bodies of regulars and militia. Twenty wagons laden with bomb shells passed through Geneva for the frontier from the 1st to the 3d inst. Capt. Kennedy with three of our vessels is at Fort Erie ready to co-operate as occasion may require.

From the Vermont Historical Collections. Vol. VI, Page 510.

(From the Northern Sentinel, August 19th, 1814.)

Extract of a letter from an officer of the 11th Regiment to his friend in Burlington, Vt., dated Buffalo, 2nd August, 1814. (Probably written by Lieut. F. A. Sawyer.)

"The late engagement was probably the most sanguinary ever fought on this continent. We engaged the enemy the 25th July, at 6 p. m., near the Falls of Niagara, and continued the fight till half-past 11 at night, when by very inferior numbers the enemy was compelled to retire, leaving us in quiet possession of the field of battle.

The First Brigade, as usual, bore the brunt of the action. We maintained our ground for an hour and a half against the whole forces of the enemy, which were four times our number, before we were supported by a solitary individual of Gens. Ripley's and Porter's brigades. They, however, joined in time to prevent us from being entirely cut up, and contributed a little in giving the enemy a hearty drubbing.

On leaving camp no one anticipated a general engagement. It was the impression that the brigade was ordered out to disperse 400 or 500, as it was supposed, of the enemy's militia and Indians, who were hanging on the rear for the purpose of annoying our piquets and kidnapping those who might be led by curiosity to visit the Falls. As we advanced a few of the enemy would form and then retire. This manœuvre was continued until we had advanced within half musket shot of the enemy's lines, when the battle commenced. The enemy's position was a most excellent one. Their line of infantry was posted behind a fence, which formed a semi-circle and encompassed a field which our troops were compelled to accept of if they made the attack. Their flanks were protected by woods filled with militia and Indians, and in their rear, at a desirable distance, was a height on which their artillery was planted. Nature could not have formed a more advantageous position. Under these disadvantages our troops attacked them. The 9th and 25th were ordered to attack their flanks, while the 11th and 22nd met their front. We endeavored to form a line in the face and eyes of all their infantry and artillery, but they opened such a deadly and destructive fire upon us that we were compelled to retire a few paces and form in the skirts of a wood, and before we opened upon them more than two-thirds of the two regiments were cut down. However, we then maintained our ground until a reinforcement joined us, when we advanced and drove the enemy in every direction. Col. Miller with his regiment charged and took their artillery, consisting of nine pieces, but they repossessed themselves (on the next morning, when our army had left the field,) of all but two brass six-pounders. For an hour the two lines were within four rods of each other, firing with as much deliberation as if it had been a sham fight, and now and then for a change the point of the bayonet was used. Here, for the first time, I witnessed a charge. It did not prove destructive enough. Towards the close of the action, as there was hardly a company remaining of our regiment and but one man in my platoon, I volunteered in the 9th, and was assigned to Capt. Hull's company. He was killed in the last charge we made upon the enemy. Capt. Pentland and two or three subalterns were also wounded. The latter part of the action was most severe. Gens. Brown and Scott remained untouched, as well as the greater part of the field officers, until the action was nearly at an end. This part of the action proved more destructive to the enemy than to us, as our men did much better execution when in close contact with them. Our fire at length proved so destructive that the enemy's bugle sounded the retreat for the last time, and our troops were left in undisturbed possession of the heights. After having taken off all our own and some of the enemy's wounded, we were ordered to camp. It is a circumstance much to be regretted that our troops did not keep possession of the field until next morning, as it is believed it might have been effected without much hazard on our part, and then the enemy would not have had the shadow of a claim to the victory, for never was an enemy more completely beaten than in this action, nor never was one gained by harder knocks. We may date all mishaps from the time our beloved General (Scott) was wounded. None could fight more gallantly than he. He had three horses shot under him. Gen. Brown was brave, even to imprudence. He and Gen. Scott were continually in front of the line encouraging the men, both by example and precept. It would be impossible to give you an account of the killed and wounded on their side, if it was proper. Neither can I guess at it, though I am a Yankee. Of our regiment is Capt. Goodrich killed; Capt. Bliss, Lieuts. Hall, Cooper, Webster and Stephenson, and Ensigns Thompson and Bradford wounded. But two captains of our regiment were in the action. Capt. Weeks, with five or six other officers of the regiment, were at Buffalo sick. Our company suffered more severely than any other one. At the commencement of the action it was fifty strong, and next morning but thirteen could be mustered for duty. Gen. Drummond joined the enemy but an hour previous to the action, with 1,400 men. They had 800 or 1,000 more in the field than we did.

From the Baltimore Federal Gazette.
(Issue of 6th August, 1814.)

Extract from a letter from J. B. Varnum to Abraham Bradley, dated at Buffalo, 27th July, 1814:

"Our army behaved most gallantly, fought to desperation, but the enemy was too numerous for them. Our First Brigade was almost annihilated; but one field officer escaped death or severe wounds. It is impossible to say what is the full extent of our loss. A small proportion of our wounded fell into the hands of the enemy besides, I fear, some prisoners. The enemy was so severely cut to pieces that they did not pursue our army.

Lieut. MacEwen to His Wife.
(From A. Brymner's "Excerpts.")

FALLS OF NIAGARA, 29th July, 1814.

I came here yesterday on my way to Fort Erie, where the enemy is determined to make a stand. They have done a great deal of harm in this part, and among the sufferers is poor Muirhead, who has been burnt out of his house—Street's Mills and many more.

From Niles' Register, 27th August, 1814.

RICHMOND, August 11.

A letter from Major Hindman of the United States Artillery, after giving an account of the gallant conduct of Captain Ritchie of that corps, who was killed in the battle of the 25th, says: "The British General, Riall, our prisoner, has written for his (Captain R.'s) word and promises that I shall return it to his friends."

Colonel Hercules Scott, 103d Regt., to His Sister.

FALLS OF NIAGARA, 30th July, 1814.

MY DEAR HELEN,—I am much to blame in thus long having delayed replying to your several letters which I have from time to time received, but for a long time past I have been so much employed in one way or other I have not had a moment to myself. For nearly a month past I have been lying in the woods: the enemy having entered this province in force, all the troops in the neighborhood have taken the field. On the 5th of this month a severe action was fought within about 5 miles of this place, wherein our troops were defeated with a heavy loss. In the first action I was not engaged, but we had another severe one on the 25th, when we had rather the advantage. Thank God, I escaped with only the loss of one horse shot under me. We have been following the enemy and hope to drive them out of the country. I wish you were beside me just now for 10 minutes just to see the grandest falls in the world. No description that I have ever seen comes up in any degree to the original. * * * * *

Believe me, yours ever affectionately,

H. SCOTT.

Lieut. Wm. McEwen, Royal Scots, to Mrs. McEwen.

STREET'S CREEK, 31st July.

This place from the quarters we occupied yesterday is one continuous ruin. We have not seen a soul all the way we have come. We are making every preparation to move towards Fort Erie, where the enemy is in considerable force waiting for one more trial. If once more defeated here, they will be quiet for the remainder of the summer.

From Niles' Register, 27th August, 1814.

Extract from a letter from General Scott, dated Williamsville, August 2d, 1814: "I am doing pretty well under my wounds. That in the shoulder (musket ball through the point of the left shoulder and clavicle) gives me great pain. I hope, however, [to] recover the use of my arm, which is at present helpless. T[he] wound was received just at the close of the action."

Extract from a Letter from Sailing Master J. E. McDonald [to] Capt. Kennedy, U. S. Navy.

ERIE, Pa., July 27, 1814.

SIR,—Agreeably to your instructions, I sailed on the 23d ins[t.] on board the schooner *Diligence* with sixteen volunteers, which with the six seamen from the *Lady Prevost*, made a party of 2[4] men, for Long Point. At daylight on the morning of the 25th [I] landed, with 18 men. We ascended a high and steep bank and advanced about half a mile into the country to Charlotteville, [a] small village. At this place the enemy had commenced a very large block house. We broke open the doors of an inn and th[e] jail and seized the jailor, from whom I was in hopes I should b[e] able to collect the information wanted. At this moment an alarm gun was fired by the enemy, which was answered by several others We then retired with the jailor to the boat. When distant from the shore about half a mile, nearly 300 of the enemy had collected on the bank, which number seemed constantly increasing while w[e] were in sight.

Hon. James Fisk to the Secretary of War.

BARRE, Vt., 27th June, 1814.

SIR,—I learn from unquestionable authority that droves o[f] cattle are continually passing from the northern parts of this State into Canada to the British. This business is principally carried o[n] in that part of this State which lies east of Lake Memphramago[g] and west of the Connecticut river, and can only be checked by a[n] armed force—probably one company of horse might be sufficient Whether the object be worthy of attention you must judge.

Major-General Izard to the Secretary of War.
(Extract.)

CAMP NEAR PLATTSBURG, July 31, 1814.

The letter from Mr. Fisk of Vermont only confirms a fac[t] which is not only disgraceful to our countrymen but seriously detri mental to the public interest. From the St. Lawrence to the ocea[n] an open disregard prevails for the laws prohibiting intercourse with the enemy. The road to St. Regis is covered with droves of cattl[e] and the river with rafts destined for the enemy. The revenu[e] officers see these things but acknowledge their inability to put a stop to such outrageous proceedings. On the eastern side of Lake Champlain the high roads are found insufficient for the supplies of cattle which are pouring into Canada. Like herds of buffaloes, they press through the forest making paths for themselves. The collectors of Plattsburg and Burlington have applied to me for assistance. I have offered to supply them with what men and means they might require. Plans have been proposed and acceded to. But when the time of execution arrives the civil officers decline acting. Nothing but a *cordon* of troops from the French Mills to Lake Memphramagog could effectually check the evil. Were it not for these supplies the British forces in Canada would soon be suffering from famine, or their government be subjected to immense expense for their maintenance.

(From "Official Correspondence with the Department of War relative to the military operations of the American army under the command of Major-General Izard on the Northern frontier of the United States in the years 1814 and 1815."

PHILADELPHIA, 1816.)

Lt.-Gen. Drummond to Sir Geo. Prevost.

HEADQUARTERS, NIAGARA FALLS, 31st July, 1814.

SIR,—I have the honor to acknowledge the receipt of Your Excellency's letter (duplicate) of the 20th, and your private communication of the 23rd, the latter stating Your Excellency's view in sending Major Coore to my headquarters.

In reply to the latter I beg briefly to state that in this quarter the great object at present is the defeat and expulsion of the enemy's force which has taken post at Fort Erie, and to this object my sole attention must be given. I am sanguine that with the force I am collecting it will not be found difficult of attainment. I have in the meantime been under the necessity of considerably reducing the garrisons of the forts. Defended, however, by the 89th and 100th Regts., 4 companies of the 41st and 50 marines, they are secure against a *coup de main*. Moreover, if the enemy's squadron should even make its appearance without a co-operating army, and ignorant of the state of their garrisons, I much doubt whether any force that might be embarked on board it would at once proceed to attack the forts. I shall, of course, lose no time in reinforcing those garrisons the moment my present object is accomplished, and if I am fortunate in my operations at Fort Erie this whole frontier may be considered as secure, and I shall immediately direct my attention to Burlington and York. With regard to Kingston, I beg permission most earnestly to recommend to Your Excellency to concentrate a very large force at that place, not alone for the protection of that most important depot, but the moment the squadron is ready to sail to strike that blow which can alone extinguish the war in this province.

Maj.-Gen. Conran having joined this division, it will move forward towards the enemy to-morrow.

Sir G. Drummond to Sir Geo. Prevost.

HEADQUARTERS, CAMP BEFORE
FORT ERIE, 4th Aug., 1814.

SIR,—I have the honor to acquaint Your Excellency that on Monday the 1st I moved my headquarters to Palmer's, (halfway betwixt Chippawa and Fort Erie,) and on the following morning the troops being closed up in the order directed in the accompanying District General Order, I took up a position on the heights opposite to Black Rock, the enemy retiring his picquets on the approach of our advanced guards.

Previous to the advance of the brigades, I gave the instructions of which I enclose a copy, to Maj.-General Conran for the crossing of a detachment of 600 men to the right bank of the river for the purpose of capturing or destroying the enemy's depots at Buffalo and Black Rock. Had this service been effected, as I sanguinely expected, the enemy's force shut up in Fort Erie would have been compelled by want of provisions either to come out and fight or to surrender it. I enclose Lt.-Col. Tucker's report, on which I do not think it necessary to offer any other observation than that the disembarkation was effected without the smallest opposition: the force of the enemy which was distinctly seen from the heights on this side the river did not exceed 150 or 200 men, chiefly militia and Indians. The officers, I am happy to find, appear to have done their duty.

The enemy having been put on his guard by this movement made against Black Rock, has in consequence increased his force at that place and Buffalo. Whatever further movement I may be inclined to make on the right bank must be made in considerable force.

On the afternoon of yesterday I advanced the Light Brigade under cover of the wood as close as possible to the fort and position, of which I obtained a very tolerable reconnoissance. In addition to a breastwork and intrenchment by which the fort has been connected with Snake Hill, the enemy has continued the north-eastern demi-bastion of the fort down to the lake and mounted a considerable number of heavy guns along the whole face. Snake Hill has also been fortified and armed with heavy guns, and the wood round the whole position *abbatied*. Three armed schooners are anchored off the place, so as to flank by their fire the roads both above and below.

On mature consideration therefore, I have determined not to assault the position until I have made some impression by guns of proper battery calibre, which I have sent for from Fort George. The fire of the long 24-pdrs. (iron) which I brought up with the troops, and which was directed during the reconnoissance of yesterday against the enemy's schooners and the fort, convinced me that with the addition of those I have ordered up, viz.: a long 18-pdr., an 8-inch mortar and a 24-pdr. carronade, I shall be able to compel the force shut up in Fort Erie to surrender, or attempt a sortie which can only terminate in his defeat.

Should a favorable opportunity occur before my batteries are established of attacking the place in any other manner, I shall avail myself of it.

I have this morning detached an officer of the Quartermaster-General's Department with a party of dragoons and a few mounted men of the Glengarry Light Infantry by the road leading upon Fort Erie by Bird's and Tyce Horn's, along the lake shore, to make an accurate reconnoissance of the enemy's position.

Should the report be favorable to the enterprise I may probably be induced to assault the place at two points after I am joined by the right wing of the Regt. DeWatteville, for which the schooners have been sent to York, and I am in hourly expectation of hearing of their arrival.

Capt. Dobbs, R. N., is with me with a party of about 30 seamen, and has already been of very essential service to the troops, particularly in the enterprise against Black Rock yesterday.

I have been duly honored with Your Excellency's letter of the 25th ulto. The force recapitulated by Your Excellency as that of the Right and Centre Divisions has a very formidable appearance on paper. I regret, however, to be obliged to observe that the inefficient state and composition of many of the regiments are such as to detract greatly from the confidence which their numbers might otherwise inspire. It is my intention to write, when I have leisure, more fully on this subject, and also, as soon as circumstances will permit, to send down to Kingston several of the corps on this frontier, which are entirely unfit for service in the field.

I transmit by this opportunity a letter which I had intended to have forwarded some days ago by Major Coore. But that officer having informed me that he has Your Excellency's confidential instructions to remain here for some time, I have acceded to his wishes to be permitted to do so.

(Secret.)

HEADQUARTERS, 2nd Aug., 1814.

SIR,—I am directed by Lieut.-Gen. Drummond to desire that you will place the following force under the command of Lt.-Col. Tucker, who must be instructed to hold it in readiness to embark this evening in batteaux for the purpose of passing over and operating on the right bank of the river, viz:

Rank and File.

4 Battn. Companies, 41st Regt.........	240 ⎫ Lt.-Col. Evans.
2 Flank " " "	140 ⎭
	380
Light Company, 89th Regt..........	63 ⎫
" " 100th Regt.........	52 ⎬ Lt.-Col. Drummond.
Flank Companies, 104th Regt.........	95 ⎭
	210
1 subaltern, a steady sergeant and 10 Arty........................	10
Total......................	600

6 or 8 guard rockets and one rocketeer.

The detachment of artillery to take with it a few 6-pound cartridges, port-fires and slow match, a smith with a sledge hammer, and axes with spikes and everything necessary for effecting the destruction of ordnance, and, (if necessary,) the burning of buildings, stores, and vessels.

This force will embark at 10 o'clock, as near to Frenchman's Creek as may be considered prudent. It is desirable to land it as near the foot of Squaw Island as possible. Proper pilots will be put into the boats, and guides will be sent to conduct the column, which is to proceed with all possible silence and secrecy by the right bank of Conguichity Creek to gain the road leading upon the 11 Mile Creek from Buffalo, which place is to be the first attacked and destroyed, and the boats and craft (if any) seized; this (rapidly) effected, the troops are to march upon Black Rock, attack whatever force the enemy may have there and get possession of his guns should he have any. Lt.-Col. Tucker will decide at the moment as to the expediency of spiking, dismounting, or destroying their guns, or manning them and serving them against the enemy's position or corps or on the schooners which are anchored on his right flank and which Capt. Dobbs of the Royal Navy with a party of seaman under his command will make an attempt to gain. It is desirable that Lt.-Col. Tucker should time his march so as to arrive at Buffalo an hour before day in order, after effecting his object at that place, to reach Black Rock just as the day begins to break, at which moment the whole of the division on the left bank will move forward towards Fort Erie for the purpose of favoring Lt.-Col. Tucker's operations against Black Rock by preventing the enemy from detaching troops to that bank. The destruction of the enemy's depot of provisions and stores at Buffalo is the first object, the capture of the guns and dispersion or capture of his troops at Black Rock, should he have either at that place, the second and scarcely less important. By this blow, if effected, and particularly if his stores and provisions fall into our hands, the enemy's force on this side will not only be reduced to the necessity of fighting under desperate circumstances or surrendering unconditionally, but it may lead immediately to the re-establishment of our naval ascendancy on Lake Erie.

The foregoing outline for Lieut.-Col. Tucker's operations is made upon the supposition that his force is passed undiscovered, and at least that his landing is effected without opposition. Should this not be the case, however, and should Lt.-Col. Tucker find himself not only discovered but opposed on approaching the shore, or attacked when landing, it may then become necessary for the Lieut.-Colonel to change his plan of operations by beginning with Black Rock, and afterwards, (if necessary,) proceeding to execute the other objects of the service. Lt.-Col. Tucker will exercise his discretion in this as in every other contingency that may arise and which may not have been contemplated in the proceeding memorandum.

The next point to be considered is the disposal of the batteaux after the troops are landed. The Lieut.-General conceives that they cannot be better disposed of than by taking a station at Strawberry Island or the lower end of Squaw Island, there to await the return of the troops. Capt. Dobbs will avail himself of any favorable opportunity which may offer of carrying into effect the enterprize against any of the enemy's schooners.

Lt.-Col. Nichol, Quartermaster-General of Militia, will accompany Lt.-Col. Tucker, who will not fail to derive the greatest benefit from his valuable local knowledge and his zeal and ability.

J. HARVEY,
Lt.-Col., D. A. G.

To Maj.-Gen. Conran.

Lt.-Col. Tucker to Maj.-Gen. Conran.

BIVOUAC NEAR FERRY HOUSE, Aug. 4th, 1814.

SIR,—I am sorry to report to you that the force entrusted to my command for purposes stated in the secret instructions with which you did me the honor to furnish me on the evening of the 2nd inst. has failed in the attempt to accomplish the important and very desirable object contemplated by Lieut.-General Drummond, owing to the enemy having destroyed the bridge over Conguichity Creek prior to our arrival at that point and there being no possibility of fording it. I lament to add that in exploring our situation we have sustained a loss of one sergeant and 11 rank and file killed, 17 wounded, and five missing.

I should have been less chagrined at our miscarriage could I consistently, with matter of fact, commend the conduct of the soldiers under my command. Unfortunately it becomes a painful but very necessary duty to apprise you that the men displayed an unpardonable degree of unsteadiness, without possessing one solitary excuse to justify this want of discipline. The officers were perfectly unaware of the sudden impulse of panic which threw their men into a tremendous confusion; their exertions and spirit, however, succeeded in re-forming our column, and I am happy to express my approbation of their conduct.

Lieut.-Col. Drummond commanded my advance and cheerfully afforded every assistance that I could wish or expect from an officer of zeal and judgment, nor am I less indebted to Lt.-Col. Evans, 41st Regt., who had charge of the reserve. These officers perfectly concurred with me in opinion that the destruction of the bridge, the position of the enemy, and the want of a proper guide to conduct us through an intricate wood, amply justified my withdrawing my force in the best possible manner, the wood being occupied partially by the enemy, who was evidently collecting a large force to retain the command of it, and who occupied two small redoubts on the left bank of the creek, which were so situated as to obstruct my advance by a footpath on the right bank, had one been discovered or pointed out to me.

I have the honor to be, &c..

JOHN GOULSTON PRICE TUCKER.

Return of killed, wounded and missing of the 2d *demi* of the Light or Reserve Brigade and 41st Regiment, under the command of Lieut.-Colonel Tucker, in an action on the 3d August, 1814:

41st Companies.—Killed—6 rank and file. Wounded—9 rank and file.

89th do.—None.

100th do.—Wounded—3 rank and file.

104th do.—Killed—1 sergeant, 5 rank and file. Wounded—1 rank and file. Missing—4 rank and file.

41st Regiment.—Wounded—4 rank and file.

Major Morgan to Maj.-Gen. Brown.

FORT ERIE, August 5th, 1814.

SIR,—Having been stationed with the 1st Battalion of the 1st Regiment of riflemen at Black Rock, on the evening of the 22nd instant, I observed the British army moving up the river on the opposite shore, and suspecting they might make a feint on Fort Erie with an intention of a real attack on the Buffalo side, I immediately moved and took up a position on the upper side of Conjocta Creek, and that night threw up a battery of some logs which I found on the ground and had them torn away. About 2 o'clock the next morning my pickets from below gave me information of the landing of 9 boats full of troops, half a mile below. I immediately got my men (240 in number) to their quarters, and patiently awaited their approach. At a quarter past 4 they advanced upon us and commenced the attack, sending a party before to repair the bridge under cover of their fire. When they had got at good rifle distance I opened a heavy fire on them, which laid a number of them on the ground and compelled them to retire. They then formed in the skirt of the woods and kept up the fire at long shot, continually reinforcing from the Canada shore, until they had 22 boat loads, and then attempted to flank us by sending a large body up the creek to ford it, when I detached Lieutenants Ryan, Smith and Armstrong with about 60 men to oppose their left wing, where they were again repulsed with considerable loss, after which they appeared disposed to give up their object and retreated by throwing six boat loads of troops on Squaw Island, which enfiladed the creek and prevented me from harassing their rear.

Their superior numbers enabled them to take their killed and wounded off the field, which we plainly saw, and observed they suffered severely. We found some of their dead thrown into the river and covered with logs and stones, and some on the field. We also collected a number of muskets and accoutrements, with clothing that appeared to have been torn to bind their wounds. We took six prisoners, who stated the British force opposed to us to consist of from 12 to 1500 men, commanded by Lieutenant-Col Tucker of the 41st Regiment. They also state that their object was to recapture General Riall with other British prisoners, and destroy the stores deposited at Buffalo. The action continued about two hours and a half. I am happy to state they were completely foiled in their attempts.

Our loss is trifling compared with theirs. We had two killed and eight wounded. I am sorry to inform you that Captain Hamilton, Lieutenants Wadsworth and McIntosh are among the latter. Their gallantry in exposing themselves to encourage their men, I think, entitles them to the notice of their country. My whole command behaved in a manner that merited my warmest approbation, and in justice to them I cannot avoid mentioning the names of the officers, which are as follows:—Captain Hamilton, Lieutenants Wadsworth, Ryan, Calhoun, McIntosh, Arnold, Shortridge, McFarland, Tipton, Armstrong, Smith, Cobbs, Davidson and Austin, with Ensign Page. If, sir, you believe we have done our duty we shall feel highly gratified.

I am, sir, &c.,
L. MORGAN,
Major 1st Rifle Regiment.

Major-General Brown.

Brigadier-Gen. Gaines to the Secretary of War.

HEADQUARTERS, FORT ERIE,
UPPER CANADA, Aug. 7th, 1814.

SIR,—I arrived at this post on the 4th instant and assumed the command. The army is in good spirits and more healthy than I could have expected.

The British army under Lieutenant-General Drummond is strongly posted opposite to Black Rock, two miles east of the fort; a skirt of thick wood separates us. I yesterday endeavored to draw him out to see and try his strength: for this purpose I sent the rifle corps through the intervening woods with orders to amuse the enemy's light troops until his strong column should get in motion, and then to retire slowly to the plain this side the woods, where I had a strong line posted in readiness to receive the enemy. Our riflemen met and drove the enemy's light troops into their lines, where they remained, although the riflemen kept the woods near two hours and until they were ordered in. They returned without being able to draw any part of the enemy's force after them.

Major Morgan reports that his officers and men acted with their usual gallantry. The enemy left 11 dead and three prisoners in our hands, and I am informed by two persons just from the

British camp that their loss was much more considerable; among their killed were five Indians. We lost five killed and three or four wounded.

General Drummond's force, from the best information we are able to collect from deserters and others, amounts to upwards 4,000, principally regulars. De Watteville's regiment has joined since the battle of the 25th ultimo, together with two or three companies of the Glengarry corps, making a total joined since the 5th of about 1,200.

August 11th, 1814.

The enemy's position remains unchanged. They have constructed two batteries with two embrasures each, and have erected a wooden breastwork 1200 to 1400 yards in our rear. In examining their works yesterday, Captain Birdsall of the 4th Rifle Regiment, with a detachment of the 1st and his company, amounting in the whole to 160 men, beat in two of their strong pickets with a loss on their part of 10 killed. Captain Birdsall had one killed and three wounded. General Drummond was much disappointed and chagrined at the failure of the enterprise of the 3rd instant against Buffalo, our riflemen having opposed and beaten him. Colonel Tucker, it seems, has been reprimanded in General Orders.

I have, &c.,

EDMUND P. GAINES.

To the Secretary of War.

From Niles' Register, Vol. 6, P. 428.

August 20th, 1814.

Brig.-Gen. Gaines arrived at Fort Erie on the 5th. Some riflemen and other detached parties had gone over. Fort Erie is strong, and our men are full of spirits and confidence. We have no official particulars of the great battle; the account has possibly gone to the enemy with the post-rider from Buffalo. One private letter says the cannon we took in that affair were rolled into the Niagara.

The enemy having been disappointed in gaining Buffalo, made a movement on our position at Fort Erie. They opened a fire on the fort from a large piece of artillery placed on the point about a mile below, which was answered from the fort and a schooner in the harbor. The enemy attacked our picquets with a large force, and marched into the open ground in the rear of the fort, and commenced a heavy fire of musketry, which was warmly returned, and a brisk discharge from several pieces of artillery soon compelled him to retreat in great confusion, leaving a number of his men on the field as the price of his temerity. The actual loss of the enemy we have not ascertained. We had a few wounded.

Sir G. Drummond to Sir Geo. Prevost.

CAMP BEFORE FORT ERIE, 8th Aug., 1814.

SIR,—Immediately after the dispatch of the Deputy-Adjutant-General's letter to Colonel Baynes, respecting the unfortunate accident which Maj.-Gen. Conran met with, and the appearance of the enemy's fleet off Niagara, a sharp affair of outposts took place, the enemy having thrown the whole of his riflemen into the woods in front of his position for the purpose of driving away the Indians, the latter having retired precipitately on the advance of the rifles, some of our most advanced picquets also fell back. On being supported, however, by the Glengarry Light Infantry in the first instance, and subsequently by the reserve, the enemy was driven back and our advanced posts quickly re-occupied. I enclose a return of casualties on this occasion.

During this operation the enemy's schooners cannonaded our position, and one of his 32-pdr. shot having struck close to myself and the Deputy-Adjutant-General, I am sorry to say Lt.-Col. Harvey received a severe wound from one of the splinters, which will, I fear, deprive him of the use of one of his eyes for a few days.

In consequence of the very exposed situation in which we have been compelled from the nature of the ground to place our breaching battery, of which the accompanying sketch will give Your Excellency some idea. I felt convinced that it would be risquing the safety of the guns to arm the battery until a traverse had been thrown up in the front and an *abbattis* on the flanks, to protect it against a sortie, which the enemy would otherwise have the opportunity of making against it with his whole force. The engineer and an officer of the Quartermaster-General's department have accordingly been employed on it, and I am in hopes that by this night the battery will be in a state of sufficient security to admit my placing the guns in it. Your Excellency will perceive, however, by a glance at the sketch, that from the position of the enemy's schooners on its flank and the battery at Black Rock in its rear, a traverse in both these directions is also necessary, for although the enemy has not as yet shewn any guns at Black Rock we have no reason to believe he will refrain from availing himself of that position.

I hope to be able to open this battery to-morrow morning, and if a good effect is produced and no unfavorable circumstances occur,

I shall probably risque an assault upon the place on the following morning, the 10th. My present idea is to make the principal attack with the 2nd Brigade, consisting of the King's and De Watteville's Regts., under Lt.-Col. Fischer, upon the right of the enemy's position by the lake road, on which side I have hitherto carefully refrained from making any demonstration, and have reason to believe that the whole of the enemy's attention has been drawn to his left. If Lt.-Col. Fischer succeeds in gaining possession of Snake Hill I cannot doubt of our success; but Your Excellency may be assured that I shall well weigh the risque and consequences of failure against the chances of success before I commit this division of the troops by an attempt which, considering the strength of the enemy's position and the number of men and guns by which it is defended, must certainly be considered as one of great hazard.

I enclose Your Excellency the latest report from Lt.-Col. Warburton, which is dated at 4 o'clock this morning, at which time the enemy's fleet was standing down the lake without having attempted anything against the forts or vessels in the river. I regret to find that His Majesty's schooner *Magnet*, which had not been able to enter the river Niagara on the appearance of the enemy's squadron and which had in consequence been run ashore at the 10 Mile Creek, has been burnt by her commander. To me this appears to have been an act of unpardonable precipitation, Lt.-Col. Warburton having moved a field-piece and troops to her support. But I am not yet in possession of the whole of the circumstances; however, I trust and believe that the whole of her stores, &c., have been landed and saved.

I omitted to mention, I believe, to Your Excellencey, that on the first appearance of the enemy's fleet I ordered Col. Grant to detach one wing of his regiment to Burlington, remaining with the other himself at York, by which means the security of both places has been effectually provided for.

With a view to the attack contemplated above, I have moved up the remainder of De Watteville's regiment from the forts, and sent the battalion companies of the 41st to replace them.

The troops have hitherto supported the privations and hardships of this severe service with great constancy and cheerfulness, and I am happy to say very few desertions have taken place. Those from the enemy to us have been numerous, and, what is remarkable, three of our deserters serving in the enemy's rifle corps have just come in. I have pardoned these men. They state a circumstance which I have strong reason for believing to be a fact, viz: That in the night action of the 25th ulto., their boasted 1st Brigade laid down their arms and called out that they had surrendered. This being believed by us to be a *ruse de guerre* was not attended to, our fire resumed and the enemy compelled to save themselves by flight.

P. S.—I have considered it necessary to order the 6th Regt. to this frontier.

Commodore Chauncey to the Secretary of the Navy.

U. S. S. *Superior*, OFF KINGSTON,
August 10, 1814.

SIR,—Great anxiety of mind and severe bodily exertions have at length broken down the best constitution, and subjected me to a violent fever that confined me for 18 days. This misfortune was no more to be foreseen than prevented, but was particularly severe at the moment it happened, as it induced a delay of five or six days in the sailing of the fleet.

In the early part of July I expected that the fleet would be made ready by the 10th or 15th, but many of the mechanics were taken sick, and among them the blockmakers and blacksmiths, so that the *Mohawk* could not be furnished with blocks and iron work for her gun and spar decks before the 24th or 25th ult., when she was reported by Capt. Jones. As considerable anxiety was manifested by the public to have the fleet on the lake, I should have asked Capt. Jones to have taken charge of it, but I was then recovering my health and was confident I should be able in three or four days to go on board myself. There was an additional reason for submitting to this delay in the difficulty I found in making the changes of commanders, neither of them being willing to be separated from his officers and men, a change of crews through the fleet being inadmissible.

In the afternoon of the 31st July, I was taken on board, but it was calm, and I did not sail before the next morning. To satisfy at once whatever expectations the public had been led to entertain of the sufficiency of the squadron to take and maintain the ascendency on this lake, and at the same time to expose the falsity of promises the fulfilment of which had been rested on our appearance at the head of the lake, I got under way at 4 o'clock in the morning of the 1st inst. and steered for the mouth of the Niagara. Owing to light winds, I did not arrive there before the 5th. There we intercepted one of the enemy's brigs running from York to Niagara with troops, and drove her ashore about six miles to the westward of Fort George. I ordered the *Sylph* in to anchor as near to the enemy as she could with safety, and destroy her. Capt. Elliot ran in in a very gallant manner to within from 300 to 500 yards of her, and was about anchoring, when the enemy set fire to her and she soon after blew up. This vessel was a schooner the last year, and called the *Beresford*: since they attired her to a brig they changed her name, and I have not been able to ascertain it. She mounted 14 guns, twelve 24-pound carronades and two long 9-pounders.

Finding the enemy had two other brigs and a schooner in the Niagara river, I determined to leave a force to watch them, and selected the *Jefferson*, *Sylph* and *Oneida* for that purpose, and placed the whole under the orders of Capt. Ridgely. Having looked into York without discovering any vessel of the enemy, I left Niagara with the remainder of the squadron on the evening of the 7th and arrived here the 9th. We found one of the enemy's ships in the offing, and chased her into Kingston.

My anxiety to return to this end of the lake was increased by the knowledge I had of the weakness of Sackett's Harbor, and the apprehension that the enemy might receive large reinforcements at Kingston, and embarking some of the troops on board his fleet make a dash at the harbor and burn it with my stores in our absence. When I left the harbor there were but about 700 regular troops fit for duty. It is true a few militia had been called in, but little could be expected of them should an attack be made. My apprehension, it seems, was groundless, the enemy having contented himself with annoying, in some trifling degree, the coasters between Oswego and the harbor, in his boats.

I cannot forbear expressing my regret that so much sensation has been excited in the public mind because this squadron did not sail so soon as the wise-heads that conduct our newspapers have presume to think I ought. I need not suggest to one of your experience that a man-of-war may seem to the eye of a landsman perfectly ready for sea when she is deficient in many of the most essential points of her armament, nor how unworthy I should have proved myself of the high trust reposed in me had I ventured to sea in the face of an enemy of equal force without being able to meet him in one hour after my anchor was weighed.

It ought in justice to be recollected that the building and equipment of vessels on the Atlantic are unattended by any of the great difficulties which we have to encounter on the lakes: there every department abounds in facilities. A commander makes a requisition, and articles of every description are furnished in twelve hours; but this fleet has been built and furnished in the wilderness, where there are no agents and chandlers, shops and foundries, &c., &c., to supply our wants, but everything is to be created, and yet I shall not decline a comparison with anything done on the Atlantic in the building and equipment of vessels. The *Guerriere*, for instance, has been building and fitting upwards of twelve months in the city of Philadelphia, and is not yet ready. The *President* went into the navy yard at New York for some partial repairs a few days after the keel of the *Superior* was laid, since then two frigates of a large class and two sloops of the largest class have been built and fitted here, and have sailed before the *President* is ready for sea, although every article of their armament and rigging has been transported from New York in despite of obstacles almost insurmountable. I will go further, sir, for it is due to the unremitted and unsurpassed exertions of those who have served the public under my command, and will challenge the world to produce a parallel instance in which the same number of vessels of such dimensions have been built and fitted in the same time by the same number of workmen.

I confess that I am mortified in not having succeeded in satisfying the expectations of the public, but it would be infinitely more painful could I find any want of zeal or exertion in my endeavors to serve them to which I could in any degree impute their disappointment.

UNITED STATES SHIP *Superior*, OFF KINGSTON,
August 10th, 1814.

SIR.—I have been duly honored with your letters of the 19th and 24th of July. I do assure you, sir, that I have never been under any pledge to meet General Brown at the head of the lake; but, on the contrary, when we parted at Sackett's Harbor I told him distinctly that I should not visit the head of the lake unless the enemy's fleet did. I can ascribe the intimation of General Brown, that he expected the co-operation of the fleet, to no other motive than a cautious attempt to provide an apology to the public against any contingent disaster to which his army might be exposed.

But, sir, if any one will take the trouble to examine the topography of the peninsula, (the scene of the General's operations) he will discover that this fleet could be of no more service to General Brown and his army than it could to an army in Tennessee.

General Brown has never been able to penetrate nearer to Lake Ontario than Queenston, and the enemy is in possession of all the intermediate country, so that I could not even communicate with the army but by a circuitous route of 70 or 80 miles.

Admitting General Brown could have invested Fort George, the only service he could have derived from the fleet would have een our preventing the supplies of the enemy from entering the Niagara river, for the water is so shallow that large vessels could not approach within two miles of their works. General Brown had therefore two abundantly sufficient reasons for not expecting the co-operation of this fleet; it was not promised him, and was chimerical in itself.

My fixed determination has always been to seek a meeting with the enemy the moment the fleet was ready, and to deprive him of any apology for not meeting me. I have sent four guns on shore from the *Superior* to reduce her armament in number to an equality with the *Prince Regent's*, yielding the advantage of their 8-pounders. The *Mohawk* mounted two guns less than the *Princess Charlotte*, and the *Montreal* and *Niagara* are equal to the *General Pike* and *Madison*. I have detached on separate service all the brigs, and am blockading his four ships with our four ships in hopes that this may induce him to come out.

Commodore Chauncey to General Brown.

UNITED STATES SHIP *Superior*, OFF KINGSTON,
August 10, 1814.

SIR,—Your letter of the 13th ult. was received by me on a sick bed, hardly able to hear it read, and entirely unfitted to reply to it. I, however, requested General Gaines to acquaint you with my situation, the probable time of the fleet's sailing and my views of the extent of its co-operation with the army.

From the tenor of your letter it would appear that you had calculated much upon the co-operation of the fleet. You cannot surely have forgotten the conversation we held on this subject at Sackett's Harbor previous to your departure for Niagara. I then professed to feel it my duty as well as inclination to afford every assistance in my power to the army, and to co-operate with it whenever it could be done without losing sight of the great object for which this fleet had been created—to wit, the capture or destruction of the enemy's fleet; but this was a primary object, would be first attempted, and that you must not expect the fleet at the head of the lake unless that of the enemy should induce us to follow him there.

I will not suffer myself to believe that this conversation was misunderstood or has since been forgotten. How then shall I account for the intimation thrown out to the public in your despatch to the Secretary of War, that you expected the fleet to co-operate with you? Was it friendly or just or honorable, not only to furnish an opening for the public, but thus to assist them to infer that I had pledged myself to meet you on a particular day at the head of the lake for the purpose of co-operation, and in case of disaster to your army to turn their resentment from you, who are alone responsible, upon me, who could not by any possibility have prevented or retarded even your discomfiture? You well know, sir, that the fleet could not have rendered you the least service during your late incursion upon Upper Canada. You have not been able to approach Lake Ontario on any point nearer than Queenston, and the enemy were then in possession of all the country between that place and the shore of Ontario, and I could not even communicate with you without making a circuit of 70 or 80 miles. I would ask, of what possible use the fleet would have been to you in threatening or investing Fort George when the shallowness of water alone would prevent an approach with these ships within two miles of that fort or Niagara? To pretend that the fleet could render the least assistance in your projected capture of Burlington Heights, on your route to Kingston, is still more romantic, for it is well known the fleet could not approach within 9 miles of those Heights.

That you might find the fleet somewhat of a convenience in the transportation of provisions and stores for the use of the army, and an agreeable appendage to attend its marches and countermarches, I am ready to believe, but, sir, the Secretary of the Navy has honored us with a higher destiny—we are intended to seek and to fight the enemy's fleet. This is the great purpose of the government in creating this fleet, and I shall not be diverted in my efforts to effectuate it by any sinister attempt to render us subordinate to or an appendage of the army.

We have one common object in the annoyance, defeat and destruction of the enemy, and I shall always cheerfully unite with any military commander in the prosecution of that object.

Colonel Hercules Scott to His Brother.

BEFORE FORT ERIE, 12th August, 1814.

MY DEAR JAMES,—I shall now give you a short account of our military transactions in this quarter. About 5 weeks ago the enemy crossed over into this Province at Fort Erie with about 6,000 men with 12 pieces of cannon. General Riall, who commanded at Fort George, marched out to meet them, with only 1,500 men. He attacked the enemy near Chippawa, and after a severe action was defeated, with the loss of 700 killed, wounded and missing. This action was ill-advised and the movements ill-executed. After this action General R. returned to Fort George, which the enemy invested, but in a partial manner. Reinforcements arriving from below he came out of the Fort and marched towards Burlington, where I had assembled a considerable force and advanced to meet him. Finding that we had been reinforced, the enemy retired and we followed them. On the 25th of last month they attacked our advanced guard in the evening. This brought on an action, which began about 7 in the evening and lasted till 11 at night. The enemy made several severe and determined attacks and were as often repulsed. In the last they gained possession of 5 out of 7 of our guns, but the fire kept upon them was so severe that it afterwards appeared they had not been able to carry them off, for we found them next morning on the spot they had been taken. No boast of a "Great Victory," but in my opinion it was nearly equal on both sides. Their loss in men was equal ours—878 killed, wounded and missing, besides 61 officers. We found on the field five of the enemy's iron guns, and they carried off one of our brass 6-pounders. The troops engaged behaved well, particularly the 89th Regt., with small detachments of the Royals, 8th, and 103rd. These were in the action during the whole time and lost more than one-half the number they had in the field. Gen. Drummond commanded in the action, but I am sorry to say I could not then or now observe the smallest appearance of generalship. I fear he has got his command, like many others, from the interest of friends, not from his own merit. Since the action the enemy have retired to Fort Erie. We have advanced within two miles, and after innumerable delays have in *9 days* constructed a *4* gun battery, which I expect will open to-morrow, but in my opinion is not adequate to the reduction of the place. Time will show how we get on. We had a severe loss the other day in Gen. Conran. He had only joined a few days when we were deprived of his valuable services by a fall from his horse. He broke his leg. In the few days he was with the the army he had gained the esteem and confidence of every officer and man in the army. We are since the above accident again under the immediate command of Gen. Drummond. For one I can safely say, my confidence is gone. For my part I like to see a General that can first form a plan and then has steadiness to carry his plan into execution. Thank God, I have hitherto escaped. I had only one horse shot under me on the 25th. I shall write you again soon, but probably shall have another brush first in storming this same Fort Erie. Should I fall I have to request that you will give to Archibald five hundred a year to enable him, when he thinks proper, to live in his own country. I have made no will since I have been in this country. I made one in India but do not know what is become of it, so that it will entirely depend on yourself if you comply with my request or not. I also wish you to give one thousand each to Helen and David. I have some funds in this country but cannot at present say the amount. I shall leave a memorandum for some one here to have my accounts settled and the balance remitted through my friend, Mr. Mure of Quebec, who has some of my baggage in his charge.

Since writing the above our battery has opened against the Fort, and continued the whole of yesterday without having the smallest effect. It is at much too great a distance. I expect we shall be ordered to storm to-morrow. I have little hope of success from this manœuvre. I shall probably write you more, that is, if I get over this present business.

My dear James, yours ever sincerely,
H. S.

14th Augt.

Lt.-Gen. Drummond to Sir George Prevost.

HEADQUARTERS,
CAMP BEFORE FORT ERIE, 12th Aug., 1814.

I had hoped to have been able this morning to have tried the effect of the guns, which have been placed in battery against the enemy's fort and schooner, but the very limited means at the disposal of the engineer officers, and the absolute necessity of constructing a traverse in the rear of the battery against any guns the enemy may have at Black Rock, and of throwing a strong *abbattis* in front of the battery, and securing it on its flanks by similar *abbattis* against a sortie which the enemy would have it in his power to make upon it with his whole force, together with other circumstances connected with the enterprise which Capt. Dobbs of the Royal Navy, with a party of seamen and marines, will this night undertake against the enemy's schooners, have induced me to defer opening the guns until to-morrow morning.

The enemy has unavoidably had so much time for preparation, and has in his position so considerable a number of heavy guns, that I much fear we shall find the fire of our battery unable to effect much. That of his schooners, if Capt. Dobbs succeeds, will be removed or perhaps turned in our favor, but we shall still be exposed to the enemy's batteries at Black Rock should he, as is confidently believed, have established any on that commanding ridge. From the nature of the ground in front of Fort Erie, Your Excellency must be aware, that without cutting down an immense tract of forest wood it would not be possible to establish my batteries in any situation that would not be taken in reverse from batteries at

Black Rock. I am, however, far from approving of the site on which the battery has been placed by Capt. Romilly, and I have had reason in other respects to be so little satisfied with that officer in the field that I have sent him to Fort George to superintend the duties of the Engineer Department at that post. Lieut. Philpot, assisted by Lieut. Portlock, Royal Engineers; by Lieut. Stevens, Royal Marine Artillery, and by Capt. Barney, 89th Regt., whom I have for the moment attached to the Engineer Department, has conducted the works much to my satisfaction, and should it be found necessary to change the situation of the battery I feel confident in its being quickly and ably effected by these officers.

The enemy makes daily efforts with his riflemen to dislodge our advanced picquets and to obtain a reconnoissance of what we are doing. These attacks, tho' feeble and invariably repulsed, yet harass our troops and occasion us some loss. I enclose returns of those of the 10th and of this day. Your Excellency will observe with concern that on both occasions we have lost an officer killed. I am happy to report that on every occasion the troops show great steadiness, and invariably inflict a loss on the enemy more considerable than their own. The Indians went forward with great spirit the day before yesterday, and in the affair of this day it has just been reported to me they surprised, took, and scalped every man of one of the enemy's picquets.

I cannot forbear of taking this occasion of expressing to Your Excellency my most marked approbation of the uniform exemplary good conduct of the Glengarry Light Infantry and Incorporated Militia, the former under command of Lt.-Col. Battersby, and the latter under Major Kerby: of the services of the latter officer, I regret to say that I have this day been deprived by two wounds, which I trust will prove slight. These two corps have constantly been in close contact with the enemy's outposts and riflemen during the severe service of the last fortnight: their steadiness and gallantry as well as their superiority as light troops have on every occasion been conspicuous.

I am sorry to acquaint Your Excellency that Colonel Stuart of the Royal Scots, whom I had ordered up from York on my being deprived of Major-General Conran's services to assist in the direction of the details of this division, and who arrived here yesterday, is this day attacked with ague and so ill as to be unable to leave his bed. I particularly regret this in consequence of the extraordinary circumstance of Colonel Scott, the next senior officer, having begged permission to resign the command of the brigade to which he had been appointed and to serve in command of his regiment, under a *junior officer*. I can therefore derive no assistance from that officer. I am very anxious that another General officer should be sent up to this Province as soon as possible.

I have ordered up the 82nd Regt. from York as soon as the first division of the 6th approaches that place.

Commodore Chauncey has left three of his brigs to watch our vessels in the Niagara. They continue cruising off that place.

To-morrow I hope to be able to make a satisfactory communication to Your Excellency of the result of Capt. Dobbs' attempt against the enemy's schooners off Fort Erie, and of the effect produced by the fire of our battery.

I fear I have omitted to represent to Your Excellency the very great assistance which this division of the army has derived from the detachment from H. M. squadron on Lake Ontario, consisting of the *Star* and *Charwell* brigs, and *Netley* and *Magnet* schooners, under Captain Dobbs, R. N. Without their valuable aid in the transport of troops and stores I certainly should not have been able to have attempted offensive operations so soon after my arrival. I feel infinite obligations to Sir James Lucas Yeo for his prompt acquiescence in my request to him to detach these vessels, and I feel the appointment of an officer of such conciliating manners and such zeal and professional ability as Capt. Dobbs to command as an additional favour. Everything is to be expected from the gallantry and exertions of Capt. Dobbs and the party of seamen and marines who have undertaken the enterprise alluded to in the former part of this letter, and who have on every occasion been most forward in volunteering on any service in which they could be useful.

P. S.—Since writing the above the enemy has opened two guns from Black Rock, by the fire of which one sergeant has been killed and four men wounded, of the 2nd Brigade.

G. D.

Lt.-Gen. Drummond to Sir Geo. Prevost.

CAMP BEFORE FORT ERIE, 13th Aug., 1814.

SIR,—I have great satisfaction in acquainting Your Excellency with the capture of two of the three armed schooners which were anchored off Fort Erie, and which very much annoyed our left flank. This enterprise was executed in very gallant style by Capt. Dobbs and a party of about 70 seamen and marines, who embarked last night in six batteaux which I had caused to be carried across to Lake Erie for that purpose. I enclose a copy of an order which I have given on the occasion.

I have this morning opened the fire of the battry on Fort Erie, and, although the distance is found to be great, I hope a sufficient effect will be produced.

Morning District General Order.
HEADQUARTERS,
CAMP BEFORE FORT ERIE, 13th Aug., 1814.

Lieut.-Gen. Drummond congratulates the army on the brilliant achievement executed last night by Capt. Dobbs of the Royal Navy and a party of 70 seamen and marines, who in the most gallant style boarded and after a short struggle carried two of the enemy's armed schooners, anchored close to Fort Erie. Accident alone prevented the capture of the third schooner. Those captured are the *Somers* and *Porcupine*. The former mounts two long 12-pounders, the latter one 12. They were commanded by lieutenants, and had on board 35 men each. The Lieut.-General laments to find that Lieut. Radcliffe, commander of H. M. schooner *Netley*, has fallen on this occasion. He will be buried at 12 o'clock, with such marks of respect as circumstances will permit. Besides Mr. Radcliffe our loss has been only one seaman killed and four wounded. The enemy's loss was one seaman killed, three officers and four seamen wounded. The whole enterprise reflects the greatest credit on the ability and spirit of Capt. Dobbs and the gallant party under his command. The Lieut.-General felt convinced that it could not fail, from the spirited manner in which it was undertaken. He takes this occasion of informing the troops that he has a similar service for them to execute, and he invites corps and individuals desirous of volunteering their services on the occasion to intimate their wishes without delay through their respective Brigadiers to the Deputy-Adjutant-General, for the information of the Lieut.-General commanding.

This Order to be read to the corps immediately.

J. HARVEY,
Lt.-Col., D. A. G.

Captain Alexander Dobbs, R. N., to Sir James L. Yeo.
NIAGARA RIVER NEAR FORT ERIE,
Somers SCHOONER, Aug. 13th, 1814.

SIR,—Having succeeded in getting my gig and five batteaux across from the Niagara River to Lake Erie, a distance of eight miles by land, I last night attacked the three enemy's schooners that had anchored close to Fort Erie for the purpose of flanking the approaches to that fort. Two of them were carried sword in hand in a few minutes, and the third would certainly have followed had not the cables been cut, which made us drift to leeward of her among the rapids. The schooners taken are the *Ohio* and *Somers*, commanded by lieutenants and mounting three long 12-pounders, with a complement of 35 men each. My gallant friend, Lieut. Radcliffe, and one seaman fell in the act of boarding, which with four wounded is our loss. The enemy had one man killed and seven wounded; among the latter is Lieut Conkling, commanding the squadron, as well as two of his officers. The steady and gallant conduct of the officers, seamen and marines employed on this service was such as to have insured me success against a greater force, and has called forth a very handsome General Order from His Honour, Lt.-Gen. Drummond. I beg leave particularly to mention Mr. Grinded, mate of the *Star*, and Mr. Hyde, mate of the *Charwell*, not only for their gallant conduct in the attack, but for their skill in bringing the vessels into this river through shoals and rapids and under a constant and heavy fire.

Killed and wounded in an attack on two of the enemy's schooners under Fort Erie on the night of Aug. 12th:

Killed—C. Radcliffe, acting commander, and J. Acton, seaman. Wounded—J. Hudson and J. Bowen, seamen; T. Roach and J. Dickson, private marines.

Lieut. Conkling to Captain Kennedy.

FORT ERIE, UPPER CANADA, August 16th, 1814.

SIR,—With extreme regret I have to make known to you the circumstances attending the capture of the *Ohio* and *Somers*. On the night of the 12th between the hours of 10 and 12 the boats were seen a short distance ahead of the *Somers* and were hailed from that vessel: they answered "provision boats," which deceived the officers on the deck, as our army boats had been in the habit of passing and repassing through the night, and enabled them to drift athwart his hawser and cut his cables, at the same time pouring in a heavy fire before he discovered who they were. Instantaneously they were alongside of me, and notwithstanding my exertions, aided by Mr. McCally acting sailing master, (who was soon disabled,) I was unable to repulse them but for a moment. I maintained the quarter deck until my sword fell in consequence of a shot in the shoulder, and all on deck either wounded or surrounded with bayonets. As their force was an overwhelming one I thought further resistance vain, and gave up the vessel, with the satisfaction of having performed my duty and defended my vessel to the last.

List of Killed and Wounded.
Ohio.

Killed—John Fifehill, boatswain's mate, shot through the body.
Wounded—Reuben Wright, shot through the arm.
Sailing-Master McCally, shot through the thigh and bayonetted through the foot.
Sergeant Eastman of the 11th Regiment of the army, wounded in the neck by a musket ball.
—— Granger, 11th Regiment, wounded in the arm.
—— Wreath, 11th Regiment, wounded in the arm.
—— Whillers, 21st do., wounded, cut in the arm.

Somers.

Wounded—Samuel Taylor, shot in the arm and cut in the head.
Charles Ordean, cut in the shoulder; also one of the *Ohio's* marines, whose name the sergeant cannot find, now in the hospital, badly wounded.

The enemy's loss in killed and wounded is much more considerable. Amongst the killed is the commanding officer of the *Netley*, (lying here,) Captain Ratcliff: he fell in attempting to come over my quarters. Notwithstanding the number of muskets and pistols which were fired, and the bustle inseparable from enterprises of this kind, neither the fort nor the *Porcupine* attempted to fire as we drifted past them, nor did we receive a shot until past Black Rock, though they might have destroyed us with ease.

Respectfully your obedient servant,

A. M. CONKLING.

P. S.—We expect to be sent to Montreal, and perhaps to Quebec, directly.

General Gaines to the Secretary of War.

HEADQUARTERS, FORT ERIE, August 13th, 1814.

SIR,—It has become my painful duty to announce to you the loss of that brave and excellent officer, Major Morgan of the 1st Rifle Regiment. He fell at the head of his corps in an affair with the enemy on the 12th instant, after a display of gallantry worthy of the corps and meriting the gratitude of his country.

I had desired him to send a detachment of from 80 to 100 men to cut off a working party, supported by a guard of the enemy's light troops, engaged in opening an avenue for a battery in our rear, having directed him to have his corps ready in support in case the enemy should be reinforced. The detachment was commanded by Captain Birdsall, who attacked and drove the enemy, but when about to return to camp he discovered a large force approaching.

The firing having continued longer than the Major expected, he moved up the moment the enemy's reinforcements made their appearance. A warm conflict ensued, in which they were forced back, but discovering additional reinforcements and receiving my order to fall back on the appearance of a large force, the Major gave the signal with his bugle to retire: at this moment he received a ball in his head. He was brought from the field together with his, men who were killed and wounded. Of the former were two riflemen and a New York volunteer, who, unsolicited, accompanied the riflemen with a small party of his corps, under the command of Lieut. Goodfellow, who, I am informed, has distinguished himself on similar occasions, and for whom permit me to request a commission in one of the Rifle regiments.

(Secret.)

HEADQUARTERS,
CAMP BEFORE FORT ERIE, 14th Aug., 1814.

ARRANGEMENT.

Right Column—Lt.-Col. Fischer:

    King's Regiment.
    Volunteers—Regt. DeWatteville.
    Light Companies—89th and 100th Regts.
    Detachment Royal Artillery, one officer and 12 men, and a rocketeer with a couple of 12-pound rockets.
    Capt. Eustace's picquet of cavalry.
    Capt. Powell, Deputy-Asst.-Quartermaster-General, will conduct this column, which is to attack the left of the enemy's position.

Centre Column—Lt.-Col. Drummond:

    Flank Companies—41st Regiment.
      do   do —104th   do
    Royal Marines—50.
    Seamen—90.
    Detachment Royal Artillery, one subaltern and 12 men.
    Capt. Barney, 89th Regt., will guide this column, which is to attack the fort.

Left Column—Col. Scott, 103rd Regt:

    103rd Regt.
    Capt. Elliott, Deputy-Asst.-Quartermaster-General, will conduct this column, which will attack the right of the enemy's position towards the lake, and endeavor to penetrate by the opening between the fort and the entrenchment, using the short ladders at the same

time to pass the entrenchment which is reported to be defended only by the enemy's 9th Regt., 250 strong.

The infantry picquets on Buck's road to be pushed on with the Indians to attack the enemy's picquets on that road. Lt.-Col. Nichols, Quartermaster-General of Militia, will conduct this column.

The rest of the troops, viz:
1st Battalion Royals.
Remainder of DeWatteville's Regt.
Glengarry Light Infantry and Incorporated Militia
Will remain in reserve under Lt.-Col. Tucker and are to be posted on the ground at present occupied by our picquets and covering parties.

Squadron of 19th Dragoons in rear of the battery nearest to the advance, ready to receive charge of prisoners and conduct them to the rear.

The Lieut.-General will station himself at or near the battery, where reports are to be made to him.

Lt.-Col. Fischer, commanding the right column, will follow the instructions he has received, copy of which is communicated to Col. Scott and Lt.-Col. Drummond for their guidance.

The Lieut.-General *most strongly recommends a free use of the bayonet*. The enemy's force does not exceed 1500 fit for duty, and those are represented as much dispirited.

The ground on which the columns of attack are to be formed will be pointed out, and the orders for their guidance will be given by the Lieut.-General commanding.

J. HARVEY,
D. A. G.

(*Secret.*)

HEADQUARTERS,
CAMP BEFORE FORT ERIE, 14th Aug., 1814.

SIR,—Lieut.-General Drummond having selected you to command the (volunteer) force intended to be employed in assaulting the right of the enemy's position, I am directed to desire that you will accordingly march immediately in order to enable you to pass through the woods before dark. On reaching Baxter's you will halt for the night, using every precaution which your experience and prudence can suggest, aided by the necessary personal vigilance of the officers of every rank under your command, to prevent *desertion* and the consequent discovery of your situation and intentions to the enemy. No fire must be lighted, nor any loud chatting by your sentries or patroles permitted. Frequent (hourly) roll-calls must take place, and no officer allowed to quit his company, section, or sub-division for a single moment except while employed in performing duty on visiting videttes or patroles, and which duties officers of every rank must be required to perform. The surprise of the enemy and perhaps the success of the attack may depend upon this. You are to advance to the attack precisely at two o'clock. You are to enter the enemy's position between Snake Hill and the lake, which is presented as sufficiently open, but this is not to prevent your making your arrangements for assaulting any other point of the position by means of the short ladders or hay-bags with which you will be furnished. In order to *ensure secrecy* the Lieut.-General most strongly recommends that the flints are taken out of the firelocks with the exception of a reserve of select and steady men who may be permitted to retain their flints, (if you think it necessary or advisable,) not exceeding one-third of your force. This reserve, with the detachment of artillery, should take post on Snake Hill. The Lieut.-General is unwilling, however, to suppose the probability of such necessity, as it can only originate in a check, which he is persuaded if the troops are steady and resolute cannot happen. Turning to the left after entering the position, the whole of the enemy's diminished and dispirited troops will be found either in the trench extending from Snake Hill to the fort or in rear of the White House near the lake shore, and in either case will, as well as the batteries, be completely taken in reverse and exposed to your attack under very favorable circumstance which you could desire. The rest must be left to the valour of the troops. I am to apprize you that two columns will advance from this side as soon as it is ascertained that that under your command has entered it—one to attack the fort, composed of flank companies under Lieut.-Col. Drummond and a party of seamen and marines. The other to assault the line of entrenchments extending from the fort down to the lake. A demonstration will be made a few minutes before two o'clock by an attack upon the enemy's picquet opposite to the centre of his entrenchment. The advantages which will arise from taking out the flints are obvious. Combined with darkness and silence it will effectually conceal the situation and number of our troops, and those of the enemy being exposed by his fire and his white trousers, which are very conspicuous marks to our view, it will enable them to use the bayonet with effect which that valuable weapon has been ever found to possess in the hands of British soldiers. A detachment of Royal Artillery will accompany the column for the purpose of either spiking or turning the enemy's guns against himself, according as may be found expedient.

If repulsed the troops are to retire upon the battery on this side and on the reserve on Snake Hill and the cavalry, which will be posted on the Lake Road, on the other.

If the British troops meet within the place they will recognize each other by the words "Prince Regent," answered by "Twenty," the countersign of the day. Capt. Powell, Quartermaster-General's Dept., and Major Coore, A. D. C. to His Excellency the Commander of the Forces, will accompany you. As proposals of surrender may probably be made to you, you are to attend to none which are not unconditional, not suffering yourself for a moment to be diverted from the prosecution of your attack. Clemency to prisoners it is unnecessary to recommend to you, but in removing them to the rear you must be careful not to detach too many men. The cavalry will be found useful in receiving and escorting prisoners. By making a considerable number of prisoners you will find, in the event of the contest being protracted until daylight, that the enemy will be so reduced in numbers as not to be able to make any stand against the force under your command (particularly if you have taken possession of Snake Hill) and that which will be detached to co-operate with you from this side. His force is at present understood to be about 1,500 fit for duty. I shall be found at or near the battery.

Much is necessarily left to your judgment and discretion, on which Lieut.-Gen. Drummond has the fullest reliance.

J. HARVEY,
Lt.-Col., D. A. G.

Gen. Armstrong to Gen. Wilkinson.

SACKETT'S HARBOR, September 18, 1813.

"De Watteville's Regiment was made up in Spain, is composed of Poles, Germans, Spaniards and Portuguese, and completely disaffected."

Lieut.-Gen. Drummond to Sir Geo. Prevost.

CAMP BEFORE FORT ERIE, Aug. 15th, 1814.

SIR,—Having reason to believe that a sufficient impression had been produced on the works of the enemy's fort by the fire of the battery I had opened on it on the morning of the 13th, and by which the stone building had been much injured and the general outline of the parapet and embrasures very much altered, I determined on assaulting the place, and accordingly made the necessary arrangements for attacking it by a heavy column directed to the entrenchments on the side of Snake Hill, and by two columns to advance from the battery and assault the fort and entrenchments on this side. The troops destined to attack by Snake Hill, (which consisted of the King's Regiment and that of De Watteville, with the flank companies of the 89th and 100th Regiments, under Lieut.-Col. Fischer of the Regiment De Watteville,) marched at four o'clock yesterday afternoon in order to gain the vicinity of the point of attack in sufficient time. It is with the deepest regret I have to report the failure of both attacks, which were made two hours before daylight this morning. A copy of Lieut.-Col. Fischer's report herewith enclosed will enable Your Excellency to form a tolerably correct judgment of the cause of the failure of that attack. Had the head of the column, (which had entered the place without difficulty or opposition) been supported, the enemy must have fled from his works, (which were all taken as was contemplated in the instructions in reverse) or have surrendered. The attack on the fort and entrenchments leading from it to the lake was made at the same moment by two columns, one under Lieut.-Col. Drummond, 104th Regt., consisting of the flank companies of the 41st and 104th Regts., and a body of seamen and marines under Capt. Dobbs of the Royal Navy, on the fort: the other, under Col. Scott, 103d, consisting of the 103d Regt., supported by two companies of the Royals, was destined to attack the entrenchments. These columns advanced to the attack as soon as the firing upon Col. Fischer's column was heard, and succeeded after a desperate resistance in making a lodgment in the fort through the embrasures of the demi-bastion, the guns of which they had actually turned against the enemy who still maintained the stone building, when most unfortunately some ammunition which had been placed under the platform caught fire from the firing of the guns to the rear, and a most tremendous explosion followed, by which almost all the troops which had entered the place were dreadfully mangled. Panic was instantly communicated to the troops, (who could not be persuaded that the explosion was accidental,) and the enemy at the same time pressing forward and commencing a heavy fire of musquetry, the fort was abandoned and our troops retreated towards the battery. I immediately pushed out the 1st Battalion, Royals, to support and cover the retreat, a service which that valuable corps executed with great steadiness. Our loss has been very severe in killed and wounded, and I am sorry to add that almost all those returned " missing" may be considered as wounded or killed by the explosion, and left in the hands of the enemy. The failure of these most important attacks has been occasioned by circumstances which may be considered as almost justifying the momentary panic which they produced, and which introduced a degree of confusion into the columns which in the darkness of the night the utmost exertions of the officers were ineffectual in removing. The officers appear invariably to have behaved with the most perfect coolness and bravery, nor could anything exceed the steadiness and order with which the advance of Lieut.-Col. Fischer's brigade was made until, emerging from a thick wood, it found itself suddenly stopped by an *abbattis*, and within a heavy fire of musquetry and guns from behind a formidable entrenchment.

With regard to the centre and left columns, under Col. Scott and Lieut.-Col. Drummond, the persevering gallantry of both officers and men until the unfortunate explosion could not be surpassed. Col. Scott of the 103d and Lieut.-Col. Drummond of the 104th Regiments, who commanded the centre and left attacks, were unfortunately killed, and Your Excellency will perceive that almost every officer of those columns was either killed or wounded, by the enemy's fire or by the explosion.

My thanks are due to the undermentioned officers, viz: To Lieut.-Col. Fischer, who commanded the right attack: to Major Coore, aide-de-camp to Your Excellency, who accompanied that column: Major Evans of the King's, commanding the advance; Major Villatte of De Watteville's; Capt. Basden, light company, 89th; Lieut. Murphy, light company, 100th. I beg also to add the name of Capt. Powell of the Glengarry Light Infantry, employed on the staff as Deputy-Assistant in the Quartermaster-General's Department, who conducted Lieut.-Col. Fischer's column and first entered the enemy's entrenchments, and by his coolness and gallantry particularly distinguished himself: Major Villatte of De Watteville's Regiment, who led the column of attack and entered the entrenchments, as did Lieut. Young with about 50 men of the light companies of the King's and De Watteville's Regiments. Capt. Powell reports that Sergt. Powell of the 19th Dragoons, who was perfectly acquainted with the ground, volunteered to act as guide and preceded the leading sub-division in the most intrepid style. In the centre and left columns, the exertions of Major Smelt of the 103d Regt., who succeeded to the command of the left column on the death of Col. Scott: Capts. Leonard and Shore of the 104th flank companies: Capts. Glew, Bullock and O'Keefe, 41st flank companies: Capt. Dobbs, of the Royal Navy, commanding a party of volunteer seamen and marines, are entitled to my acknowledgements (they are all wounded). Nor can I omit mentioning in the strongest terms of approbation the active, zealous and useful exertions of Capt. Elliott of the 103d Regt., Deputy-Assistant-Quartermaster-General, who was unfortunately wounded and taken prisoner, and Capt. Barney of the 89th Regt., who had volunteered his services as a temporary assistant in the Engineer Department and conducted the centre column to the attack, in which he received two dangerous wounds. To Major Phillot, commanding Royal Artillery, and Capt. Sabine, who commanded the battery as well as the field guns, and to the officers and men of that valuable branch of the service, serving under them, I am to express my entire approbation of their skill and exertions. Lieut. Charlton of the Royal Artillery entered the fort with the centre column, fired several rounds upon the enemy from his own guns, and was wounded by the explosion. The ability and exertions of Lieut. Philpot of the Royal Engineers and the officers and men of that department claim my best acknowledgements. To Lieut.-Col. Tucker, who commanded the reserve, and to Lieut.-Col. Pearson, Inspecting Field Officer, and Lieut.-Col. Battersby of the Glengarry Light Infantry, and Capt. Walker of the Incorporated Militia, I am greatly indebted for their active and unremitting attention to the security of the outposts. To the Deputy-Adjt.-Gen. and Deputy-Quartermaster-Gen., Lieut.-Col. Harvey and Lieut.-Col. Myers, and to the officers of their departments respectively, as well as to Capt. Foster, my military secretary, and the officers of my general staff, I am under the greatest obligations for the assistance they afforded me. My acknowledgements are due to Capt. D'Alton of the 90th Regt., Brigade Major to the Right Division, and to Lieut.-Col. Nichol, Quartermaster-General of Militia: the exertions of Dep.-Commissary-Gen. Turquand and the officers of that department, for the supply of the troops; and the care and attention of Staff Surgeon O'Malley and the medical officers with the division to the sick and wounded, also claim my thanks.

Lt.-Col. Fischer to Col. Harvey.

CAMP BEFORE FORT ERIE, Aug. 15th, 1814.

SIR,—I have the honor to report to you for the information of Lieut.-Gen. Drummond, that in compliance with the orders I received, the brigade under my command, consisting of the 8th and De Watteville's Regiment, the light companies of the 89th and 100th, with a detachment of artillery, attacked this morning at two o'clock the enemy's position at Snake Hill, and to my great concern failed in the attempt. The flank companies of the brigade who were formed under the orders of Major Evans of the King's Regiment for the purpose of turning the position between Snake Hill and the lake, which was found impenetrable, and was prevented from supporting Major De Villatte of De Watteville's and Captain Powell of the Quartermaster-General's Department, who actually

with a few men had turned the enemy's battery. The column of support, consisting of the remainder of De Watteville's and the King's Regiment forming the reserve, in marching too near the lake found themselves entangled between the rocks and the water, and by the retreat of the flank companies, were thrown into such confusion as to render it impossible to give them any kind of formation during the darkness of the night, at which time they were exposed to a most galling fire of the enemy's battery and the numerous parties in the *abbattis*, and I am perfectly convinced that the great number of missing are men killed or severely wounded at that time when it was impossible to give them any assistance. After daybreak the troops formed and retired to camp. I enclose a return of the casualties.
I have, &c.,
J. FISCHER.

Killed, Wounded and Missing of the Right Division at Fort on the Morning of 15th August, 1814.

Killed—2 lieut.-colonels, 1 captain, 1 lieut., 1 sergeant, 1 drummer, 51 rank and file.

Wounded—1 dep.-assist.-quartermaster-general, 1 major, 8 captains, 11 lieuts., 2 ensigns, 1 master, 12 seamen, 20 sergeants, 3 drummers, 250 rank and file.

Missing—1 dept.-assist.-quartermaster-general, 1 captain, 3 lieuts., 2 ensigns, 1 midshipman, 1 adjutant, 7 seamen, 41 sergeants, 3 drummers, 479 rank and file. Of the number returned missing the greater part are supposed to have been killed by the explosion of a magazine.

Officers killed, wounded and missing:

Killed—1st or Royal Scots, Capt. Torrens; 8th Regt., Lieut. Noel; 103d, Col. Scott; 104th, Lieut.-Col. Drummond.

Wounded—General Staff, Capt. Powell, Navy Captain Dobbs, Lieut. Stevenson, Mr. Harris, master; Royal Scots, Captain Rowan, Lieut. Vaughan; 8th Regt., Lieut. Young; 41st Flank Companies, Capts. Glew and Bullock, Lt. Hailes, Ensign Townshend; 89th Regt., Capt. Barney; 100th, Volunteer Frazer; 103d, Major Smelt, Capts. Gardner and Colclough, Lieuts. Fallon, Charlton, Cuppage, Meagher, Burrows and Hazen, Ensign Nash; 104th Flank Companies, Capt. Leonard, Lieut. McLaughlan.

Missing—General Staff, Capt. Elliott, Royal Navy; Mr. Hyde, midshipman; 41st Flank Companies, Lieut. Gardner, Ensign Hall; 100th Light Co., Ensign Murray; 103d Regt., Capt. Irwin, Lieut. Kaye, Ensign Henry, Lieut. and Adjt. Pettit.

Lt.-Gen. Drummond to Sir Geo. Prevost.

CAMP BEFORE FORT ERIE, Aug. 16, 1814.

(Private.)

DEAR SIR,—I have had a most painful and distressing duty to perform in reporting to Your Excellency the disastrous result of the attack which I directed to be made yesterday morning on the enemy's works and Fort Erie, an attack which there was no probability of a doubt but must have succeeded had the troops fulfilled that part allotted to them.

It signifies not to the public to whom the culpability of failure in military matters is attachable, the commander at all times falls under censure, however high his character may have been. The agony of mind I suffer from the present disgraceful and unfortunate conduct of the troops committed to my superintendence wounds me to the soul.

The right column of attack was entrusted to Lt.-Col. Fischer, and from the reports I had of its steady conduct on the line of march every hope was entertained of a continuance of it in the hour of trial. Capt. Powell, D. A. Q. M. G., led the column. The forlorn hope consisted of a sub-division of the light company of the King's Regt. under Lieut. Young, and Sergt. Powell of the 19th Light Dragoons accompanied it, being acquainted with the ground. This sub-division was supported by the light company of De Watteville's Regt. The 100th Light Company followed. Next, the second sub-division of the King's Light Company. Then the grenadiers of De Watteville's and the light company of the 89th. This corps was supported by the volunteers of De Watteville's (nearly the whole regiment) and the King's Regt.

It appears that part of the forlorn hope and about half of De Watteville's Light Company, by wading through the water, though the footing was excessively rough and rocky along the lake shore, turned the left flank of an *abbattis* which extended from the enemy's battery on Snake Hill (the left of their position) to the lake, and part penetrated through the *abbattis* itself, and thereby gained the rear of the enemy's works. The fire of the enemy by this time being extremely heavy, both from artillery and musketry, it would seem as if a simultaneous shock of panic pervaded the greater part of those not immediately in advance, and the forlorn hope, not finding itself sufficiently supported, was reluctantly under the necessity of relinquishing the advantages they had gained and of retiring again through the water under a most galling fire. They lost many men, and De Watteville's light company nearly half their numbers. The light company of the 89th, notwithstanding they were nearly overwhelmed by the grenadiers of Watteville's in the precipitancy of their retreat, was the only body that preserved its order and remained firm upon its ground. By this act of steadiness they fortunately lost scarcely a man. The main body of De Watteville's retreated in such confusion they carried the King's Regt. before them like a torrent.

Thus by the misconduct of this foreign corps has the opportunity been totally lost for the present of striking such a blow at the enemy's force in this neighborhood as would altogether prevent his appearing again in any force on the Niagara frontier, at least during the present campaign.

The attacking columns of the left were entrusted to Col. Scott and Lieut.-Col. Drummond. An unfortunate explosion, supposed by accident, of some expense ammunition in the demi-bastion of the works, by the destruction of many valuable officers and men, threw the remainder into such confusion and dismay that they likewise made a precipitate retreat, and the enemy remained in possession of his works.

Major Coore, Your Excellency's A. D. C., who volunteered his services, accompanied Lt.-Col. Fischer's column and, I have much pleasure in acquainting you, afforded much assistance to that officer.

Capt. Powell's zeal and gallantry was most conspicuous. His exertions have at all times been so unremitting as to merit my warmest approbation.

I am now reduced to a most unpleasant predicament with regard to force, as the Royals, the King's, 41st. 89th, 100th, and now the 103rd, are so much weakened as certainly not to be fit to keep the field.

I have thought advisable to order the 82nd from Burlington and York without delay, and the 6th, now on its march to York, also to proceed to this frontier.

I had intended to order another regiment from Kingston, but from the badness of the roads since the recent rains I could not calculate upon their arrival here before our squadron will be able to take the lake, and as even at present the diminution of stores and provisions is beginning to be felt, I entreat Your Excellency will impress upon the Commodore the necessity of conveying to the Right Division, the very first moment the squadron can leave harbor, a full supply of each, as well as a reinforcement of troops, which I should wish to be the 90th or any equally strong regiment, instead of the Canadian Fencibles or 97th, both comparatively weak in point of numbers.

I take the opportunity of transmitting this letter by Your Excellency's A. D. C., Major Coore.

General Order.

HEADQUARTERS,
MONTREAL, August 25th, 1814.

In promulgating to the troops an extract from a District General Order issued by Lieutenant-General Drummond to the right division of this army in consequence of the capture of two of the enemy's schooners, co-operating in the defence of the enemy's position at Fort Erie, the commander of the forces avails himself of the opportunity it presents to acknowledge the high sense he entertains of the valuable services rendered to the right division by Captain Dobbs of the Royal Navy and the officers and seamen of the vessels placed under his command for that purpose by Commodore Sir James Yeo.

This event, so ably planned and so gallantly executed, was followed by a general attack of the enemy's forts and entrenchments.

Lieutenant-General Drummond reports that the spirit with which it was undertaken enabled our troops to surmount every obstacle, Fort Erie and the entrenchments were entered, the guns turned on the barrack blockhouse, (the enemy's last refuge) when unfortunately a most violent explosion occurred in the battery, in its effect destroying and disabling many a valuable officer and soldier, and caused so considerable a consternation as to induce the remaining troops to abandon the works and all those advantages which they had gained by their determined conduct, and precipitately to retire on our first approaches.

From other causes, almost inseparable to night operations carried on in a close and difficult country, the right column failed in the object it had to accomplish.

With deep regret the Commander of the Forces records the loss His Majesty's service has sustained on this occasion.

Return of Killed, Wounded and Missing of the Right Division, in the Assault of Fort Erie on the 15th August, 1814.

Killed—1 colonel, 1 lieutenant-colonel, 1 captain, 1 lieutenant, 1 sergeant, 1 drummer, 51 rank and file.

Wounded—1 major, 9 captains, 11 lieutenants, 2 ensigns, 1 master, 20 sergeants, 3 drummers, 262 rank and file.

Missing—2 captains, 3 lieutenants, 2 ensigns, 1 adjutant, 1 midshipman, 41 sergeants, 3 drummers, 486 rank and file.

Officers killed—1st Royal Scots—Captain Torrens: 8th King's—Lieut. Noel: 103rd Regt.—Colonel Scott: 104th Regt.—Lieut.-Col. Drummond.

149

Officers wounded—Royal Navy—Captain Dobbs and Lieut. Stevenson, slightly; Mr. Harris, master, severely.

1st Royal Scots—Capt. Rowan, severely; Lieut. Vaughan, slightly.

8th King's—Lieut. Young, slightly.

41st Flank Companies—Captains Glew and Bullock, severely; Lieut. Hailes, slightly; Ensign Townsend, severely.

89th Regt.—Capt. Barney, acting assistant engineer, severely.

100th Regt.—Lieut. Murray, wounded and prisoner; volunteer Fraser, severely.

103rd Regt.—Major Smelt and Capt. Gardner, severely; Captain Colclough and Lieut. Charlton, severely and prisoner; Lieut. Fallon, severely; Lieut. Cuppage, Jr., dangerously; Lieut. Meagher, slightly; Lieuts. Burrows, Hazen and Ensign Nash, severely.

104th Flank Companies—Capt. Leonard and Ensign McLaughlin, severely.

Officers missing—General Staff—Capt. Elliot, deputy-assistant-quartermaster-general.

Royal Navy—Mr. Hyde, midshipman.

41st Flank Companies—Lieut. Gardner and Ensign Hall.

103rd Regt.—Capt. Irwin, Lieut. Kaye, Ensign Huoy, Lieut. and Adjutant Pettit.

EDWARD BAYNES,
Adjutant-General.

Gen. Gaines to the Secretary of War.

HEADQUARTERS,
FORT ERIE, U. C., August 15th, 1814.

SIR,—My heart is gladdened with gratitude to heaven and joy to my country, to have it in my power to inform you that the gallant army under my command has this morning beaten the enemy commanded by Lieutenant-General Drummond, after a severe conflict of near three hours, commencing at 2 o'clock this morning. They attacked us on each flank, got possession of the salient bastion of the old Fort Erie, which was regained at the point of the bayonet with a dreadful slaughter. The enemy's loss in killed and prisoners is about 600; near 300 killed. Our loss is considerable, but I think not one-tenth as great as that of the enemy. I will not detain the express to give you the particulars. I am preparing my force to follow up the blow.

Killed, Wounded and Missing of the Left Division of the United States Army, Commanded by Brigadier-General Gaines, in the Action of the 15th August, 1814, at Fort Erie, Upper Canada.

Adjutant-General's Office,
FORT, ERIE, Aug. 14th, 1814.

Corps of Bombardiers.

Killed—1 private.

Artillery.

Killed—1 captain, 1 subaltern, 2 privates; wounded—severely, 1 lieutenant, 3 privates; slightly, 6 privates; missing—1 lieutenant, 3 privates.

1st Brigade.

9th Regiment—slightly wounded—1 private.

11th do—killed—3 privates; wounded—dangerously, 1 sergeant, 1 private; severely, 4 privates; slightly, 4 privates.

19th Regiment—killed—5 privates; wounded—dangerously, 1 subaltern; severely, 1 sergeant, 4 privates; slightly, 1 corporal, 8 privates. (This regiment was stationed in the fort.)

22nd Regiment—killed—two privates; wounded—severely, 5 privates.

2nd Brigade.

21st Regiment—killed—2 privates; wounded—severely, 1 subaltern, 3 privates; slightly, 3 privates; missing—2 privates.

1st and 4th Rifle Corps.

Wounded—severely, 1 captain, 1 private; missing—1 private.

Names of Officers.

Artillery—Capt. Williams and Lieut. McDonough, killed; Lieut. Watmough, wounded severely; Lieut. Fontaine, missing.

19th Regt.—Lieut. Bushnell, Ensign Cissna, wounded.

23rd Regt.—Lieuts. Brown and Belknap, wounded.

4th Rifles—Capt. Birdsall, wounded.

Report of the Killed and Wounded During the Cannonading and Bombardment.

Commencing at sunrise on the morning of the 13th instant and continuing without intermission till 8 o'clock p. m., recommenced on the 14th at daylight with increased warmth, and ending one hour before the commencement of the action at Erie on the morning of the 15th:

ADJUTANT-GENERAL'S OFFICE, August 15th, 1814.

Corps of Artillery—wounded—severely, 2 privates; slightly, 1 captain, 2 subalterns, 1 sergeant, 1 corporal, 3 privates.

11th Regt.—wounded—severely, 2 sergeants, 2 privates: slightly, 3 privates.

19th Regt.—wounded—severely, 1 subaltern.

21st Regt.—killed—4 privates: wounded—severely, 3 privates; slightly, 2 privates.

22nd Regt.—killed—1 sergeant: wounded—severely, 2 corporals, 2 privates: slightly, 3 privates.

23rd Regt.—killed—1 private: wounded—severely, 1 private.

Rifle Regiments, 1st and 4th—killed—1 corporal, 2 privates: wounded—severely, 3 privates: slightly, 1 private.

Officers Wounded.

Artillery—Capt. Biddle, Lieuts. Zantzinger and Watmough.
Infantry—Lieut. Patterson, 19th Regt.

Killed.

George Carryl, 23rd Regt., Orderly to General Gaines.

ROGER JONES,
Asst.-Adjt.-Gen.

Brigadier-General Gaines to the Secretary of War.

H. Q., FORT ERIE, U. C., Aug. 23d, 1814.

SIR,—Loss of sleep and constant exposure to weather gave me some days ago a violent cold, which has put it out of my power to do anything more than the state of the service here rendered indispensable: hence my apology for delaying until this day my report of the battle of the 15th inst.

General Drummond is quietly engaged in collecting reinforcements. His camp appears to be fortified. I attempted to look at it a few days past and it cost me a fine young officer, Lieut. Yates of the 4th Rifle Regiment, killed, and Lieut. Kearsley of that excellent corps with Lieut. Childs of the 9th, wounded, with the loss of 2 or 3 privates killed and 5 or 6 wounded. The loss of the enemy I was unable to ascertain; he would not leave his defences, and I did not think fit to leave mine at all exposed. Several deserters say that the 6th and 82d Regiments arrived last night. If this be true, their strength is about the same as it was before the battle of the 15th. Their Colonel Scott is dead. About twenty deserters from the De Watteville Regiment and some few from the other corps concur in the report that their loss in killed, wounded and missing on the 15th was upwards of a thousand.

Brigadier-General Gaines to the Secretary of War.

H. Q., LEFT WING 2D DIVISION,
FORT ERIE, U. C., Aug. 23d, 1814.

SIR,—I have the honor to communicate for the information of the department of war, the particulars of the battle fought at this place on the 15th inst. between the left wing of the 2d Division of the Northern army under my command and the British forces in the Peninsula of Upper Canada commanded by Lieut.-General Drummond, which terminated in a signal victory in favor of the United American arms. Our position on the margin of the lake at the entrance of the Niagara River being nearly a horizontal plain, twelve or fifteen feet above the surface of the water, possessing few natural advantages, had been strengthened in front by temporary parapet, breastworks, entrenchments and *abattis*, with two batteries and 6 field pieces. The small unfinished Fort Erie with a 24, 18 and 12-pounders formed the N. E., and the Douglass battery with an 18 and 6-pounder the S. E. angle of our right: the left is defended by a redoubt battery with 6 field pieces, just thrown up on a small ridge: our rear was left open to the lake, bordered by a rocky shore of easy ascent: the battery on the left was defended by Capt. Towson: Fort Erie by Capt. Williams, with Major Trimble's command of the 19th Infantry: the batteries on the front by Captains Biddle and Fanning: the whole of the artillery commanded by Major Hindman. Parts of the 11th, 9th and 22d Infantry (of the late veteran brigade of Maj.-Gen. Scott) were posted on the right under the command of Lieut.-Col. Aspinwall; Gen. Ripley's brigade, consisting of the 21st and 23d, defended on the left; Gen. Porter's brigade of the New York and Pennsylvania Volunteers with our distinguished riflemen occupied the centre.

I have therefore omitted stating to you that during the 13th and 14th the enemy had kept up a brisk cannonade, which was sharply returned from our batteries without any considerable loss on our part. At 6 p. m. one of their shells lodged in a small magazine in Fort Erie, which was fortunately almost empty; it blew up with an explosion more awful in its appearance than injurious in its effects, as it did not disable a man or damage a gun. It occasioned but a momentary cessation of the thunders of the artillery on both sides; it was followed by a loud and joyous shout of the British army, which was instantly returned on our part, and

Captain Williams, amidst the smoke of the explosion, renewed the contest by an animated roar of his heavy cannon.

From the supposed loss of our ammunition and the consequent depression such an event was likely to produce upon the minds of our men, I felt persuaded that this explosion would lead the enemy to assault, and made my arrangements accordingly. The annexed paper, No. 1, is a copy of Lieut.-Gen. Drummond's plan of attack.

The night was dark and the early part of it raining, but the faithful sentinel slept not. One-third of the troops were up at their posts. At half-past 2 o'clock the right column of the enemy approached, and though enveloped in darkness, black as his designs and principles, was distinctly heard on our left and promptly marked by our musquetry, under Major Wood, and artillery, under Captain Towson. Being mounted at the moment, I repaired to the point of attack, where the sheet of fire rolling from Towson's battery and the musquetry of the left wing of the 21st Infantry, under Major Wood, enabled me to see the enemy's column of about 1,500 men approaching on that point. His advance was not checked until it approached within ten feet of our infantry: a line of loose brush representing an *abattis* only intervened: a column of the enemy attempted to pass round the *abattis* through the water, where it was nearly breast deep: apprehending that this point would be carried, I ordered a detachment of riflemen and infantry to its support, but having met with the gallant commander, Major Wood, was assured by him that he could defend his position without reinforcements.

At this moment the enemy were repulsed, but instantly renewed the charge and were again repulsed. My attention was now called to the right, where our batteries and lines were soon lighted by a most brilliant fire of cannon and musquetry. It announced the approach of the centre and left columns of the enemy, under Colonels Drummond and Scott. The latter was received by the veteran 9th, under the command of Capt. Foster, and Captains Boughton and Harding's companies of New York and Pennsylvania Volunteers, aided by a 6-pounder judiciously posted by Major McRea, chief engineer, who was most active and useful at this point. They were repulsed. That of the centre, led by Col. Drummond, was not long kept in check. It approached at once every assailable point of the fort, and with scaling ladders ascended the parapet, but was repulsed with dreadful carnage. The assault was twice repeated and as often checked, but the enemy having moved round in the ditch, covered by darkness added to the heavy cloud of smoke which had rolled from our cannon and musqetry enveloping surrounding objects, repeated the charge, re-ascended the ladders, and with their pikes, bayonets and spears fell upon our gallant artillerists. The gallant spirits of our favorite Capt. Williams and Lieuts. McDonough and Watmough, with their brave men, were overcome: the two former and several of their men received deadly wounds. Our bastion was lost. Lieut. McDonough being severely wounded, demanded quarter: it was refused by Col. Drummond. The lieutenant then seized a handspike and nobly defended himself until he was shot down with a pistol by the monster who had refused him quarter, who often reiterated the order, "give the damned Yankees no quarter." This officer, whose bravery if it been seasoned with virtue would have entitled him to the admiration of every soldier—this hardened murderer—soon met his fate. He was shot through the breast by ——— of the ——— regiment while repeating the order to give no quarter. The battle now raged with increased fury on the right, but on the left the enemy was repulsed and put to flight: thence and from the centre I ordered reinforcements. They were promptly sent by Brig.-Gen. Ripley and Gen. Porter. Captain Fanning of the corps of artillery kept up a spirited and destructive fire with his field pieces on the enemy attempting to approach the fort. Major Hindman's gallant efforts, aided by Major Trimble, having failed to drive the enemy from the bastion with the remaining artillery and infantry in the fort, Capt. Birdsall of the 4th Rifle Regiment gallantly rushed in through the gateway to their assistance, and with some infantry charged the enemy, but was repulsed and the captain severely wounded. A detachment from the 11th, 19th and 22d Infantry under Capt. Foster of the 11th were introduced over the interior bastion for the purpose of charging the enemy: Major Hall, Assistant-Inspector-General, very handsomely tendered his services to lead the charge. The charge was gallantly made by Capt. Foster and Major Hall, but owing to the narrowness of the passage up the bastion, admitting only 2 or 3 men abreast, it failed. It was often repeated and as often checked. The enemy's force in the bastion was, however, much cut to pieces and diminished by our artillery and small arms.

At this moment every operation was arrested by the explosion of some cartridges deposited in the end of the stone building adjoining the contested bastion: the explosion was tremendous: it was decisive: the bastion was restored.

At this moment Capt. Biddle was ordered to cause a field piece to be posted so as to enfilade the exterior plain and salient glacis. The captain, though not recovered from a severe contusion in the shoulder received from one of the enemy's shells, promptly took his position and served his field piece with vivacity and effect. Capt. Fanning's battery likewise played upon them at this time with great effect. The enemy were in a few moments entirely defeated, taken, or put to flight, leaving on the field 221 killed, 174 wounded, and 186 prisoners, (581), including 14 officers killed and 7 wounded and prisoners. A large portion are so severely wounded that they cannot survive. The slightly wounded, it is presumed, were carried off.

To Brig.-Gen. Ripley much credit is due for the judicious disposition of the left wing previous to the action, and for the steady, disciplined courage manifested by him and his immediate command, and for the promptness with which he complied with my orders for reinforcement during the action. Brig.-Gen. Porter, commanding the New York and Pennsylvania Volunteers, manifested a degree of vigilance and judgment in his preparatory arrangements as well as military skill and courage in action, which proves him worthy the confidence of his country and the brave volunteers who fought under him. Of the volunteers, Captains Boughton and Harding, with their detachments posted on the right and attached to the line commanded by Capt. E. Foster of the veteran 9th Infantry, handsomely contributed to the repulse of the left column of the enemy, under Col. Scott.

The judicious preparations and steady conduct of Lieut.-Col. Aspinwall, commanding the First Brigade, merit approbation. To Major McRea, chief engineer, the greatest credit is due for the excellent arrangement and skilful execution of his plans for fortifying and defending the right, and for his correct and seasonable suggestions in regaining the bastion. Major Wood of the Engineers also greatly contributed to the previous measures of defence. He had accepted the command of a regiment of infantry, (the 21st,) for which he had often proved himself well qualified, but never so conspicuously as on this occasion.

Towson's battery emitted a constant sheet of fire. Wood's small arms lighted up the space and repulsed five terrible charges made between the battery and the lake. Brig.-Gen. Ripley speaks in high terms of the officers and men engaged, particularly Captains Marston and Ropes: Lieutenants Riddle of the 15th, (doing duty with the 21st,) and Hall: Ensigns Benn, Jones, Cummings and Thomas of the 21st : and Keally and Green of the 19th.

Major Hindman, and the whole of the artillery under the command of that excellent officer, displayed a degree of gallantry and good conduct not to be surpassed. The particular situation of Capt. Towson and the much lamented Captain Williams and Lieutenant McDonough, and that of Lieut. Watmough as already described, with their respective commands, rendered them most conspicuous. The courage and good conduct of Lieut. Zantzinger and

Lieut. Chiles is spoken of in high terms by Major Hindman and Captain Towson, as also that of Sergeant-Major Denbon. Captains Biddle and Fanning on the centre and right of their intrenchments threw their shot to the right and left and front, and annoyed the Indians and light troops of the enemy approaching from the woods. Lieut. Fontaine in his zeal to meet the enemy was unfortunately wounded and made prisoner. Lieut. Bird was active and useful, and, in fact, every individual of the corps did their duty.

The detachment of Scott's gallant brigade, consisting of parts of the 9th, 11th and 22d Infantry, did its duty in a manner worthy the high reputation the brigade had acquired at Chippawa, and at the Falls of Niagara. The 9th, under the command of Capt. E. Foster, was actively engaged against the left of the enemy, and with his and Lieut. Douglass's corps of bombardiers commanding the water battery, and of that of the volunteers under Captains Boughton and Harding, effected their repulse. The good conduct of Lieuts. Childs, Cushman and Foote, and Ensign Blake, deserves commendation.

The officers killed are Captain Williams and Lieut. McDonough of the artillery. Wounded—6 other subaltern officers, severely.

Lieut. Fontaine of the artillery, who was taken prisoner, writes from the British camp that he fortunately fell into the hands of the Indians, who after taking his money treated him kindly. It would seem then that these savages had not joined in the resolution to give no quarters.

Brigadier-General Ripley to General Gaines.

FORT ERIE, August 17th, 1814.

SIR,—I take the liberty of reporting to you the course of operations on the left flank of the camp during the action of the 15th instant.

From indications satisfactory to me I was persuaded very early of the enemy's design of attacking us in our position. Before any alarm, I caused my brigade to occupy their alarm posts. On the first fire of the picket, Captain Towson opened his artillery upon them from Fort Williams in a style that does him infinite credit. It was continued with very great effect upon the enemy during the whole action.

The enemy advanced with fixed bayonets and attempted to enter our works between the fort and the water. They brought ladders for the purpose of scaling, and in order to prevent their troops from resorting to any other course excepting the bayonet, had caused all the flints to be taken from their muskets. The column that approached in this direction consisted of Colonel Fischer's command and amounted in number to at least 1,500 men, and according to representations of prisoners they were 2,000 strong. The companies posted at the point of the works which they attempted to escalade were Captain Ross's, Captain Marston's, Lieutenant Bowman's and Lieutenant Larned's of the 21st Regiment, not exceeding 250 men, under the command of Major Wood of the Engineer corps. On the enemy's approach, they opened their musketry in a manner the most powerful. Fort Williams and this little band emitted one broad uninterrupted sheet of light. The enemy were repulsed. They rallied, came on a second time to the charge, and a party waded round our line by the lake and came in on the flank, but a reserve of two companies posted in the commencement of the action to support this point marched up and fired upon the party, who were all killed or taken. Five times in this manner did the enemy advance to the charge; five times were their columns beaten back in confusion by a force one-sixth of their numbers, till at length finding the contest unavailing they retired. At this point we made 147 prisoners.

During the contest in this quarter the lines of the whole of the left wing were perfectly lined in addition to the reserves, and I found myself able to detach three companies of the 23rd Regiment from the left to reinforce the troops at Fort Erie, viz: Captain Wattle's, Lieutenant Cantine's and Lieutenant Brown's companies, and one of the 19th under Captain Chunn. They were in the fort during the time of the explosion, and their conduct is highly spoken of by Major Brooke, their commanding officer. Indeed from the high state to which that regiment has been brought by Major Brooke, I am convinced that no troops will behave better.

In submitting to your view the conduct of the troops under my command on this occasion, I find everything to applaud and nothing to reprehend. The utmost coolness and subordination was manifested both by the 21st and 23rd Regiments. To Major Wood I feel particularly indebted. This officer's merits are so well known that approbation can scarcely add to his reputation. He has the merit with this Spartan band, in connexion with Captain Towson's Artillery, of defeating a vaunting foe of six times his force. Major Brooke did everything in his power, and it affords me pleasure at all times to call the attention of the General commanding to this amiable and accomplished officer.

The officers commanding companies immediately engaged have my highest commendation. Their conduct was most judicious and gallant. I cannot refrain from adverting to the manner in which Captain Towson's Artillery was served. I have never seen it equalled. This officer has so often distinguished himself that to say simply that he is in action is a volume of eulogium; the army only to be informed he is there, by a spontaneous assent are at once satisfied that he has well performed his part. I have no idea that there is an artillery officer in any service superior to him in the knowledge and performance of his duty.

The officers I have mentioned as commanding companies of the 21st and 23rd Regiments are particularly commended by their commanding officers. Captain Marston, a most valuable officer, commanded a first line of three companies opposed to the enemy's column. Captain Ropes commanded the companies of reserve. Major Wood reports in the highest terms of the good conduct of the subalterns, Lieutenant Riddle of the 15th, attached to the 21st, and Ensigns Bean, Jones, Cumming and Thomas of the 19th, as being extremely active and performing their duties with alacrity.

The manner in which Lieutenant Belknap of the 23rd retired with his picket guard from before the enemy's column excites my particular commendation. He gave orders to fire three times, as he was retreating to camp, himself bringing up the rear. In this gallant manner he kept the light advance of the enemy in check for a distance of two or three hundred yards. I have to regret that when entering our lines after his troops the enemy pushed so close upon him that he received a severe wound from a bayonet.

Lieutenants Bushnel and Cissney of the 19th, while gallantly engaged with the enemy at Fort Erie, were both severely if not mortally wounded. Their conduct merits the warmest approbation.

Permit me to recommend to your notice the good conduct of my staff, Lieutenant Kirby of the Corps of Artillery, my aid-de-camp, and Lieutenant Holding, Acting-Brigade-Major. Their activity and zeal was entirely to my satisfaction.

I close this long report with stating to you in the highest terms of approbation the skilfulness exhibited by Doctor Fuller, surgeon of the 23rd, and Doctor Trowbridge, surgeon of the 21st Infantry, with their mates, Dr. Gale of the 23rd and Doctors Everett and Allen of the 21st. Their active, humane and judicious treatment of the wounded, both of the enemy and of our own, together with their steady and constant attention to the duties of their station, must have attracted your attention, and I am confident will receive your approbation.

Report of the Killed, Wounded and Prisoners taken at the Battle of Erie, U. C., August 15th, 1814.

Killed—left on the field, 222; wounded—left on field, 174; prisoners—186. Grand total, 582.

Two hundred supposed to be killed on the left flank (in the water) and permitted to float down the Niagara. The number on the right flank near the woods could not be ascertained.

Given at the Inspector-General's office, Fort Erie, Upper Canada.

NATHL. N. HALL,
Asst.-Inspt.-Gen.

Brigadier-General Gaines to the Secretary of War.

HEADQUARTERS, FORT ERIE.
UPPER CANADA, August 26th, 1814.

SIR,—In my report of the battle of the 15th instant, I inadvertently omitted the names of Captain Chunn of the 19th, Lieutenants Bowman and Larned of the 21st, and Jewitt of the 11th Infantry, as also of my brigade-major, Lieutenant Gleason, each of whom bore a conspicuous part in the action, and whom I beg leave to recommend to your notice. Lieutenants Bowman and Larned commanded companies in the 21st, which so gallantly beat the enemy's right column. Captain Chunn with his company was doing duty with the same regiment. I also omitted mentioning that a part of this regiment pursued the enemy's right upwards of a mile, and took 100 prisoners. His left was also pursued and more than an hundred prisoners were taken beyond our works. These facts prove that the affair was not merely a *defence* of our position, or a mere *repulse* of the enemy, as I find it called by some. As regards myself, I am satisfied with the result and am not disposed to make any difficulty about the name by which the affair may be called, but it is due to the brave men I have the honor to command that I should say that the affair was to the enemy a sore *beating* and a *defeat*, and it was to us a *handsome victory*.

Our position is growing stronger every day by the exertions of Majors McRea and Wood and the officers and men generally. We keep up a smart cannonade. One of the enemy's pickets yesterday approached nearer to ours than usual. Major Brooke, officer of the day, added 100 men to our picket, attacked and drove them in with considerable loss: the Major brought in about 30 muskets. In this affair, however, we have to lament the loss of another gallant officer, Captain Wattles of the 23rd: our loss was otherwise inconsiderable.

(Extracts.)
Charges Preferred Against General Gaines by Col. W. A. Trimble.

General Courtmartial Convened at New York, 2nd Sept., 1816.

CHARGE II.
Misconduct and Gross Injustice in Office.

Specification 2.—In this: That the said Major-General Gaines, being in command of the army of the United States in the battle of the 15th of August, 1814, at the fortified encampment aforesaid, during said battle ordered a small detachment of infantry and riflemen into Fort Erie not to act under the orders of Major Trimble, the officer commanding the fort, but under the direction of an officer of the staff with special orders to charge the northeast bastion of the fort, then in the possession of the enemy—orders which could not be successfully executed—prevented said detachment from being usefully employed, and exposed part of it to destruction without the possibility of subjecting the enemy to equal loss.

Spec. 3.—In this: That at the fortified encampment aforesaid between the 15th and 23d of August, 1814, the said Major-General Gaines, commanding as aforesaid, required many officers to report to him the conduct of their commands at the battle aforesaid, and, actuated by injustice and a vindictive spirit, did not require Major Trimble to report the conduct of his command in said battle, although he held throughout the said battle the separate and highly important command of Fort Erie, where the battle raged with great fury and the enemy was bravely and efficiently fought by said Trimble's command, but required Major Hindman and Major Hall to report the operations in the fort, the former of which officers, being the senior officer of the artillery of the army under the said Major-General Gaines and having the general superintendence of all the artillery attached to said army, was not stationed in Fort Erie, and the command of Major Hall being confined to a small detachment, which was sent into the fort under special orders a very short time before the close of the action and which was, though bravely, worse than uselessly, employed on impracticable service, and neither of which officers had an opportunity to be acquainted with the general defence of the fort—conduct on the part of the said Maj.-Gen. Gaines calculated most unjustly to insult and wound the honorable sensibilities of Major Trimble and the officers and men of the infantry under his command, to exclude them from their rightful participation in the glory and honors of that battle, and to produce dissatisfaction and dissension in the service and injure its interests.

Spec. 4.—In this: That the said Major-General Gaines, in his principal detailed official report to the Secretary of War of the battle of the 15th of August, 1814, aforesaid, with malice and unjustly and contrary to his duty, concealed the fact that Major Trimble commanded Fort Erie during the said battle, and not only concealed said fact but endeavored to communicate the impression that he did not so command, and that in the first part of the action the fort was commanded by Captain Williams and afterwards by Major Hindman—the said Major-General Gaines having, in person, on the evening immediately preceding the action assigned the command of the fort to Major Trimble, and Major Trimble ranking both Captain Williams and Major Hindman and commanding the fort during the battle.

Spec. 5.—In this: That the said Major-General Gaines, in his aforesaid official report of the battle of Fort Erie, stated that the centre column of the enemy, led by Colonel Drummond, "approached at once every assailable part of the fort, and with scaling ladders ascended the parapet, but was repulsed with dreadful carnage. The assault was twice repeated and as often checked," whereas the whole efforts of said column of the enemy in the first part of the action and during the time alluded to in said statement, as said Maj.-Gen. Gaines knew or ought to have known, were directed against the north curtain of the fort (or north line of the redoubt connecting the bastions of the fort), and that the said Major-General Gaines in said statement and throughout said report omitted to mention that it was by the detachment of the 19th Infantry, stationed in the fort, that this service was performed: the said Major-General Gaines being careful in other parts of his report to state who were engaged in the services mentioned and alleged, herein misrepresenting the battle of Fort Erie, unjustly injuring the officers and men of the detachment of the 19th Infantry stationed in the fort, and acting with improper partiality towards other parts of the army he commanded, to the injury of the service.

Spec. 6.—In this: That the said Major-General Gaines, in his aforesaid official report of the battle of Fort Erie, represented and caused to be understood that the left column of the enemy, led by Col. Scott, was completely repulsed and finally driven from the contest by the American troops stationed to the right of Fort Erie and between the fort and the lake: and that the said Maj.-Gen. Gaines in his official report suppressed the facts that the said left column of the enemy, having advanced in the direction and within about 50 yards of an opening in the said line between the fort and the lake and being deterred from proceeding further in that direction, and from entering said opening by an incessant blaze of fire from the Douglass battery and the artillery and infantry stationed on said line, moved promptly to the right, gained the ditch of the northeast bastion of the fort and was the first to assault and enter the bastion ; that a large proportion of the prisoners remaining and taken in and near the fort belonged to the 103d Regiment; and that it was at the fort that Colonel Scott, who commanded said column, was mortally wounded, and Captain Elliott, who conducted it, was made prisoner; which facts the said Major-General Gaines at the time of making his said report ought to have known and did know ; the said Major-General Gaines by said wilful misstatements and suppression of facts materially misrepresenting the battle to his government, unjustly depriving the garrison of Fort Erie, particularly the detachment of the 19th Infantry, of the credit of important services which they had performed, contrary to his duty, and to the injury of the service.

Spec. 7.—In this: That the said Major-Gen. Gaines, in his aforesaid official report of the battle of Fort Erie, stated that Captain Fanning of the corps of artillery kept up a spirited and destructive fire with field pieces on the enemy attempting to approach the fort, whereas no part of the centre and left columns of the enemy, the columns which attacked the fort, were within range of Captain Fanning's field pieces, and, if the Indians and light troops of the enemy in front of the encampment were referred to in said statement, there was not evidence nor ground of presumption to warrant the assertion that Capt. Fanning's fire, however spirited, was destructive, and the strong presumption was that it could not have been so.

And that the said Major-General Gaines in his official report stated that "Captain Fanning's battery likewise played upon them (the enemy) at this time with great effect," whereas at the time referred to the enemy were not within scope of Captain Fanning's battery, and of course could not have been played upon it with effect.

And that the said Major-General Gaines in said report represented and gave it to be understood that Brigadier-General Porter, commanding the New York and Pennsylvania Volunteers, and said volunteers generally, were engaged in action in the aforesaid battle at Fort Erie, and mentioned him and them with high commendation for their conduct in action therein, whereas Captain Boughton's and Captain Harding's companies, detached and distantly separated from General Porter's command in said battle, and not under his command therein, were the only part of said volunteers who fought or could be said to be engaged in action in said battle, they being under the command of Lieut.-Col. Aspinwall on the right of the American position and acting with Capt. Foster of the 11th.

And that the said Major-General Gaines in his said official report stated that "Captain Birdsall of the 4th Rifle Regiment with a detachment of riflemen gallantly rushed in through the gateway" (of Fort Erie) "to their assistance," (meaning to the assistance of Major Hindman and Major Trimble,) "and with some infantry charged the enemy but was repulsed and the captain severely wounded," thereby exhibiting in detail with praise conduct *in Fort Erie*, which, though gallant, was of little or no avail, and of very short continuance.

And that the said Major-General Gaines, in his said official report, detailed, "that a detachment of the 11th, 9th and 22d Infantry, under Capt. Foster of the 11th, were introduced over the interior bastion" (of Fort Erie) "for the purpose of charging the enemy. Major Hall, Assistant-Inspector-General, very handsomely tendered his services to lead the charge. The charge was gallantly made by Capt. Foster and Major Hall, but owing to the narrowness of the passage up the bastion, admitting only two or three men abreast, it failed. It was often repeated and as often checked," thereby showing forth in detail and with praise, and calling the attention of his government to the conduct of officers and men *in Fort Erie*, who were sent into the fort only a short time before the close of the action, and, however bravely, were worse than uselessly employed on impracticable service, and for a few minutes only.

And that the said Major-General Gaines, in said official report, with malice omitted to mention the judicious arrangements and preparations which Major Trimble under the most embarrassing circumstances made for the defence of Fort Erie: the gallant manner in which the detachment of 19th Infantry, stationed in the fort, repelled the repeated assaults of the centre column of the enemy, and the prompt and skilful disposition made of said detachment, and the cool and desperate courage it displayed in the most hazardous situation and against a great superiority of force when the enemy obtained possession of the northeast bastion of the fort, that a part of said detachment was formed so as to command the gorge of said bastion, under cover of which line part of which detachment was thrown into the adjoining stone messhouse, and that thence a constant and destructive fire was kept up on the enemy, that a part of said detachment without the messhouse was posted in a situation which afforded it security and enabled it to pour into the bastion a direct and deadly fire: that the enemy repeatedly advanced from the bastion to gain possession of the fort, and twice attempted to force the door of the messhouse aforesaid, and were driven back with loss by said detachment of the 19th Infantry and a small detachment of artillery, which in the last attack were aided by Lieutenant John Brady who had just come into the fort with about twenty men of the 22d Infantry,— several of which circumstances were communicated in a written statement to the said Major-General Gaines before he forwarded or closed his said official report, and all of which circumstances and of the defence of Fort Erie generally the said Major-General Gaines might have obtained full information had he required it of Major Trimble, as it was his duty to have done, and that the said Major-General Gaines with malice omitted to allude to said circumstances in the particular manner in which they merited to be spoken of in the said report.

The said Major-General Gaines by said representations, wilfully incorrect statements and designed suppression of facts, in his said official report, ascribing services to officers and men which they did not peform, displaying services some of them performed *in Fort Erie* with disproportionate emphasis and minuteness and improper partiality, and unjustly concealing other services of much greater importance and usefulness performed in Fort Erie, grossly injuring and insulting Major Trimble and the officers and men of said detachment of the 19th Infantry, and very materially misrepresenting the battle of Fort Erie to his government, to the injury of the service.

Spec. 8.—In this: That the said Major-General Gaines, in his official report aforesaid, stated that "at this moment every operation was arrested by the explosion of some cartridges deposited in the end of the stone building adjoining the contested bastion. The explosion was tremendous—it was decisive—the bastion was restored," hereby very improperly misrepresenting the place of the explosion —the cartridges that exploded not being in the end of the stone building adjoining the contested bastion, but under the platform of the bastion, and the end of the stone building being occupied by his own troops, part of the 19th Infantry, who poured from it a constant and destructive fire on the enemy, and further, by the said statement, unjustly and to the great injury of part of his army, ascribing to an untoward accident a victory which had been insured by the valor and good conduct of his troops, who had fought the enemy without intermission and at first under the most disadvantageous circumstances for more than two hours—and the said Major-General Gaines knowing, or it being his duty to have known, that the enemy had been repeatedly repulsed and driven from the interior of the fort, that they had suffered extremely from the fire of the garrison, to which they could do but little injury, and that had they remained in the bastion but a few minutes longer their capture or destruction might have been made certain.

CHARGE IV.
Neglect of Duty and Misconduct in Office.

Spec. 1.—In this: That the said Major-General Gaines, in his principal detailed official report to the Secretary of War of the battle of Fort Erie aforesaid, stated that "the small unfinished Fort Erie with a 24, 18 and 12-pounders forms the northeast, and the Douglass Battery, with an 18 and 6-pounder near the edge of the lake, the southeast angle of our right," there being, as it was the duty of the said Major-General Gaines to have known, six pieces of cannon in Fort Erie and but one, an 18-pounder, in the Douglass Battery.

Spec. 2.—In this: That the said Major-General Gaines, in his said official report, stated that "the front of our position had been strengthened by temporary *abatis*," &c., there being at the time, as it was the duty of the said Major-General Gaines to have known, on what he denominated the front of our position no *abatis* nor anything representing *abatis*.

Spec. 3.—In this: That the said Major-General Gaines, being in command of the army of the United States at Fort Erie and the adjoining fortified encampment, between the 5th and 15th of August, 1814, and having good reason to expect an attack from the army of the enemy under the command of Lieut.-General Drummond, greatly superior in numbers to his own army, neglected to strengthen and improve the defence and works of his said position to the extent he had the means and it was his duty to strengthen and improve them.

Spec. 4.—In this: That the said Major-General Gaines, being in command as aforesaid on the 14th of August, 1814, and having every reason to expect an attack from the enemy's army, under Lieut.-Gen. Drummond, neglected to make that arrangement and provision for the defence of Fort Erie which the place required, and which by a proper use of the means at his disposal he might have made; and that he intrusted the defence of that place, the key of his position, to about sixty artillerists and to about one hundred and eighteen infantry recruits who had never seen service and were placed in the fort under the most embarrassing and unfavorable circumstances.

Spec. 5.—In this: That the said Major-General Gaines, on the 15th August, 1814, at the fortified encampment aforesaid, being then and there in command as aforesaid, made no attempt to intercept, capture, or destroy the right column of the enemy after it had been effectually repulsed in the battle of the said 15th of August, from Towson's battery, and was retreating in great disorder without flints or cartridges.

Spec. 6.—In this: That the said Major-General Gaines at the time and place last aforesaid, being then and there in command as aforesaid, neglected to make a sortie on the centre and left columns of the enemy when they were in great confusion in the northeast bastion of the fort and its surrounding ditches, in which last place they could have made but little resistance to an attack on their flank or rear.

Spec. 7.—In this: That the said Major-General Gaines at the time and place aforesaid, after the explosion of some ammunition under the platform of the before mentioned bastion, suffered the centre and left columns of the enemy, in great confusion and disorder and partly unarmed, to retire from Fort Erie over a plain without making or having made any effort or attempt to capture them.

Spec. 8.—In this: That the aforesaid Major-General Gaines at the time and place aforesaid, being then and there in command as aforesaid, neglected to avail himself of the advantages gained by the valour of his troops in the action fought between the American and British forces at Fort Erie and Towson's battery, on the said 15th August, the situation and condition of the British forces being such as would have exposed them to inevitable destruction had the American army been properly commanded.

Finding.

1st Nov., 1816.

The court do therefore honorably acquit him (General Gaines) of the same, and the court feel it to be due to the good of the service to pronounce that most of the charges appear to it as frivolous, and the whole of them without support or foundation.

(Sgd.) WINFIELD SCOTT,
Brevet Major-General, President.

Lieut. MacMahon to Mr. Wm. Jarvis.

CAMP BEFORE FORT ERIE, 22nd August, 1814.

DEAR SIR,—I have received and laid before the President your letter of the 17th, and am sorry that it is not in my power under present circumstances to prepare warrants for the payment of your office accounts to the 30th June. I have, however, obtained the letter of credit for fifty pounds sterling, which in the event of the warrants not being granted, you desire, and which you will receive herewith.

Since the assault of the fort on the morning of the 15th nothing of any moment has taken place between the armies. Cannonading and skirmishing daily takes place, in which there are always lives lost. The day before yesterday a serious one for the enemy took place with the Western Indians, in which the former lost about fifty, killed and wounded, and the latter only two. On this occasion the Indians behaved with great spirit and drove the enemy to their very works.

The result of an assault upon the fort we have great cause to lament, for our loss in valuable officers and the best of our men, which, including all ranks, was 920, was one which at the present moment we can but badly bear; and this is the more to be regretted as the loss which the enemy sustained on the occasion did not exceed 50 men. A considerable portion of the loss on our part was occasioned by the explosion of a quantity of ammunition which the enemy had placed under the platform of the bastion at which our troops had entered and made a lodgment, and but for which the place would have been ours. It was not, however, intentionally placed there for the purpose, but, seeing the opportunity and availing himself of it, a corporal of American Artillery, having got on a red coat and the cap of a British deserter, and while it was scarce daylight, got in amongst our men, who were principally in and near this bastion, and appeared to make himself very busy in working the gun, which by this time had been turned against the enemy, and in the bustle he got under the platform and effected his purpose by a slow match. He had but just time himself to slink off and get behind a stone building in the fort when this unfortunate explosion took place, which has left the 103rd Regt., who were principally at that point, but a mere skeleton. Poor Col. Drummond, whose loss is universally deplored, Colonel Scott of the 103rd, Capt. Irwin of the same corps, Capt. Torrens of the Royals, and many others, some of whom from their mutilated state could not be identified, have fallen in this affair. Colonel Drummond was mortally wounded before the explosion, as was Col. Scott, but the other officers which I have mentioned were all blown up. Capt. Elliott of the Quartermaster-General's department was also blown up, but I am glad to say was only slightly wounded; he is prisoner. The 103rd have lost on that unfortunate morning, killed, wounded, &c., 370, and out of 18 officers present 14 were killed and wounded. De Watteville's Regiment, which were before held in high estimation, lost on that morning their claim to distinction. That corps with the King's and some of the flank companies of other regiments composed the right column, under Colonel Fischer of the former corps, which was destined to attack an important point of the enemy's works, and it marched with the greatest steadiness and order till within about three hundred yards of the point of attack, when suddenly the Dutchmen caught a panic which no exertions of the officers could remove, and that regiment, being strong and rather near the head of the column, when they turned all the other corps in rear, who were weak, were compelled to give way.

The enemy kept up a most tremendous fire of musquetry and artillery from half-past two o'clock until daylight, when our troops retired, during which time a single shot was not discharged by us, the whole dependence being placed in the bayonet when the troops should enter the works for the accomplishment of the object, and to prevent the possibility of men breaking through the orders the flints were all taken out of the musquets. The enemy maintained their ground with bravery, but then they had all the firing to themselves, and few of our men came in contact with them. We were for a day or two greatly dispirited, but it is now dispelled and the troops in high spirits once more. We are preparing again for offensive operations.

Believe me, dear sir, faithfully yours,
EDW. MACMAHON.

William Jarvis, Esq.

Extract from a Letter from Col. J. Le Couteur to Col. H. Le Couteur.

17 CHAPEL STREET,
BELGRAVIA, 29th July, 1869.

MY DEAREST HALKETT,—I was greatly interested in that part of your letter in which you tell of my gallant friend's death, Col. Scott of the 103d, at the storming of Fort Erie.

After we were blown up, some three or four hundred men, by the springing of the mine or magazine in Fort Erie, on recovering my senses from being blown off the parapet some twenty feet into the ditch, which was filled with burnt and maimed men, the Yankees relined their works and fired heavily into the ditch.

My colonel, Drummond of Keltie, had commanded the right attack, Col. Scott the left attack. Finding that the ditch was not to be held under such disarray and such a fire, several of us jumped over the scarp and ran over the plain to our lines. Lieut. Fallon of the 103d, who was desperately wounded, was caught by his sling belt in a log and thought to die there; however, I said to my grenadier friend, " Jack, my boy, put your arm over my neck and I will take you round the waist and run you into the lines." The Yankees were then pelting us with grape and musketry. As we jogged on I saw an officer carried on his back in some sort of a stretcher and I said to the four men, "Who is that officer?" "Col. Scott, sir, shot through the head," where I saw the bullet mark in the noble man's forehead. When I got my friend into the lines, regardless of who was by, in a fit of sorrow, I threw my sabre down exclaiming, "This is a disgraceful day for Old England." Col. M., who heard me, said, "For shame, Mr. Le Couteur! The men are sufficiently discouraged by defeat." Col. Pearson said, "Don't blame him! It is the high feeling of a young soldier." To my surprise the commander-in-chief, Sir Gordon Drummond, had heard all this as he was close behind and asked me, "Where is Col. Scott?" "Oh! Sir! He is killed, just being brought in by his men." "Where is Col. Drummond?" "Alas! Sir! He is killed too! Bayonetted!" And I burst into tears at the loss of my beloved commander and three parts of my men. Sir Gordon immediately gave me orders to collect all the stragglers, line the works, and prepare to resist an attack should the Yankees assault our works, which they did not do.

Poor Drummond's body remained in the American lines blown up. Col. Scott received a soldier's funeral—a most amiable and gallant officer; indeed, there were no two more heroic men in our army.

Dr. Young, Surgeon of 103rd Regiment, to Mr. James Scott, Writer to the Signet, Edinburgh.

QUEBEC, 20th December, 1814.

DEAR SIR,—I wrote you in August last announcing the death of your much lamented brother, the late Col. Scott. Part of the regiment arrived here a few days ago and the rest are on their way for this place, where we are to winter. On their arrival I expect to be able to settle all the concerns of your brother in the regiment and send you a statement of them. The affairs of the regiment have been in much confusion of late from the loss of so many of the principal officers, viz.: your brother and the adjutant and Capt. Irwin, the acting paymaster, &c., and the corps have not been together, and they have suffered severely from sickness.

I informed you in my last that your brother on being wounded was attended by some of our men and one of the assistant surgeons of the 89th Regt. He inquired for me, and as I was not present he directed that all his effects should be given to me. In consequence of this Lieut.-Col. Smelt desired me to take charge of his property and to settle his affairs, and if I required it that he would give me every assistance in his power, and to write you the particulars of his last moments. Altho' I had the honor of being more in your brother's confidence than any one in the regiment, he never hinted anything to me concerning his affairs in this country in case of his fall. I suppose he considered them of too trivial a nature, as he had left his will at home. The night of the attack I slept on the ground with him under a piece of canvas suspended from a branch of a tree, but not sufficient to protect us from the inclemency of a dreadful rainy night. I asked him his opinion of the attack; he spoke unfavorably of it, yet tho' drenched with rain he was in high spirits, and his last words to me before he led off the corps were: "We shall breakfast together in the fort in the morning." Alas! when I saw him again he was mortally wounded and he could not speak to me, but the slight pressure from his hand and the languid expression of his countenance seemed to say, "I am dying! Farewell! I leave you my best wishes."

Extract from Dr. Young's Letter of Aug. 18th, 1814, to Mr. Scott.

Your brother was wounded in the fort. He was carried off by a sergeant of grenadiers and one of the men. His remains were interred on the evening of the day on which he fell. We had a coffin made by the regimental carpenters, who have since enclosed his grave with a wooden paling. His funeral was attended by three officers and myself, the whole that remained untouched after the attack.

Sir George Prevost to Lieut.-General Drummond.
(Secret.)

HEADQUARTERS, MONTREAL, 25th July, 1814.

SIR,—I have had the honor of your letter of the 20th inst. transmitting four letters (originals) from Major-General Riall, with their enclosures from Lieut.-Colonel Tucker of the 41st and Major Evans of the King's Regiment. The events detailed in these, which have lately taken place on the Niagara frontier, are highly creditable to the steadiness and gallantry of the troops, and to the skill and judgment of the officers in command of them.

The general features of the campaign have been so much the subject of my late communications that but little remains for me to add.

Your local knowledge will give you great advantage and much is left to your discretion, upon which I have the fullest reliance.

Should the enemy remain at Queenston after the concentration of our forces upon the 12 or 20-Mile Creek has taken place, would it not be expedient to cross over some troops to Fort Niagara for the purpose of being detached from thence to Lewiston to deprive the Americans of that *debouche* to retreat.

The movement from the fort ought to be simultaneous with the advance upon Queenston Heights. It appears to me that the sooner you commence molesting General Brown's line of communication and by which he obtains his supplies, the easier will his task prove.

It is now stated that Commodore Chauncey's squadron will not be ready to take the lake before the end of the month. If that information prove correct and Brown's army remains stationary at Queenston, I have hopes it will not escape without a severe retribution for the evils it has inflicted. I have enumerated in the margin the corps with and destined for the Right and Centre Divisions; the expansion of the force to the Right Division must depend on the success of your operations, never losing sight of the principal object of the campaign, the destruction of Sackett's Harbour.

Major-General Powers' brigade consisting of the 3rd, 5th, 27th and 58th Regiments, from Bordeaux, is in the river, and part of it has arrived at Quebec. It left Bordeaux on the 5th June.

(Memo. in the Margin.)

Proposed force of the Right Division:
    1st Battn. Royals.
    6th Regt.
    1st Battn. King's.
    41st Regt.
    82d   do.
    89th do.
    100th do.
    103d do.
    104th flank companies.
    Canadian Fencibles.
    Glengarry Light Infantry.
    De Watteville's Regiment.
    Exclusive of cavalry, artillery, militia and Indian warriors.

Proposed force of the Centre Division:
    16th Regt.
    90th do.
    97th do.
    104th do.
    Nova Scotia Fencibles.
    Exclusive of artillery, cavalry and militia.

Sir George Prevost to Lord Bathurst, Secretary of State for the Colonies.
(No. 183.)

HEADQUARTERS, MONTREAL, 5th August, 1814.

MY LORD,—I had the honor of addressing Your Lordship on the 13th of last month, for the purpose of reporting that the enemy crossed the Niagara River on the 3rd, and of stating the events that had resulted from that movement.

As soon as I became acquainted with the intention of His Majesty's government strongly to reinforce the army in the North American Provinces, the troops in Lower Canada not immediately employed in opposing the advance of the United States commanded by Major-General Izard against the Richelieu frontier, were pushed forward under Major-General Conran to replace those Lieutenant-General Drummond had drawn from York and Kingston, with the view of strengthening the Right Division, to the command of which Lieutenant-General Drummond had repaired with characteristic promptitude before my wishes on the subject could be made known to him.

I have the high satisfaction of transmitting to Your Lordship Lieutenant-General Drummond's detail of the distinguished exertions of that division of the army near the Falls of Niagara on the 25th of last month, when the skill and the valour and discipline of his troops were eminently conspicuous, and I beg leave to join the Lieutenant-General in soliciting His Royal Highness the Prince Regent's gracious reward of the officers particularized in his report.

Major-General Conran arrived at Fort George with a wing of De Watteville's Regiment on the 29th ulto.—the remainder of that corps, with the 6th and 82nd Regiments, were fast approaching York. I have just received a report that His Majesty's ships *York* and *Vengeur* are at anchor in the river, and that the transports under their convoy with troops from France are arriving at Quebec.

This despatch will be delivered to Your Lordship by Captain Jervois, aide-de-camp to Lieutenant-General Drummond. Having shared in the events of the 25th, he can satisfy Your Lordship's enquiries respecting them, and he is well calculated to give Your Lordship full information upon the state of the Upper Province.

Sir George Prevost to Lord Bathurst.
(No. 184.)

HEADQUARTERS, MONTREAL, 5th August, 1814.

MY LORD,—Intelligence has just reached me that Commodore Chauncey's squadron was under weigh and cruising out of Sackett's

Harbor on the 1st inst., probably for the purpose of proceeding off Niagara in order to co-operate with Major-General Brown.

This fleet will arrive too late to be any material service to the American army. It is perhaps intended to receive on board all the troops which can be procured from that frontier in order to convey them to Sackett's Harbour, there to be reinforced by the disposable part of that garrison and then to attempt the execution of part of General Armstrong's plan of operations towards the close of this campaign, particularly the interruption of the intercourse between the two Provinces.

Your Lordship may rely on my adopting every practicable precautionary measure to prevent the success of such a design.

The transports with the two last brigades of troops from Bordeaux are approaching Quebec, where arrangements have been made for their being pushed forward without a moment's delay. But notwithstanding every exertion, it will be impossible to collect the whole force in the neighborhood of this place before the end of the present month.

This circumstance is the less to be regretted as our fleets on the lakes cannot attain a sufficient strength to co-operate with the divisions of the army assembling for the destruction of Sackett's Harbour and the occupation of Plattsburg before the 15th of next month, and without their aid and protection nothing could be undertaken affording a reasonable hope of substantial advantage.

The State of Vermont having shown a decided opposition to the war and very large supplies of specie daily coming in from thence, as well as the whole of the cattle required for the use of the troops, I mean for the present to confine myself in any offensive operations which may take place to the western shore of Lake Champlain.

Sir George Prevost to Lieut. General Drummond.

HEADQUARTERS, MONTREAL, 13th August, 1814.

SIR,—I have had the honor to receive your letters of the 31st ulto. and 4th inst. I have only to observe in reply that your suggestion respecting Kingston has been anticipated by the arrangements which have been made for assembling in the first instance General Kempt's brigade at this place and the allotment of it for the service you mention.

I have remarked with pain and mortification the conduct of the troops under the command of Lieut.-Colonel Tucker in the enterprise entrusted to him on the right bank of the Niagara river, and must confess I had expected a very different result.

The enemy appear to have made extraordinary exertions since the last action, for the defence of the position they have taken up. The caution, therefore, with which you have acted in the previous measures to an attack upon them I cannot but commend as being the best calculated to obtain the end wished for—the defeat and expulsion of the enemy without an unnecessary effusion of blood.

I am in hopes that the fire of your batteries, which I observe by a letter from Colonel Harvey of the 6th inst. were to open on the 7th, will have all the effect you expect from them, particularly their vertical fire and rockets, which will be most likely to intimidate the enemy.

Precautionary measures ought immediately to be taken to replace from the depots at Kingston the small arm and great gun ammunition which shall be expended on the Niagara frontier.

The reports received from Kingston of the return of Chauncey to Sackett's Harbour on the 9th, lead me to hope that the 6th and 82nd Regiments will have no difficulty in joining you. Strengthened by such a description of men as they are composed of, you will be competent to resist any efforts of the enemy, however they may be reinforced, and I trust finally to expel them.

The measures you shall adopt for that purpose will, I am satisfied, be prudent and proper.

Whilst such important operations have been pending, Major Coore has acted right in availing himself of my instructions to remain at your headquarters.

Sir George Prevost to Lieut.-General Drummond.
(An Intercepted Letter.)

MONTREAL, Aug. 26, 1814.

SIR,—I have the honor to acknowledge the receipt of your official letters of the 15th and 16th with their enclosures, and a private one of the 17th inst.

I do most deeply regret the sequel of the gallant enterprise which put into your possession two of the enemy's schooners. You appear to have been inclined to precipitate the attack of Fort Erie by a desire to reap the full benefit of the spirit of emulation produced by that daring achievement. If the object had been accomplished, a scrutiny of the operations to attain it would have been equally excited, and it is not in reproach of its failure that I observe to you that night attacks made with heavy troops are very objectionable, principally because chance and not skill too frequently decide the contest, and that at night difficulties and dangers are ever magnified, particularly when they present themselves unexpectedly, and in the latter case the best disciplined troops are placed only on a level with raw and unformed soldiers.

It is to be inferred from Lieut.-Colonel Fischer's report and your statement that the Right Column was not sufficiently prepared for the obstacles it had to surmount in attaining the point of attack, otherwise neither hesitation nor consternation would have presented themselves.

I acknowledge that I feel apprehensive you have rather yielded to than approved the eagerness of the Right Division to increase its fame, before you were sufficiently prepared for the enterprise. Your skill and excellent judgment will profit by experience in your future operations, by guarding you against public opinion, however clamorous, when it would sacrifice your well-earned reputation and the honor and safety of the army placed under your command.

I sincerely hope the candor with which I have disclosed my sentiments on your last operation will be to you their best apology. They flow from a source unpolluted by any invidious feeling.

The 37th is ordered to Kingston, from whence General Stovin is desired to send you the 97th or any other corps you may have demanded. Major-General Kempt with the remainder of the troops will soon follow. My views in sending that officer to Kingston will be developed to you by the Adjutant-General.

Sir George Prevost to Lieut.-General Sir Gordon Drummond.
(An Intercepted Letter.)

MONTREAL, Aug. 26th, 1814.

SIR,—Major Coore has this moment delivered to me your letter of the 16th. I view with pain the agony of mind you experience from the unfortunate termination of the night attack you had been induced to make on the 15th, and would gladly soothe your feelings on the occasion by anything I could offer in addition to the sentiments you will find expressed in the letter I addressed to you this morning, but all I have heard since has confirmed my prejudices to highly important operations being performed in the dark. Too much was required from De Watteville's Regiment so situated and deprived, as I am told they were, of their flints. The attempt has proved a costly experiment, and its result will be severely felt.

As you have fixed on the 90th, orders shall be given for that regiment to proceed to you without delay. I had intended the 97th for that service as being men of a hardy description, but the numbers of the 90th will probably make them equally useful to you. When this regiment, together with the 6th and 82nd, shall have joined you, you will, I have no doubt, be enabled to efface the recollection of the late disaster and to effect the expulsion of the enemy from the Province.

Sir George Prevost to Vice Admiral the Honorable Alexander Cochrane.

HEADQUARTERS, MONTREAL, 30th July, 1814.

SIR,—Since writing to you on the 20th June last communicating the wanton destruction of private property on the north shore of Lake Erie, a repetition of similar outrages has taken place on the Niagara frontier. The enemy crossed the Niagara river with 6,000 men on the 3d of July, and having immediately afterwards got possession of Fort Erie advanced towards Chippawa, where Major-General Riall had collected about 1,500 troops, exclusive of militia and Indians. With this small force, he on the 5th anticipated the attack which the enemy had intended to make on his position on the following day, and after a severe contest of several hours, in consequence of the great inferiority in his numbers, he was obliged to retire to his lines at Chippawa with great loss. Two days afterwards, his position being turned, he retreated to Fort George, and the American army advanced to Queenston.

In this situation it remained for nearly three weeks, occasionally making a demonstration for attacking the forts, but evidently waiting for the co-operation of the fleet from Sackett's Harbour. During this time the possession by the enemy of Queenston and St. David's with a force far superior to any we could oppose to it, enabled them to follow up with impunity the same disgraceful mode of warfare to which they have hitherto so frequently resorted, the wanton destruction of private property. The villages of Queenston and St. David's were committed to the flames by them and totally destroyed.

Lieutenant-General Drummond arrived at Fort George on the 24th, and the enemy, despairing of any co-operation from the fleet, began on the following day to retreat from Queenston. Major-General Riall being immediately pushed forward with the advance to harass them on their retreat, was attacked by their whole force on the evening of that day, and General Drummond shortly afterwards coming up with the remainder of our disposable troops on that frontier, a general action commenced, which terminated at midnight by the total discomfiture of the enemy. I have not yet received the official details of the action, but the enclosed will give you the substance of the information which has reached me respecting it.

You will observe by it that the enemy on the last moment of retiring added another act of wanton outrage to those before committed, by the destruction of Messrs. Clarke and Street's mills, the most useful and valuable in the country, and the loss of which will be long and severely felt by the peaceful and unoffending inhabitants, who were accustomed to resort to them with their grain.

These events so dishonorable to the American character, so little merited by the forbearance I have practiced, I deem it my duty to bring under your consideration as affording ample grounds of justification for any conflagrations which may have taken place on the coast, and as calling loudly for a severe retribution, which I trust when opportunities offer you will not fail to inflict.

Sir George Prevost to Lord Bathurst.
(No. 187.)

HEADQUARTERS, MONTREAL, 14th August, 1814.

MY LORD,—Since I had the honor of addressing Your Lordship on the 5th inst., it has been ascertained that the enemy's squadron sailed from Sackett's Harbour on the 4th with reinforcements of troops for General Brown's army, which were disembarked on the 6th a few miles below the fort of Niagara, near a road leading to Buffalo.

The fleet afterwards made its appearance off York and Kingston, and are now blockading the latter port. The naval ascendency possessed by the enemy on Lake Ontario enables him to perform in two days what our troops going from Kingston to reinforce the Right Division require from sixteen to twenty of severe marching to accomplish: their men arrive fresh, whilst ours are fatigued and with an exhausted equipment. The route from Kingston to the Niagara frontier exceeds two hundred and fifty miles, and passes in several places through a tract of country impracticable for the conveyance of extensive supplies. By our exertions the Right Division has been placed beyond the apprehension of any material want before the period fixed by Sir James Yeo for taking the lake with his augmented force: until then our best endeavors will be used to prevent the enemy from making a serious impression on the Upper Province. Whilst Kingston is blockaded, Your Lordship must be aware that no movement against Sackett's Harbour can take place. It will require extreme vigilance to prevent the interruption of our intercourse from hence with that post, and to secure the highly important supplies which are at this moment on their way for an ulterior service and for the armament of the large ship, as well as the transport of the frame and stores of one of our frigates.

* * * * * * * *

The accompanying despatch from Lieut.-General Drummond addressed to me, together with the reply I made, will show Your Lordship the exact state of our affairs on the Niagara frontier on the 6th inst., at which time the enemy did not manifest any disposition to recross the Niagara River, an event not to be regretted provided our resources are sufficient (as I trust they are) to compel them to lay down their arms or to attempt such a retreat as cannot fail to prove disastrous to them.

It is with regret I state to Your Lordship that it appears by Lieut.-Colonel Harvey's letter of the 6th, referred to in my reply to General Drummond's despatch, that Major-General Conran, who had just assumed the command of the Right Division, had been so much injured by a severe fall from his horse as to be incapable of serving for some time. Another Major-General has been immediately ordered forward to supply his place.

Sir George Prevost to Lord Bathurst.
(No. 189.)

HEADQUARTERS, MONTREAL, 27th August, 1814.

MY LORD,—The successful result of the gallant enterprise against the enemy's small vessels laying off Fort Erie, as detailed in the enclosed extract of a despatch from Lieut.-General Drummond, having encouraged the expectation that a favorable period had arrived for attacking the enemy in their entrenchment, the Lieut.-General was induced to order an assault upon Fort Erie and the works connected with it before the break of day on the 15th inst.

It is with deep concern I have now to acquaint Your Lordship that notwithstanding there was the fairest prospect of success at the commencement of the attack, our troops were afterwards obliged to retire without accomplishing their object and with very considerable loss.

To Lieut.-General Drummond's official report on this subject (a copy of which I have the honor of transmitting) I beg leave to refer Your Lordship for the causes of our failure. It is, however, highly satisfactory to know that until the unfortunate explosion took place, and until His Majesty's troops by their near approach to the *abatis* in front of the intrenchments met such difficulties in penetrating as were found to be insurmountable without the aid of light, they behaved with their usual gallantry and discipline, and had gained by their determined efforts advantages which accident alone appears to have compelled them to forego.

By accounts from Major-General Drummond to the 18th inst., I find he has since the 15th been joined by the 82nd Regiment and that the 6th was on the way and would probably be with the Right Division by this time. These regiments and reinforcements which are proceeding to the Right Division will fully supply the late losses and enable the Lieut.-General again to commence offensive operations against the enemy's position.

(Extract.)
No. 190.

HEADQUARTERS, MONTREAL, 27th August, 1814.

MY LORD,—

* * * * * * * *

The vacillatory communications I have received from Sir James Yeo put it out of my power to state to Your Lordship exactly when the first-rate ship building at Kingston will be launched, but from the representations of Major Coore, my aide-de-camp, who is just returned from the Right Division, it is not probable can take place before the middle of next month, and in consequence all hopes of seeing our squadron on Lake Ontario before the first week in October have vanished.

The most pressing and important service to be performed by the Commodore as soon as his squadron shall have acquired the ascendence is the conveyance of fresh troops, with a large proportion of provisions and supplies of every description, to York and the Niagara frontier before the navigation closes, and to bring from those places to Kingston the exhausted corps, the disabled and the sick who can endure transport.

In the accompanying copy of a letter from Lieut.-General Drummond on the subject of supplies, Your Lordship will find there is ample cause for the anxiety I experience respecting our naval preparations, as well as for the delay in the arrival of provisions sufficient for ten thousand men for six months, which Your Lordship in your secret dispatch of the 3d of June did me the honor to announce as ordered to be immendiately shipped for Quebec.

The resources of the Upper Province being exhausted, a large supply of provisions of every nature must be thrown into it before the navigation of the St. Lawrence and Lake Ontario becomes impracticable. Unfortunately our magazines do not afford salt provisions for the purpose, and of that important article much will be required, more, I apprehend, than it will be possible to transport from Quebec to Kingston unless winter is more backward in its approach than usual, or that the supply is nearer at hand than I contemplate.

In fact, my Lord, two-thirds of the army in Canada are at this moment eating beef provided by American contractors, drawn principally from the States of Vermont and New York. This circumstance, as well as the introduction of large sums of specie into this Province, being notorious in the United States, it is to be expected that Congress will take steps to deprive us of those resources, and under that apprehension large droves are daily crossing the lines coming into Lower Canada.

The accompanying report from Commissary-General Robinson will enable Your Lordship to judge of some of the difficulties which attend the operations in this country, and to see that the supplies of our army are not the least, but that they augment as war is protracted.

Commissary-General W. H. Robinson to Sir George Prevost.

MONTREAL, 27th August, 1814.

SIR,—I have the honor to report to Your Excellency that I this day received a letter from Deputy-Commissary-General Couche, covering a communication from Deputy-Commissary-General Turquand, which excites in my mind the greatest alarm on account of the want of provisions on the Niagara line. I had been led to believe the right division consisted of about nine thousand men entitled to draw provisions, including Indians, and that there was an ample supply to serve that number to the 1st October. But I now learn with extreme concern that fourteen thousand rations are issued daily, one-half of these to Indians and their families, and that the present state of the magazines does not admit of a hope that the army can, with every exertion of the commissariat attached to the right division, be victualled beyond the middle of next month, though I have every reliance on the zeal and abilities of Commissary-General Turquand.

The season of the year is unfavorable there for procuring flour, as the crop of last year must be consumed and that of the present harvest is not yet available, even if the mills had not been destroyed by the enemy.

With respect to cattle, I need not inform Your Excellency that the constant drain upon the country for fresh meat for the troops, the depredations of the enemy and the Indians, have entirely exhausted the Upper Province of any kind of meat. Foreseeing the evils I have now the honor to represent, I have not failed to throw a large quantity of provisions into Kingston, a return of which is enclosed as late as the 20th inst.

The difficulties in accomplishing this object are well known to Your Excellency even if nothing but provisions had been required, but when it is considered the immense quantity of naval stores that have been transported to meet the common expenditure of an extensive dockyard to construct frigates and ships of the first rate, with their armament, ordnance and other stores, besides all the hospital, barrack, engineer, and regimental stores, with the innumerable other articles requisite for the supply of forts, garrisons, and camps, I feel confident that the exertions of my department will be acknowledged, and that they have exceeded the expectations of Your Excellency as much as I confess they have done my own. For the impediments of the navigation, the scarcity of workmen, laborers and *voyageurs*, are not to be described—in fact they are incalculable, yet they have been surmounted hitherto and at a time when the supply of all the posts in this district, the arrival of troops, and the general increase of every establishment and of the military force throughout the Canadas, forming, it may be said, a new era in the present war, have all called for new and incessant efforts, as all these circumstances necessarily create fresh labors in the commissariat. Deputy-Commissary Couche has endeavored by every means to forward supplies to the head of Lake Ontario, and several small vessels were despatched while the enemy's squadron were unable to leave Sackett's Harbor, but as the exertions of the enemy have been more successful than ours in completing ships sufficient to command the navigation of the lake, that resource is for the moment cut off and only batteaux can be employed. These are a very useful conveyance, not only from the danger of the enemy's small vessels which can approach the shore without difficulty, but also from the want of proper steersmen, pilots, and middlemen.

Mr. Couche has, however, succeeded in despatching twenty-four batteaux loaded with flour and pork, which have been chiefly manned by the soldiers of the Nova Scotia Fencibles and a few pilots, with great difficulty procured from the country. But this feeble means of transport will never effect the forming a sufficient depot at York, Burlington Heights and Niagara, and unless the commissariat can be aided to a great extent by the Royal Navy the most disastrous consequences must ensue, which no efforts, no arrangement of mine, can avert.

My only hope rests upon the prospect of our fleet being very soon superior to that of the enemy, when the first object, I trust, will be to convey provisions from Kingston to the head of the lake, of the necessity of which it would be useless for me to dwell upon after the foregoing representations, for Your Excellency is aware that the road between Kingston and Niagara is not practicable for loaded wagons, therefore land carriage is out of the question, and the most ample assistance from the Royal Navy will be imperiously demanded as the only means of supporting the right division of the army.

On my part I shall continue the transport of provisions from hence to Kingston, but I am sorry to say I am not enabled to send any more salt meat at present, having already drained the stores of Lower Canada for the supply of Kingston as far as prudence would admit. The arrival of the June convoy will probably relieve my anxiety, though from its being so late I have many apprehensions, when the season of the year increases the difficulties of transport, as to the distribution of the expected supplies to all the posts from Quebec to Niagara, yet, if I am led to expect, the superiority on the lake is shortly obtained by the completion of the 100-gun ship now on the stocks and the required assistance from the squadron is afforded, the right division may be supported, but it never can be effected without cordial and efficient aid from the Royal Navy.

Sir G. Drummond to Sir J. Yeo.

HEADQUARTERS,
CAMP BEFORE FORT ERIE, 18th Aug., 1814.

SIR,—I feel it incumbent on me to represent to you, that in consequence of the operations of this division being by the late unfortunate events protracted so much beyond the period which had been expected, and the consequent necessity of bringing forward to this position a greater force than was intended, its wants in provisions, ammunition, and stores of every kind, have become so alarmingly great and urgent that nothing but the assistance of the whole of H. M. squadron on Lake Ontario can enable it to continue its operations against the enemy, or even to retain its present position on this frontier. I enclose for your information a copy of the latest return of the provisions with this division. Of the utter impossibility of getting up an adequate or timely supply from Kingston in the present interrupted state of our communication, (a blockading squadron of the enemy's vessels being left off Niagara for the important object of obstructing it,) you are yourself perfectly aware. All, therefore, that can be done by your forces is to hasten the equipment of the new ship, and, the moment the squadron can sail, to push up to this point with every article of provisions and stores which the department of the army at Kingston may apply to you to receive. If in the meantime any material supplies could by your force be pushed on to York, they will be most acceptable and invaluable.

Lieut.-Gen. Drummond to Sir Geo. Prevost.

HEADQUARTERS,
CAMP BEFORE FORT ERIE, 21st Aug., 1814.

SIR,—Nothing important has occurred since my letter of the 15th. The troops have been refreshed, ammunition has been brought up, and a long 18-pdr. is on its way from Fort George. I have employed the engineer officers in selecting a site for a battery much nearer to the fort, and in different reconnoissances necessary to be made for this purpose we have had frequent occasions to drive in the enemy's picquets, which has always been done with loss on his part. Yesterday a feeble effort was made by the enemy to support his picquets, when our Indians behaved with uncommon spirit and drove back the whole of his riflemen, supported by some hundreds of his regular troops, without its being necessary for our troops to advance to their support. From the number of scalps that were taken by the Indians and the number of dead and wounded which were seen carried into the fort, the enemy must have lost 40 or 50 men in this affair. It also appears that a party of his riflemen must have fled with great precipitation, from the numbers of rifle-arms which have been brought in. The casualties of our Indians were only two wounded. Our troops are in the best spirits, those of the enemy very much depressed by the display of intrepidity on the part of our troops in the late attack, which they are in the nightly expectation of being repeated. The deserters to to us are on the average of 6 or 7 a day, and the fear of the Indians alone prevents greater numbers from coming over. We have very few desertions, and the troops bear the little privations and hardships of the service with great cheerfulness.

The battery which I propose to establish will be within 500 or 600 yards of the place; being in the centre of the woods it will require some days to cut and secure a communication to the spot. In the meantime gabions and fascines are constructing, and whenever the necessary previous arrangements are made the battery, (which I propose to consist of three heavy long guns and one 8 inch mortar, supported by the fire of a couple of guns in the present battery,) will be quickly thrown up and armed, and I hope by that time the arrival of the 6th Regt. and the remainder of the 82nd will place me in a situation to avail myself of the opening into the enemy's fort and works which the artillery and engineer officers most confidently assure me its fire will certainly make in a very short time.

Within these last few days the enemy has endeavored to alarm me for the security of my communication to the rear, and has made a show of moving troops and boats in the direction of Schlosser, as if his object was an attempt on the two captured schooners, which are in the creek at Chippawa. In addition to their crews of seamen and marines, there is a detachment of 50 men with a 6 pdr. field piece at Chippawa, and I have ordered a couple of companies of militia to assemble there every night. It is my intention to order the remains of the 103d Regt. to this post on the arrival of the 6th. This post I have ordered to be placed in a defensible state and a new permanent bridge constructed according to the enclosed plans; in the meantime a temporary bridge passable for waggons and a scow for artillery have been constructed, and one of the guns, 12-pdr. from the schooners, has been placed in the old battery, which has been restored by the seamen. I have no apprehensions for the security of Chippawa or of my communications.

I must now speak to Your Excellency of the wants of this division and the mode of transporting the supplies.

Ammunition.—The battery of field guns on this frontier having, by some extraordinary mistake, been ordered by the commanding officer of artillery in Canada to be kept supplied with only 200 rounds per gun. To show the absolute unfitness of the person in the important situation of the assistant commissary in the field train department with this division, I enclose copy of a letter which he has addressed to the senior officer at Fort George for my information. Various instances of neglect have been reported to me and have fallen under my observation, (but which I have not now time to particularize,) make me desirous that Mr. Assistant Commissary Gordon should be immediately relieved here in his important charge by a proper officer, and that a sufficient number of inferior officers may be appointed to make the department efficient.

Artillery.—It is absolutely necessary that at least another efficient company should be sent up. Weak as the regiments are here, they are obliged to furnish additional gunners and drivers to enable us to man our guns. Regular officers of drivers are much wanted, the only regular officer (Lieut. Jack) having gone down, there remains only one Provincial officer of that corps with this division.

Artificers.—A company of sappers and miners is equally required at this advanced season. Not only no preparations have been made, but we possess no means of making anything like adequate preparations for covering the troops which it may be necessary to retain on this frontier during the approaching winter. The Deputy-Commissary-General reports that such is the distress and suffering of the country, and the want of population as of energy in what remains, that he has not yet been able to make a single contract for the supply of fuel for the troops.

Provisions.—By the beginning of next month we are likely to begin to experience the most alarming deficiency, even in the grand essential of flour. Spirits also, I fear, will by that time fail, and if that should unfortunately be the case the health of the troops must, (particularly if they remain in the field,) suffer, and the diseases of last campaign may again thin our ranks; hitherto they are uncommonly healthy—this I am confident must in a great measure be attributed to an extra allowance of half a gill of spirits, which I have authorized and which I propose to continue as long as I have the means and the troops continue in the field. I have also found it necessary to authorize the daily issue of the ration of spirits to the staff officers, who have no greater means in the present state of this division of procuring wine, &c., than the regimental officers. Transcripts of the order are enclosed.

Barracks.—Stores of every description, particularly stoves, of which there are abundance at Kingston.

Of the various wants as above enumerated, the whole, with the exception of the artillery and artificers, can, I believe, be supplied from Kingston. As to the mode of transport, Your Excellency will at once see that it is by the *squadron alone* that relief can reach us, and from the accounts I have lately received of the state of forwardness of the new ship I really begin to fear that relief by this mode may not reach us in time. I enclose copy of a letter which I have thought it incumbent on me to address to Commodore Sir James Lucas Yeo on this subject. I have to entreat that Your Excellency will make such further communications as may appear necessary to urge the Commodore to use all possible expedition in preparing the squadron for that service, which is certainly far more important than any other on which it can be employed, as on its rapid and successful performance depends the fate of this division.

I propose that the 90th Regt. should come up in the squadron, and to send down some of the most exhausted corps on its return.

I rejoice to find that so fine a force as that under Gen. Kempt has been ordered to Kingston, and as I am sanguine in hoping that by the return of the squadron I shall be enabled, after conducting my operations on this frontier to a successful and satisfactory issue, to repair to Kingston myself in time to receive Your Excellency's orders respecting the operations of the force assembled there.

Lt.-Gen. Drummond to Sir Geo. Prevost.

HEADQUARTERS,
CAMP BEFORE FORT ERIE, 24th Aug., 1814.

SIR,—Nothing of importance has occurred since my letter of the 21st except the arrival of the 82nd Regt., which marched into camp this morning. The first division of the 6th Regt. would reach York this day, and the whole of that Regt., I have reason to hope, will be assembled on this ground by the 1st of September, by which day I expect to be able to make a successful attack on the enemy's fort or entrenched camp, notwithstanding the preparation which deserters report he is making to check our troops by means of mines and foregasses, &c. The desertions to us continue to be very considerable. As our outposts are pushed nearer to those of the enemy desertions may be expected to increase with the facility of effecting it, and I am sorry, accordingly, to report that we have lost more men within this few days than during the whole of the preceding operations. Our desertion is chiefly from De Watteville's Regt. It has just been reported to me that the enemy's schooner which was drove away by our fire has returned from the direction of Presqu' Isle.

The enemy's brigs on the lower lake have resumed their station from which they were driven by a violent gale on the 20th. Capt. Dobbs has, however, been able to detach some seamen in batteaux to York with deserters, and to bring back supplies.

I have employed Lt.-Cols. Nichol and Dickson in going through the country to endeavor by their personal influence and exertions and the messages with which they are charged from me to induce the farmers to thresh out their grain earlier than usual, to enable us to hold out until our wants can be relieved by the squadron. I hope their efforts may be successful, but Your Excellency must be aware that this is at best but a precarious dependence.

Having long seen the necessity of the appointment of a provost marshal with this division, I beg to recommend that a commission of that kind be accordingly prepared, and if Your Excellency has no candidate for the situation that it be conferred on Cornet Amos McKenney of the Niagara Light Dragoons, the officer at present acting in that situation and apparently well qualified.

I beg to acknowledge the receipt of Your Excellency's letter of the 16th.

With regard to Maj.-Gen. Conran, I greatly lament to acquaint Your Excellency that two of the small bones of his leg are found to be broken. It is therefore quite impossible to reckon on his services during the present campaign. I have accordingly given him permission to proceed downwards to York, and to continue his progress to the Lower Province should he find it advisable. His loss to me and to the service is a severe one indeed.

Lt.-Col. Harvey, I am happy to inform Your Excellency, has recovered from the effects of his wound and has resumed the duties of his situation.

I rejoice to find that a company of artillery is proceeding to Kingston. It is on this frontier, however, that the deficiency in that arm is felt by me at the present moment. To enable me to carry on operations in the field I am obliged to draw from the forts more of that corps than can in strict prudence be spared.

Anselm Foster, Adjutant of the First Lincoln Militia, to Captain Jacob A. Ball.

* * * I am also directed by Major Robertson to desire you to see that the following general order is put into execution with all possible despatch. The wheat or flour to be delivered at the nearest mills where there are persons to pay the amounts specified in the order. You will keep a correct account of what is delivered and by whom, and forward me a report of your progress, for the information of the commanding officer.

Militia General Order.

The commanding officers of regiments of Lincoln Militia are particularly enjoined to instruct the officers commanding companies to enforce, if required, from five to twelve bushels of wheat from each inhabitant belonging thereto who is known to have such a quantity to spare independent of a supply for his own family. He will receive for the same the very liberal price of two and a half dollars per bushel, two dollars for an equal quantity of rye, and at the rate of fourteen dollars for flour. It is hoped that the voluntary compliance of every individual will render coercion unnecessary.

Given under my hand at headquarters, near Fort Erie, this 25th of August, 1814.

GORDON DRUMMOND,
Lt.-Genl. and President.

Lt.-Gen. Drummond to Sir Geo. Prevost.

HEADQUARTERS,
CAMP BEFORE FORT ERIE, 27th Aug., 1814.

SIR,—No express having arrived from below for several days, I am in ignorance how far the 6th Regt. may have advanced on its route, but have every reason to hope the 1st division would leave York on or about the 25th, and may therefore be expected here the day after to-morrow.

On the evening of the 25th the enemy, hearing us at work in the wood, (or perhaps apprized by our deserters,) moved out in considerable force and made an effort to drive back our picquets to discover what we were doing at that point. The gallantry of part of the 82nd Regt., (which happened to be on duty,) defeated his plan, and he was repulsed by our picquets after a sharp contest of ten minutes. The enemy must have suffered very considerably. Our loss was two killed and thirteen wounded, of the 82nd Regt.

The desertions from the enemy continue, (particularly from the 23rd Regt). I enclose a return of the number who have come in since the 25th ulto.

I also enclose a sketch by which Your Excellency will perceive the position of the enemy's enfilading batteries on the side of Black Rock, and also the line of our picquets and the position of the battery now constructing.

Previous to any further assault on Fort Erie, I have some thoughts of attempting to remove the annoyance we experience from the guns at Black Rock, by crossing over a force to storm those batteries. This movement must be made in considerable force, as the enemy is understood to have a large body of militia and some regulars and all the rifle corps on that side. At all events, I cannot decide upon the operation until the arrival or approach of the 6th Regt.

Our new battery is more than half completed, and the engineer officer informs me will be ready to receive its guns to-morrow night.

I am sorry to inform Your Excellency that Col. Talbot arrived in camp yesterday with an account of the enemy having detached a party of militia, accompanied by some white people painted and dressed as Indians, headed by a man named Walker, to plunder Col. Talbot's property and seize him. He effected his escape, fortunately, tho' in the house when they entered it. He states that the whole of his property has been carried off or destroyed, and all his horses carried away. There is reason to believe that this party has committed the same outrages throughout the whole of that small settlement. Mr. Burwell, a member of the House of

Assembly, and several other respectable inhabitants, have been carried off by them. They threaten to return in a few days and take away the cattle and complete the destruction of the settlement.

Return of Deserters from the American Army since the 25th July, 1814.

Total—Seventy.

J. B. GLEGG, Maj., A. A. G.

Lt.-Gen. Drummond to Sir Geo. Prevost.

HEADQUARTERS,
CAMP BEFORE FORT ERIE, 30th Aug., 1814.

SIR,—The new battery, consisting of two long 18-pdrs., one 24-pdr. carronade, and one 8-inch howitzer, was armed in the course of last night and opened its fire with very good effect, at daylight this morning. Having reason to believe from the trial already made that whenever I am disposed to attack the place it will not be difficult to open the breach in the fort, I have directed the commanding officer of artillery not to throw away his ammunition, of which I am far from having a superabundance, but to confine his fire for the present merely to the annoyance of the enemy, an object in which we have every reason to believe we have hitherto been very successful. The accounts of every deserter agrees in representing their daily casualties occasioned by our fire at not less than from ten to fifteen in killed and wounded.

The first division of the 6th Regt. reached the Beaver Dams yesterday, and will be within eight miles of camp this day. The second division is only two days' march behind it. By the 2nd, therefore, the regiment will be assembled here. I have ordered up from Fort George six batteaux, in addition to the 18 which I before had on this side the Chippawa. I must, however, apprize Your Excellency that I am by no means come to a final decision as to the mode of attack most advisable to be adopted. If my force was sufficient to admit of being divided I should certainly pass a strong detachment to the right bank of the river. I do not think that less than a thousand men should be risqued on that side even for a single day, and I could not spare such a detachment without leaving myself weaker on this side than would be prudent. Moreover, I have information that the enemy, in expectation of such a movement, has removed all his stores from Buffalo and the Eleven Mile Creek into the interior.

On this side he has been unceasingly employed in strengthening his position by every means in the power of an active, laborious and ingenious enemy to devise and execute. He has had his whole force at work day and night, and has thrown up such an accumulation of mounds of earth, of batteries and breastworks, as will certainly cost us many men to dislodge him from, and which bid defiance to our shot. Nevertheless I am very much disposed to the opinion that an assault in open day is more preferable to a night attack, on many accounts. The enemy, since our last attack, are known to be constantly on their guard by night. By day I think they may be taken very much off their guard. By night it has been found that mistakes may arise that cannot easily happen by day. Moreover, the impression produced on the minds of the enemy by our late attack, and which would be strengthened and confirmed by one made in open day, would be highly favorable to us.

I do not give Your Excellency the opinions of the senior officers of the artillery and engineer departments on a point so immediately belonging to their respective departments, because, promising as is the one and zealous as are both, yet they neither of them possess that degree of experience necessary to qualify them to give a good practical opinion on such a subject. It is not to them, therefore, that I can look for such an opinion.

The information just received from Lieut.-Col. McDouall renders it necessary that the decision I am to make on this point should not be delayed, as the arrival of the enemy's squadron with troops from Lake Huron may be expected every day. I hope, therefore, in my next to communicate to Your Excellency the arrangements for the attack, of the success of which I feel every confidence.

The necessity which I find for two general officers with the right division, from the extent of the frontiers and the great increase of force, added to the state of my own health, and the information that Major-General Kempt is moving upon Kingston, have induced me to order Major-General Stovin to join the headquarters of this division. Major-General De Watteville I have not heard of beyond Kingston, yet, finding the sailing of the squadron remote, I have ordered the 90th Regiment to march up to join this division.

Lieut.-Gen. Drummond to Sir Geo. Prevost.
HEADQUARTERS,
CAMP BEFORE FORT ERIE, 2nd Sept., 1814.

SIR,—Major-General De Watteville arrived yesterday. The 6th Regt. marched into camp this morning, and has voluntarily undertaken to labor this night on the construction of a battery, which it has been thought advisable to advance in front of our right picquet to within about 550 yards of the fort. It is intended to open the rear face and complete the destruction of the stone buildings. This battery will, I hope, be ready to open on the morning of the 4th. I propose to arm it with three heavy long guns, an 8-inch howitzer and a heavy mortar. Its fire, combined with that of the other batteries, will probably decide the mode of attack, which I feel it to be of much importance not to defer. I enclose a Buffalo paper of the 30th, in which Your Excellency will find the cause of my deciding not to pass troops to the other shore. I allude to the call made to the militia of the opposite frontier, numbers of whom I have occasion to believe have already come forward. It is also reported that the enemy's 6th and 13th Regiments and a body of riflemen are also at hand.

A large brig, from whence I have not yet learned, has arrived and anchored off Buffalo since my last. If from Lake Huron, she will have brought them an account of the failure of their expedition against our possessions in that quarter.

On Lake Ontario, the enemy's blockading squadron not having been seen for some days, I sent the *Vincent* across to York, where she has arrived in safety, and Capt. Dobbs has directed the *Charwell* to push across the first morning the wind is fair. By their aid I got quit of many encumbrances, (prisoners and sick,) and shall receive the supplies which are waiting at York for this division.

I am happy to report that a large detachment of batteaux laden with provisions and stores, which Major-General Stovin having properly sent off from Kingston on first learning our alarming situation, have passed York in safety and are by this time, I hope, at Fort George.

Capt. Romilly is now from sickness wholly incapable of service. I have therefore to hope that Your Excellency will see the necessity of ordering up another engineer officer of that rank. Independent of the important charge which attaches to that department on this frontier, there is at the present moment another highly important scheme to be prepared, which requires more experience and judgment and involves a greater degree of responsibility than any of the young men of that department at present with this division can be supposed to possess or ought to be required to assume. I allude to the selecting of a site for a work to protect the formation of our naval establishment on Lake Erie.

J. B. Yates to Governor D. D. Tompkins.

BUFFALO, Sept. 3, 1814.

DEAR SIR,—The militia are collecting at this place very rapidly. There is every probability that more will turn out than were required by the order. Everything has been done to rouse the feelings of the community, and the exertions for that purpose have apparently been attended with very great success. Brigadier-General Davis of Genesee County has ordered out his whole brigade without any requisition or authority. Yet, as it was considered that they might be usefully employed, it was thought proper not to discourage him. If he were regularly ordered out he would take the command from General Porter. This would by no means answer in the present situation of things, as it would occasion very general dissatisfaction. The command will be a large one, probably not less than 4,000 men, perhaps 5,000. Would it not be well to send him as soon as possible the brevet rank of Major-General, so as to obviate any difficulty that may occur. By a proper disposition and use of the means that are, or in a few days will be, in the power of General Brown, the enemy's force cannonading Fort Erie will probably be obliged to retire.

There is every appearance of a disposition on the part of the militia to cross the Niagara, and if they do not the disappointment will be great indeed, but I cannot for a moment doubt it. If they do the enemy must retreat or submit. The disproportion of force will be too great for them to resist. There has been a very great difficulty in procuring a sufficient quantity of arms. I wrote to Mr. Carpenter at Whitesborough, from whom I have not yet heard. I have also written to Mr. Hopper at Onondaga. The arms at Canandaigua and Batavia have been taken for the use of the detachment.

Men have been sent out to collect such as may be in the hands of individuals and have not been returned. These, together with such United States arms as can be procured and British arms taken from the enemy, will probably be sufficient to arm the men.

Pursuant to the request in your letter, I have made inquiries about Mr. Joshua Pell, living near Chippawa, and was told he was well and had removed about two or three miles back from the river.

Lieut.-Gen. Drummond to Capt. Noah Freer.

HEADQUARTERS,
CAMP BEFORE FORT ERIE, 5th Sept., 1814.

SIR,—I have the honor to acquaint you for the information of His Excellency the Commander of the Forces that on the 30th ulto. a marauding party of the enemy, consisting of about 70, came to

Oxford and made prisoners of Capts. Curtis, Hall and Carrol and Sergeant Dowland of the militia. They have likewise taken and paroled the greater part of the inhabitants from Deleware to Oxford.

They also made prisoners of Mr. Bonnell and Mr. Palmer, who were at that time purchasing cattle for the government, which to the value of 270 dollars, and 600 dollars in cash, they also made prize of.

On Mr. Burdock's house being attacked, he fired on and wounded, one of the enemy. Mr. Burdock, I am concerned to say, was wounded in return.

The traitor Westbrook accompanied the gang.

On the 1st of September the enemy was attacked by a party of militia under Lieut. Rapelje, who lay in ambush for them near Deleware. The enemy did not return his fire but fled with precipitation towards Oxford, leaving their commander mortally and several others wounded on the road. Westbrook, being in the rear, conducted them safe off through the woods. Capts. Curtis and Hall by this circumstance found means to effect their escape from the enemy, who left the greater part of their plunder, several horses, all their cattle and some arms.

Several strangers have appeared lately in the neighbourhood of Dover. One, armed, was fired at some nights since by a sentry, but the villain escaped into the bush. One Dickson and Simon Mabee, a fellow who made his escape from justice last year, entered the house of a person named John Muckle in Townsend and forcibly broke open a chest and robbed him of 200 dollars. Several persons are in pursuit of them, but hitherto without effect.

I take this opportunity of informing you that Deputy-Commissary-General Crookshank still continues unremitting in his exertions to forward supplies to Machilimackinac. Three only of the eleven canoes from Montreal have proceeded to that post, and the crews of those three, (the others having altogether refused to proceed,) he found it necessary to bribe largely for that purpose. Mr. La Mothe has returned to Montreal to procure fresh crews. But I have directed Colonel Claus to send steady Indians without delay in charge of the remaining canoes to Machilimackinac, and as the loss of the *Nancy* schooner has been a very serious one indeed, I have directed as many batteaux as are necessary to be taken from York to Nottawasaga for the purpose of transport across Lake Huron.

General Order.

HEADQUARTERS, FORT ERIE, 6th September, 1814.

The Brigadier-General commanding has received the report of Major Matteson of the New York Volunteers, on whom devolved the command of the party engaged in the affair of the 5th after the death of the gallant Colonel Wilcocks.

With sincere pleasure the Brigadier-General congratulates the army, that the steadiness and valour which have marked the conduct of this division during the whole campaign, were again most singularly manifested by the volunteers and regulars engaged on this occasion.

A party not exceeding 100 volunteers, (the enemy being of treble numbers,) drove the enemy to his works with comparatively small loss, and made him suffer severely. Previously to this a detachment of forty men from the 21st, under Ensign Thomas, had successfully skirmished with the enemy.

The conduct of Major Matteson on this occasion excites the highest approbation of the Brigadier-General, his coolness, courage and prudence, and the good conduct of his troops, were again conspicuously manifested. The New York Volunteers have on this occasion, as well as every other that has occurred during the whole campaign, reflected honour on the State. Captain Hale of the 11th Infantry, commanding picquet No. 2, and Ensign Thomas commanding the regulars, conducted themselves in a manner to the perfect satisfaction of the Brigadier-General. The loss on our side, with the exception of the gallant Wilcocks and Lieutenant Roosevelt, is trifling, but on the side of the enemy it was severe in the extreme; various deserters report that they had four officers and nearly 100 either killed or wounded: so great a disparity evinces in the strongest light the difference between the coolness of troops such as ours in a just and honorable career and of the enemy's thousands, who fight for objects which they care not for and in a cause which they deprecate.

Major Matteson speaks in the highest terms of the courage and good conduct of Captains Hull, Harding, Knap and Satterly, who volunteered to command a company, and Lieutenants Hathaway, Jones and Ensign Wickwire. He also expresses his highest opinion of the correct, brave and soldier-like conduct of Brigade-Major Dobbin, Quarter-Master Green and Adjutant Gilbert.

Lieutenant-Colonel Wilcocks, whose services and bravery have excited the warmest interest of the army in his favor, and Lieutenant Roosevelt of the New York Volunteers, have added other names to the gallant heroes who, during this unexampled campaign, have gloriously died on the field of honor. Colonel Wilcocks, at the moment he was mortally wounded, was charging and repulsing an infinitely superior force under the enemy's battery. The command devolving on Major Matteson, he succeeded in driving the enemy to their works and retired in good order to camp.

By command of Brigadier-General Ripley.

R. JONES,
Asst.-Adjt.-Gen.

District General Order.

HEADQUARTERS,
CAMP BEFORE FORT ERIE, 7th September, 1814.

Major-General De Watteville having been directed to detach a party yesterday evening to endeavor to cut off the enemy's picket No. 4, reports that this service was executed by a company of the 6th Regiment and one of the Glengarry Light Infantry, joined by infantry pickets at Platow's and the detachment of the 19th Dragoons, under Captain Eustace, the whole under the command of Captain Patteson of the 6th Regiment, and conducted by Captain Powell, Deputy-Assistant-Quartermaster-General.

The enemy's picket was surprised at daylight this morning. Of its advance party, which consisted of 21 men and an officer, not one escaped; 14, including an officer, being killed, and seven wounded and taken prisoners. The main body of the pickets fled towards the forts, pursued by our troops close under the guns of the place, and must have suffered very considerably from our fire. Our loss has been only one killed, (private, 6th,) and one slightly wounded.

The conduct of this little enterprise reflects great credit not only on Captain Patteson, commanding the detachment, and the whole of the officers and soldiers of which it was composed, but on Captain Powell, Deputy-Assistant-Quatermaster-General, by whom the enterprise was planned. Sergeant Powell, 19th Light Dragoons, has been named to the Lieutenant-General as having again distinguished himsef on this occasion.

J. HARVEY,
Lieut.-Col., D. A. G.

Lieut.-Gen. Drummond to Sir Geo. Prevost.

CAMP BEFORE FORT ERIE, 8th Sept., 1814.

SIR,—The new battery was completed and armed on the night of the 4th. After due consideration, however, and after consulting with the commanding artillery officer, I determined not to open its fire until the small supply of disposable ammunition which remained at Fort George had been brought up, and until by the arrival of the 97th Regt. I might have it in my power to take advantage of the impression it might produce by an assault on the place, should such a measure appear advisable. The ammunition now on its way from the forts leaves them with little more than 200 rounds per gun, and with very little powder, nor is there any prospect of a supply until the arrival of the squadron, or of part of the vessels from Kingston. Under these alarming circumstances it becomes absolutely necessary that I should husband every round of my remaining stock of ammunition.

I regret very much the capture of Your Excellency's despatches in answer to mine announcing the result of the attack of the 15th ulto. By that unfortunate event I am in all probability deprived of the knowledge not only of your sentiments but also of that of Your Excellency's views and plans with regard to the general operations of the campaign, and above all of your wishes and instructions with regard to the expediency of hazarding any further assault upon the enemy's strong position at Fort Erie and Your Excellency's opinion as to how far the blockade by this division may not be more politic than attempting its capture or destruction under circumstances which in the event (but doubtful) of success, forbid us to hope to accomplish without a very severe loss.

In ignorance of Your Excellency's sentiments and wishes, and in the absence of your instructions on these points, I shall continue to act according to circumstances, and shall not fail to avail myself of any favorable opportunity which may offer of attacking the enemy. But should no such offer present itself, I feel it incumbent on me to prepare Your Excellency for the possibility of my being compelled by sickness or suffering of the troops, exposed as they will be to the effects of the wet and unhealthy season which is fast approaching, to withdraw them from their present position to one which may afford them the means of cover. Sickness has, I am sorry to say, already made its appearance in several of the corps, particularly the 82nd.

The affair of the 5th was more important than I was aware of. The Deputy-Adjutant-General transmitted to Colonel Baynes, Lt.-Col. Campbell's very clear report on that occasion. Nothing could surpass the gallantry and good conduct of all the troops; their impetuosity was with difficulty restrained.

I have directed Lt.-Col. Harvey to forward to the Adjutant-General a copy of the district general order issued by my order yesterday on occasion of an enterprise planned by Capt. Powell, Deputy-Assistant-Quartermaster-General, and very well executed by detachments of the 6th and Glengarry Regts., under direction of Capt. Patteson of the 6th.

Since the 1st of this month, the day appointed for assembling, the militia have been collecting in great numbers on the opposite frontier—I am informed to the amount of 3 to 4,000. I do not understand that any part of them have as yet been prevailed upon to cross to this shore, but it is said they have promised to come over to Fort Erie for one week. If they do and any part of them should fall into my hands, I shall assuredly send them to Quebec, and hope they may not be suffered to return to their families for a considerable period. Nothing will more effectually check their enterprising spirit than such a measure. It is said the enemy has 40 boats nearly finished at Buffalo. His squadron, consisting of two brigs and four schooners, is still at anchor off that place, but does not venture near the fort.

On Lake Ontario the enemy's squadron has disappeared for some time. The *Charwell* brig, with the *Vincent* and *Netley* schooners, are at York waiting to bring over the 97th, which I hope will arrive there this day.

Major-General Brown to Major General Izard.
HEADQUARTERS, FORT ERIE, Sept. 10, 1814.

SIR,—I have been expecting with much anxiety to hear from you, and to learn the aid you can afford this army. My total effective force does not much exceed two thousand men, perhaps I may be able to fight in position twenty-five hundred. The force of the enemy which confines us to our works is believed to amount to four thousand, and the 90th or 97th—(the deserters say both these regiments)—is nigh at hand.

I will not conceal from you that I consider the fate of this army very doubtful unless speedy relief is afforded, and my opinion is that the wisest course will be to effect a juncture by landing below Niagara, marching on the American side of the strait, and crossing over from Buffalo. Will your force be such as to insure relief to this army if you land on the British side? Our united forces would, I have no doubt, be competent to drive Drummond from the field and perhaps capture him. Whatever may be your plan of operations, be so good as to make me acquainted with them so that I may know how to calculate. Your orders will be received and obeyed with pleasure.

General Porter has assembled say three thousand militia. It remains to be seen if they can be made useful.

Major-General Brown to Major-General Izard.

HEADQUARTERS, FORT ERIE, Sept. 11, 1814.

SIR,—I have nothing new of importance to communicate, and by the return of the express think proper to say so for your satisfaction. We have received but few shot or shells from the enemy within the two last days. Many deserters come in, who state that the enemy's supply is exhausted, but that they expect to be re-supplied within a short time. There is no doubt but they are erecting additional batteries. General Porter has succeeded in getting over about one thousand of his militia. More are expected to cross. Should you deem it proper to pass rapidly to this threatre of war, I do not doubt that it will be in your power to carry everything within this peninsula. However, if with the aid of the fleet and the forces at Sackett's Harbor you can succeed in carrying Kingston, you will accomplish a much more important object. In the execution of any plan you will find me disposed to exert myself, and I am convinced the remainder of my gallant army will do their duty under any circumstances. I shall be happy to receive your orders, and be made acquainted with your plan of operations. My command must find relief in some way before many days.

P. S.—Forts George and Niagara must be nearly empty. It is not probable that there are many of the enemy's regular troops between this and Kingston. Their militia are worse than ours, they are good for nothing.

My private opinion is that the enemy cannot bring into the field to exceed three thousand regulars between this and Burlington, unless the 97th or 90th have arrived. If you think proper to land north of Fort George, and I could know the moment of your landing so as to press upon the enemy, it would perhaps be the shortest cut to your object, the capture of Drummond and his army. He cannot escape provided you can promptly form a junction with my present command. We have artillery sufficient for every object in the field, and perhaps sufficient for the reduction of Niagara.

Sir Gordon Drummond to Sir Geo. Prevost.

CAMP BEFORE FORT ERIE, 11th September, 1814.

Since my last the enemy have shown a considerable number of boats and scows, which have kept up a frequent communication between Fort Erie and the opposite shore; this communication has passed chiefly by night, and from the singular circumstance of the desertion from the enemy to my camp, (my best source of information,) having almost entirely ceased, I am very much in ignorance of the nature of their movements, whether the enemy is preparing to avail himself of the increased means of transport which he has created to withdraw from his position at Fort Erie, or whether the account which is *invariably* given by deserters of his intention to act offensively against the division under my command be correct, I have not yet been able accurately to ascertain. The recent accounts of the capture of Washington, the alarm which is felt for New York, and the probable discovery (by the intercepted despatch) of our designs against Sackett's Harbour, would appear strongly to countenance the former supposition, the positive concurring declarations of deserters, however, and the fact (reported on the same authority) of a very large number of militia and volunteers, to the number it is said of 2,500, having actually crossed to the fort yesterday evening, these circumstances tend to favor the latter idea. Every preparation has been made to give the enemy a warm reception.

The batteries have almost been silent for several days from the reduced state of the ammunition. A small supply, the last I can command, has arrived from Fort George to-day. This I must reserve until the arrival of the 97th Regiment, in order that I may be enabled to avail myself of any favorable opening it may effect. No direct fire from the small number of guns which I have could produce any material effect on such mounds of earth defended by such a number of guns. Mortar fire is alone of use, and of that I have not more than 80 rounds for the two mortars.

I am much disappointed at not having yet heard of the arrival of the 97th Regiment at York. I had expected to have had them here before this time: the wind has been adverse, and the weather tempestuous and rainy. Should the rainy weather continue only for a few days, I dread the effect it must have on the men in their present situation; hitherto with the exception of one or two corps they have stood it tolerably well.

I have to acknowledge Your Excellency's letter of the 2nd inst.

I look with impatience for duplicates of your answer to my letter of the 17th ulto.

Major-General Brown, who has resumed command of the troops at Fort Erie, has this day sent in several private letters taken in the bag which was intercepted near the Presqu' Isle on the 29th.

I enclose a copy of his note.

Deeming it absolutely necessary to send down several of the corps on this frontier which have suffered much by sickness and severe service, as soon as the campaign here is over, I have directed Major-General Kempt to embark a regiment of the centre division, (the selection of which I have left to him,) and send it up on board the squadron, by the return of which I propose sending down one or more of the corps alluded to, viz: the Kings, 100th, 41st, and Royals.

Lt.-Gen. Drummond to Sir George Prevost.
CAMP BEFORE FORT ERIE, 14th September, 1814.

SIR,—I am sorry to acquaint Your Excellency that ever since the despatch of my last letter it has continued to rain almost incessantly. As the whole of the troops are without tents, and the huts in which they are placed are wholly incapable of affording shelter against such severe weather, their situation is most distressing. I am happy to say, however, that no considerable degree of sickness has as yet been the consequence, and what is, if possible, still more satisfactory, our desertion, except from the Regiment De Watteville, has by no means increased, notwithstanding the hardships to which they now are exposed.

The late heavy falls of rain have rendered the roads almost impassable, and at this late season there is little chance of them again becoming good, and when Your Excellency considers that I have no depot of provisions or of any other description of supplies nearer than Fort George, that the forage of the surrounding country to the distance of upwards of ten miles has been exhausted, that even if I could feed them I have not a sufficient number of cattle to move one-third of the heavy ordnance which I have in the batteries, should any unforeseen circumstances render a sudden movement necessary the difficulties of my situation will be sufficiently apparent to Your Excellency. It is certain the enemy has found the means of inducing his militia to cross the river, and I have reason to believe that a body of not less than 2,000 has been brought to Fort Erie. I also understand that a considerable number still remain on the opposite shore, to which weak regiments of regulars have within this day or two been joined from the troops at Fort Erie. It is said to be the intention, (as mentioned in my last,) to land this force in my rear.

The sudden and most unlooked for return to the head of Lake Ontario of the two brigs by which the Niagara has been so long blockaded and my communication with York cut off, has had the effect of preventing the junction of the 97th Regiment, which arrived at York on the 10th, and would probably have been at Niagara on the following day but for this unlucky circumstance. They have been reduced to the necessity of continuing their route by land, and accordingly marched from York on the 12th. In the present state of the roads and weather I cannot expect them here before the 17th or 18th. In the meantime I have strong grounds for thinking that the enemy will risque an attack, an event which, from the necessity of defending my batteries in the first instance with the picquets alone, I shall have to meet under every possible disadvantage, yet I am very much disposed to hope may be the most fortunate circumstance that can happen, as it will bring us into contact with the enemy at a far cheaper rate than if we were to be the assailants, and may at the same time, I trust, bring to a happy crisis a campaign which has been marked by a series of unlucky circumstances, as well as of late severe hardships and privations on the part of the troops, which I am most happy in repeating have borne them with the utmost cheerfulness, and have evinced a degree of steadiness and spirit highly honorable to them.

I have directed the Deputy-Adjutant-General to transmit to the Adjutant-General a return of casualties which have taken place since my last; those of this day were occasioned by an attack which about 400 of the enemy's militia and riflemen made on our batteries immediately after daylight. They were repulsed by the picquets, the officer who led them was killed and one man made prisoner.

I enclose a report of an alarming nature which has just been received from Lt.-Col. Warburton, commanding at the forts. Previous to this a considerable part of one of the other bastions had fallen down, (from the effect of the weather,) the restoration of which has been effected by great exertions. Situated as I at present am, and considering the large disposable force the enemy has on or can pass to the other bank of the river, and the weakness of the present garrison of Fort Niagara, I cannot but regard the circumstance reported by Lieut.-Col. Warburton as a very awkward one.

P. S.—Another report, (copy enclosed,) has just been received from Lieut.-Col. Warburton.

Sir Gordon Drummond to Sir George Prevost.

CAMP BEFORE FORT ERIE, 17th September, 1814.

SIR,—I have the honor to acquaint Your Excellency that the enemy made a sortie with his whole force at 3 o'clock this afternoon, and having under cover of a heavy fall of rain and favored by the thick woods which approach close to our position, gained, unperceived, the right of our batteries, he rushed upon them in such overwhelming force that the picquets and covering parties were forced back, and the momentary possession of the right and centre batteries obtained. The gallantry of the supporting brigade quickly recovered them, but not before the guns in the right battery had been disabled. The loss on our side has been considerable; that of the enemy great. Upwards of 200 prisoners are in our hands, including a number of officers, among them Lieut.-Colonel Wood, their chief engineer, mortally wounded.

A more detailed account will be transmitted to-morrow, together with a return of casualties.

Major-General Stovin arrived a short time before the attack. The 97th Regiment is within eight miles.

P. S.—The enemy's force, including militia, could not have been less than 5,000. Our troops behaved admirably.

G. D.

District General Order.

HEADQUARTERS,
CAMP BEFORE FORT ERIE, 18th September, 1814.

Lieutenant=General Drummond, having received the reports of the general officers in the immediate direction of the troops engaged yesterday, begs to offer his best acknowledgements for their very gallant conduct in repulsing the attack made by the enemy upon our batteries with his whole force, represented to consist of not less than five thousand men including militia. The brilliant style in which the battery No. 2 was recovered and the enemy driven beyond our entrenchments, by seven companies of the 82d Regiment under Major Proctor, and three companies of the 6th Regiment detached under Major Taylor, excited Lieutenant-General Drummond's admiration, and entitled those troops to his particular thanks. On the right the enemy's advance was checked by the 1st battalion of the Royal Scots, supported by the 89th, under the direction of Lieutenant-Colonel Gordon of the Royals, and in the centre he was driven back by the Glengarry Light Infantry, under Lieutenant-Colonel Battersby and directed by Lieutenant-Colonel Pearson, inspecting field officer. To these troops the Lieutenant-General's best thanks are due, as also to the remainder of the reserve under Lieutenant-Colonel Campbell, consisting of the remaining companies of the 6th Regiment, the flank companies of the 41st and the Incorporated Militia, which supported the troops engaged.

The Lieutenant-General deeply laments the unfortunate circumstances of weather, which enabled the enemy to approach unperceived close to the right of the position and to capture a considerable number of the Regiment De Watteville, stationed at that point. The severe loss in killed and wounded which the 8th or King's and De Watteville's Regiment have suffered, affords incontestable proof that No. 2 battery was not gained without a vigorous resistance; it is equally obvious that the blockhouse on the right was well defended by the party of the King's Regiment stationed in it.

Lieutenant-General Drummond feels greatly indebted to Major-General De Watteville for his judicious arrangements, and he also desires to offer his thanks to the respective commanding officers of brigades and corps and the officers and men of the Royal Artillery and Engineers, for their exertions. To Major-General Stovin, who joined the army a short time before the attack, the Lieutenant-General is indebted for his assistance, and also to the officers of his personal staff.

Lieutenant-General Drummond greatly regrets the wounds which have deprived the army for the present of the services of Colonel Fischer, Lieutenant-Colonels Pearson and Gordon.

Lieutenants-Colonels Fischer, Pearson, and Gordon have permission to proceed to the rear for the recovery of their wounds.

J. HARVEY,
Lieut.-Col., D. A. G.

Major-Gen. De Watteville to Sir Gordon Drummond.

CAMP BEFORE FORT ERIE, Sept. 19th, 1814.

SIR,—I have the honor to report to you that the enemy attacked on the 17th in the afternoon, at 3 o'clock, our position before Fort Erie, the Second Brigade, under Col. Fischer, composed of the 8th and De Watteville's Regiments, being on duty. Under cover of a heavy fire of his artillery from Fort Erie and much favored by the nature of the ground, and also by the state of the weather, the rain falling in torrents at the moment of his approach, the enemy succeeded in turning the right of our line picquets without being perceived, and with a very considerable force attacked both the picquets and their support in their flank and rear: at the same time another of the enemy's columns attacked in front the picquets between No. 2 and No. 3 batteries, and having succeeded in penetrating by No. 4 picquet, part of his force turned to his left and thereby surrounded our right and got almost immediate possession of No. 3 battery. The enemy then directed his attacks with a very superior force towards No. 2 battery, but the obstinate resistance made by the picquets, under every possible disadvantage, delayed considerably his getting possession of No. 2 battery, in which, however, he at last succeeded. As soon as the alarm was given, the 1st Brigade, being next for support, composed of the Royal Scots, the 82nd and 6th Regiments, under Lieut.-Col. Gordon, received orders to march forward, and also the light demi-brigade under Lieut.-Col. Pearson, the 6th Regiment remaining in reserve under Lieut.-Col. Campbell. From the concession road, the Royal Scots and the 89th moved by the new road and met the enemy near the blockhouse on the right of No. 3 battery, whom they engaged, and by their steady and intrepid conduct checked his further progress. The 82nd Regt. and three companies of the 6th were detached to the left in order to support Nos. 1 and 2 batteries; the enemy having at that time possession of No. 2 battery and still pushing forward, seven companies of the 82nd, under Major Proctor, and three companies of the 6th, under Major Taylor, received directions to oppose the enemy's forces, and immediately charged them with the most intrepid bravery, driving them both across our entrenchments and also from No. 2 battery, thereby preventing them from destroying it or damaging its guns in a considerable degree: Lieut.-Col. Pearson with the Glengarry Light Infantry under Lieut.-Col. Battersby, pushed forward by the centre road and carried with great gallantry the new entrenchment, then in full possession of the enemy. The enemy being thus repulsed at every point was forced to retire with precipitation to their works, leaving prisoners and a number of their wounded in our hands. By five o'clock the entrenchments were again occupied, and the line of picquets established as it had been previous to the enemy's attack. I have the honor to enclose a return of casualties, and the report of the officer commanding the Royal Artillery respecting the damage done to the ordnance and the batteries during the time they were in the enemy's possession.

Lt.-Gen. Drummond to Sir George Prevost.

CAMP BEFORE FORT ERIE, 19th Sept., 1814.

SIR,—My letter to Your Excellency of the 17th, gave a short account of the result of an attack made by the enemy on my batteries and position on that day. I have now the honor to transmit a copy of Major-General De Watteville's report, together with a return of killed, wounded and missing on that occasion. To the information which Your Excellency will derive from those documents I have to add that as soon as the firing was heard I proceeded toward the advance and found the troops had moved from camp, and the Royals and 89th had been pushed by Major-Gen. De Watteville into the woods on the right towards No. 3 battery, and that the 82nd was moving to the support of the batteries on the left. At this moment it was reported to me that the enemy had gained possession of batteries Nos. 2 and 3 and that our troops were falling back, a report which the approach of the fire confirmed. Your Excellency will have in recollection that the whole line of operations lay in a thick wood. I immediately directed Lieut.-Col. Campbell to detach one wing of the 6th Regt. to support the 82d in an attack, which I ordered to be made for the recovery of battery No. 2. I directed Major-Gen. De Watteville to superintend the movement. Major-Gen. Stovin took the direction of the troops and guns left in reserve. I threw forward the Glengarry Light Infantry into the woods in front of the centre to check the advance of the enemy and support the troops retiring from that point. Both these movement were executed to my entire satisfaction, and being combined with a judicious attack made by Lt.-Col. Gordon with part of the 1st Brigade, consisting of the 1st Battalion of the Royal Scots, supported by the 89th, the enemy was everywhere driven back and our batteries and entrenchments regained, not, however, before he had disabled the guns in No. 3 battery and exploded its magazine. The enemy did not again attempt to make a stand, but retreated in great disorder to the fort and was followed by our troops to the glacis of the place. To Major-Gen. De Watteville's report I must refer Your Excellency for the cause of the enemy's success in the first instance, viz: the overwhelming number of the enemy, to which we had only the King's and De Watteville's to oppose. The spirit which the troops displayed in all the subsequent operations deserves the highest commendation, and entitles them to my warmest approbation. I have only to regret that the scene of action, (a thick wood,) was so unfavorable to the display of the valuable qualities which are inherent in British troops. The charge made by the 82d Regt. under Major Proctor, and detachment of the 6th under Major Taylor, led to the recovery of the battery No. 2, and very much decided the precipitate retrograde movement made by the enemy from the different points of our position, of which he had gained a short possession. Major-Gen. De Watteville reports most favorably of the steadiness evinced by the 1st Battalion, Royal Scots, under Lieut.-Col. Gordon, (commanding 1st Brigade,) and the remains of the 2d Battalion, 89th, under Capt. Basden. I myself witnessed the good order and spirit with which the Glengarry Light Infantry, under Lieut.-Col. Battersby, pushed into the wood, and by their superior fire drove back the enemy's light troops. Lieut.-Col. Pearson, inspecting field officer, accompanied this part of his demi-brigade, and, I am sorry to say, received a severe, though I hope not a dangerous, wound. To Major-Gen. De Watteville, who commanded in camp and by whom the first directions were given and arrangements made, I am under great obligations for the judgment displayed by him, and for his zeal and exertions during the action. My acknowledgments are also due to Major-Gen. Stovin, who arrived at my headquarters a few hours before the attack, for the assistance I received from him. I cannot sufficiently appreciate the valuable assistance which I have received from Col. Myers, Dep.-Quartermaster-Gen., and Lieut.-Col.

Harvey, Dep.-Adj.-Gen., during the present service, and which have been of the more important as from my own state of health of late, (in consequence of my wound,) I have not been able to use those active exertions which I otherwise might. I avail myself of this opportunity of again expressing my sincere concern at the loss which this division of the army sustained by the accident which deprived it of the services of Major-Gen. Conran, from whose energy and ability much was justly to be expected. To Major Glegg, Assist.-Adj.-Gen., and to Capts. Chambers and Powell, Dep.-Assist.-Quartermaster-Gen., to Capt. Foster, Military Secretary, Lieut.-Col. Hagerman, Provincial Aide-de-Camp, and to Lieut. Nesfield, 89th Regt., acting aide-de-camp, who have rendered me every assistance in their respective situations, my best acknowledgments are due. They are likewise due to Major D'Alton, Brigade Major with the right division, for his uniform correctness, zeal and attention to his duty. To Lieut.-Col. Campbell of the 6th Regt. I am also much indebted, as well in his capacity of commanding officer of that excellent corps as in that of senior officer of the reserve of this division. Col. Fischer of De Watteville's Regt. and Lieut.-Col. Ogilvie of the King's are entitled to my best thanks. The zeal and exertions of Major Phillot, commanding the Royal Artillery, Captains Walker and Sabine, and the officers and men of that corps, have been unremitting, and merit every commendation. I have reason to be pleased with the activity and zeal which Major Lisle and the officers and men of the squadron of the 19th Dragoons have uniformly displayed. The enemy, it is now ascertained, made the sortie with his whole force, which, including the militia volunteers by which he has lately been joined, could not consist of less than 5,000. About 200 prisoners fell into our hands, and I cannot estimate the enemy's loss in killed and wounded at less than that number. The dreadful state of the roads and of the weather, it having poured with rain almost incessantly for the last ten days, rendered every movement of ordnance or heavy stores exceedingly difficult. By great exertions the commanding artillery officer has succeeded in moving the battery guns and mortars with their stores, &c., towards Chippawa, to which place I mean to withdraw them for the present.

Major-General Brown to the Secretary of War.

HEADQUARTERS,
FORT ERIE, September 18, 1814.

SIR,—I have the satisfaction to announce to you a brilliant achievement yesterday, effected by the forces under my command. A sortie was made upon the enemy's principal batteries—these were carried; we blew up his principal work, destroyed his battering pieces and captured 400 prisoners. The enemy resisted our assault with firmness, but suffered greatly; his total loss cannot be less than 800 men.

In such a business we could not but expect to lose many valuable lives; they were offered up a voluntary sacrifice to the safety and honor of this army and nation.

I will forward to you the particulars of this splendid affair, with a return of the killed and wounded, in the course of a few days.

Gen. Brown to Gov. Tompkins.

HEADQUARTERS, FORT ERIE, Sept. 20, 1814.

MY DEAR SIR,—Your Excellency is no doubt aware how much the army under my command has suffered from the fire of the enemy's batteries, of which the first and second were not more than 500 yards distant. Soon after my arrival, I ascertained they were day and night employed in erecting a third, to the right of the others, which would rake obliquely our whole encampment. About the 12th this new work was nearly completed, and in it were mounted some long 24-pounders. Being very impatient under the fire of the old, and knowing that our difficulties would increase from the opening of the new, battery, I determined to hazard a sortie with a view of carrying them and destroying the cannon. On the 17th inst. an order was given to this effect and executed in the most gallant style.

The batteries were carried, the principal work blown up, and the cannon effectually destroyed. It was a desperate conflict. The loss of the enemy cannot be less than 800 men. Our own is severe, in officers particularly. The militia of New York have redeemed their character—they behaved gallantly. Gen. Davis was killed, and General Porter slightly wounded in the hand.

Of the militia that were called out by the last requisition, fifteen hundred men have crossed. This reinforcement has been of immense importance to us; it doubled our effective strength, and their good conduct cannot but have the happiest effect upon the nation. The brave men deserve well of their country: and I flatter myself that the legislature about to convene will notice them as becomes the representatives of a generous people.

Brigadier-General Porter to Major-General Brown.

FORT ERIE, September 23rd, 1814.

SIR,—In executing the duty you have imposed upon me of reporting the conduct of the officers and men composing the left column, which you were pleased to place under my command in the *sortie* of the 17th instant, the pleasure I derive in representing to you the admirable conduct of the whole is deeply chastened by sorrow for the loss of so many brave and distinguished men.

Being obliged from the nature of the ground to act on foot, it was impossible that my own personal observation should reach to every officer. Some part of this report must therefore rest upon the information of others.

It is the business of this communication to speak of the conduct of individuals, yet you will permit me to premise, although well known to yourself already, that the object of the left column was to penetrate by a circuitous route between the enemy's batteries, where one-third of his force was always kept on duty, and his main camp, and that it was sub-divided into three divisions—the advance of 200 riflemen and a few Indians commanded by Colonel Gibson, and two columns moving parallel to and 30 yards distant from each other. The right column was commanded by Lieutenant-Colonel Wood, headed by 400 infantry under Major Brooke of the 23rd, and followed by 500 volunteers and militia, being parts of Lieutenant-Colonels Dobbins', McBurney's and Fleming's regiments, and was intended to attack the batteries.

The left column of 500 militia was commanded by Brigadier-General Davis, and comprised the commands of Lieutenant-Colonels Hopkins, Churchill and Crosby, and was intended to hold in check any reinforcements from the enemy's camp: or both columns, (circumstances requiring it, which frequently happened,) to co-operate in the same object.

After carrying by storm in the handsomest syle a strong blockhouse in the rear of the third battery, making its garrison prisoners, destroying the three 24-pounders and their carriages in the third battery, and blowing up the enemy's magazine, and after co-operating with General Miller in taking the second battery, the gallant leaders of the three divisions all fell nearly at the same time: Colonel Gibson at the second battery, and General Davis and Lieutenant-Colonel Wood in an assault upon the first.

Brigadier-General Davis, although a militia officer of little experience, conducted himself on this occasion with all the coolness and bravery of a veteran, and fell while advancing upon the enemy's entrenchments. His loss as a citizen as well as a soldier will be severely felt in the patriotic county of Genesee. Colonel Gibson fully sustained the high military reputation which he had before so justly acquired. You know how exalted an opinion I have always entertained of Lt.-Col. Wood of the engineers. His conduct on this day was what it has uniformly been on every similar occasion, an exhibition of military skill, acute judgment and heroic valor. Of the other regular officers, Lt.-Col. McDonald and Major Brook, senior in command, will report to you in relation to their respective divisions. Permit me to say, however, of these two officers, that much as was left to them by the fall of their distinguished leaders, they were able to sustain their parts in the most admirable manner, and they richly deserve the notice of the government.

Of the militia, I regret that the limits of a report will not permit me even to name all those who on this occasion established claims to the gratitude of their fellow citizens, much less to particularize individual merit. Lieut.-Cols. Hopkins, McBurney, Churchill and Crosby, and Majors Lee, Marcle, Wilson, Lawrence, Burr, Dunham, Kellogg and Ganson, are entitled to the highest praise for their gallant conduct, their steady and persevering exertions. Lt.-Col. Dobbins being prevented by indisposition from taking the field, Major Hall, Assistant-Inspector-General, volunteered his services to join Major Lee in command of the volunteer regiment, and Major Lee and every other officer speaks of the gallant and good conduct of this young officer.

Captain Fleming, who commanded the Indians, was, as he always is, in the front of the battle. There is not a more intrepid soldier in the army. I should be ungrateful were I to omit the names of Captains Knapp and Hull of the volunteers and Captain Parker and Lieut. Chatfield of the militia, by whose intrepidity I was during the action extricated from the most unpleasant situation. Capts. Richardson, Bull and Kennedy, and Lieuts. Parker and Brown, and Adjutants Dobbin, Bates and Robinson, particularly distinguished themselves. The patriotic conduct of Capt. Elliott, with twenty young gentlemen who volunteered from Batavia, and of Major Hubbard, with fourteen men exempted by age from military duty, should not be omitted. They were conspicuous during the action.

You will excuse me if I seem partial to my own family, consisting of my Brigade-Major Frazer, my volunteer aide-de-camp, Riddle, (both first lieutenants in the 15th Infantry,) Captain Biggar of the Canadian volunteers, Messrs. Williams and Delapierre, volunteer aids for the day, all of whom, except Mr. Williams, were wounded.

Lieuts. Frazer and Riddle were engaged for most of the preceding day with fatigue parties, cutting roads for the advance of the column through the swamp, and falling timber to the rear and within 150 yards of the enemy's right, which service they executed with so much address as to avoid discovery, and on the succeeding day they conducted the two columns to the attack. Frazer was severely wounded by a musket ball while spiking a gun on the second battery; Riddle, after the first battery was carried, descended into the enemy's magazine, and after securing (with the assistance of Quartermaster Greene of the volunteers, whose good conduct deserves much praise,) a quantity of fixed ammunition, blew up the magazine and suffered severely by the explosion. I must solicit through you, sir, the attention of the general government to these meritorious young men. Captain Bigger is an excellent officer and rendered me much assistance, but was dangerously wounded. The other young gentlemen are citizens and deserve much credit for their activity and for having voluntarily encountered danger. My aide-de-camp, Major Dox, was confined at Buffalo by sickness.

On the whole, sir, I can say of the regular troops attached to the left column, of the veteran volunteers of Lieut.-Col. Dobbins' regiment, that every man did his duty, and their conduct on this occasion reflects a new lustre on their former brilliant achievements. To the militia the compliment is justly due, and I could pay them no greater one than to say, that they were not surpassed by the heroes of Chippawa and Niagara in steadiness and bravery.

The studied intricacy of the enemy's defences, consisting not only of the breastwork connecting their batteries but of successive lines of entrenchments for a hundred yards in the rear, covering the batteries and enfilading each other, and the whole obstructed by *abattis*, brush, and felled timber, was calculated to produce confusion among the assailants and led to several conflicts at the point of the bayonet. But by our double columns temporary irregularities in the one was always corrected by the other. Our success would probably have been more complete but for the rain, which unfortunately set in soon after we commenced our march, which rendered the fire of many of our muskets useless, and by obscuring the sun led to several unlucky mistakes. As an instance of this, a body of 50 prisoners, who had surrendered, were ordered to the fort in charge of a subaltern and 14 volunteers: the officer mistaking the direction conducted them towards the British camp in the route by which we had advanced and they were retaken, with the whole of the guard excepting the officer and one man, who fought their way back. Several of our stragglers were made prisoners by the same mistake. But, sir, notwithstanding these accidents, we have reason to rejoice at our signal success in inflicting a vastly disproportionate injury on the enemy, and in wholly defeating all his plans of operation against this army.

Major-General Brown to the Secretary of War.

HEADQUARTERS, FORT ERIE, Sept. 29th, 1814.

SIR,—In my letter of the 18th inst. I briefly informed you of the fortunate issue of the sortie which took place the day preceding. But it is due to the gallant officers and men to whose bravery we are indebted for our success on this occasion, that I should give you a more circumstantial and detailed account of this affair.

The enemy's camp I had ascertained to be situated in a field surrounded by woods, nearly two miles distant from their batteries and entrenchments, the object of which was to keep the part of the force which was not upon duty out of the range of our fire from Fort Erie and Black Rock. Their infantry was formed into three brigades, estimated at 12 or 15 hundred men each. One of these brigades with a detail from their artillery was stationed at their works, (these being about 500 yards distant from old Fort Erie and the right of our line.) We had already suffered much from the fire of two of their batteries and were aware that a third was about to open upon us. Under these circumstances, I resolved to storm the batteries, destroy the cannon, and roughly handle the brigade upon duty before those in reserve could be brought into action.

On the morning of the 17th, the infantry and riflemen, regulars and militia, were ordered to be paraded and put in readiness to march precisely at 12 o'clock. Gen. Porter with the volunteers, Colonel Gibson with the riflemen, and Major Brooks with the 23d and 1st Infantry and a few dragoons acting as infantry, were ordered to move from the extreme left of our position upon the enemy's right by a passage opened through the woods for the occasion. Gen. Miller was directed to station his command in the ravine which lies between Fort Erie and the enemy's batteries, by passing them by detachments through the skirts of the wood, and the 21st Infantry under Gen. Ripley was posted as a corps of reserve between the new bastions of Fort Erie—all under cover and out of the view of the enemy.

About 20 minutes before 3 p. m. I found the left columns under the command of Gen. Porter, which were destined to turn the enemy's right, within a few rods of the British entrenchments. They were ordered to advance and commence the action. Passing down the ravine, I judged from the report that the action had commenced on our left. I now hastened to Gen. Miller and directed him to seize the moment and pierce the enemy's entrenchments between batteries Nos. 2 and 3. My orders were promptly and ably executed. Within 30 minutes after the first gun was fired, batteries Nos. 3 and 2, the enemy's line of entrenchments, and his two blockhouses were in our possession. Soon after, battery No. 1 was abandoned by the British. The guns in each were spiked by us or otherwise destroyed, and the magazine of No. 3 was blown up.

A few minutes before the explosion, I had ordered up the reserve under Gen. Ripley. As he passed me at the head of his column, I desired him, as he would be the senior in advance, to ascertain as near as possible the situation of the troops in general, and to have a care that not more was hazarded than the occasion required; that the object of the sortie effected, the troops would retire in good order, &c. Gen. Ripley passed rapidly on. Soon after I became alarmed for General Miller and sent an order for the 21st to hasten to his support towards battery No. 1. Col. Upham received the order and advanced to the aid of Gen. Miller. Gen. Ripley had inclined to the left, where Maj. Brooks' command was engaged, with a view of making some necessary inquiries of that officer, and in the act of doing so was unfortunately wounded. By this time the object of the sortie was accomplished beyond my most sanguine expectation. Gen. Miller had consequently ordered the troops on the right to fall back. Observing this movement, I sent my staff along the line to call in the other corps. Within a few minutes they retired to the ravine and from thence to camp.

Thus one thousand regulars and an equal portion of militia, in one hour of close action blasted the hopes of the enemy, destroyed the fruits of fifty days' labor, and diminished his effective force 1000 men at least. I am at a loss to express my satisfaction at the gallant conduct of the officers and men of this division, whose valor has shone superior to every trial. Gen. Porter, in his official report herein enclosed, has very properly noticed those patriotic citizens who have done so much honor to themselves by freely and voluntarily tendering their services at a dangerous and critical period.

As the scene of the action was in the wood in advance of the position I had chosen for directing the movements, the several reports of the commandants of corps must guide me in noticing individuals.

General Miller mentions Lieut.-Col. Aspinwall, Lieut.-Col. Beedle, Major Trimble, Capt. Hull, Capt. Ingersol, Lieut. Crawford, Lieut. Lee, and particularly Ensign O'Fling, as entitled to distinction.

Lieut.-Col. McDonald, upon whom the command of the rifle corps devolved upon the fall of the brave and generous Gibson, names Adjutants Shortridge of the 1st and Ballard of the 4th Regiment as deserving the highest applause for their promptness and gallantry in communicating orders. Of the other officers of the corps, he reports generally that the bravery and good conduct of all was so conspicuous as to render it impossible to discriminate.

Major Brooks, to whom much credit is due for the distinguished manner in which he executed the orders he received, speaks in high terms of Lieuts. Goodell, Ingersol, Livingston, and Ensigns Brant and O'Fling of the 23d, particularly of the latter. Also of Capt. Simms, Lieutenants Bissel, Shore and Brinot of the 1st Infantry, and Lieut. Watts of the dragoons.

Lieut.-Col. Upham, who took command of the reserve after Gen. Ripley was disabled, bestows great praise upon Major Chambers of the 4th Regiment of riflemen attached to the 21st Infantry, as also upon Capt. Bradford and Lieut. Holding of that regiment.

My staff, Col. Snelling, Col. Gardner, Major Jones, and my aide-de-camp, Major Austin, and Lieut. Armstrong, were, as usual, zealous, intelligent, and active:—they performed every duty required of them to my entire satisfaction.

Major Hall, Assistant Inspector-Gen., led a battalion of militia and conducted it with skill and gallantry. Lieut. Kirby, Aid-de-Camp to Gen. Ripley, was extremely active and useful during the time he was in the action.

Lieutenants Frazer and Riddle were in Gen. Porter's staff; their bravery was conspicuous, and no officers of their grade were more useful.

The corps of artillery commanded by Major Hindman, which has been so eminently distinguished throughout this campaign, had no opportunity of taking a part in the sortie. The 25th Infantry, under Col. Jessup, was stationed in Fort Erie, to hold the key of our position.

Col. Brady, on whose firmness and good conduct every reliance could be placed, was on command at Buffalo with the remains of the 22d Infantry. Lieut.-Col. McRea and Lieut.-Col. Wood of the corps of engineers have rendered to this army services the most important. I must seize the opportunity of again mentioning them particularly. On every trying occasion I have reaped much benefit from their sound and excellent advice. No two officers of their grade could have contributed more to the safety and honor of this army. Wood, brave, generous, and enterprising, died as he had lived, without a feeling but for the honor of his country and the glory of her arms: his name and example will live to guide the soldiers in the path of duty so long as true heroism is held in estimation. McRea lives to enjoy the approbation of every virtuous and generous mind, and to receive the reward due to his services and high military talents.

It is proper here to notice that although but one-third of the enemy's force was on duty when his works were carried, the whole were brought into action while we were employed in destroying his cannon. We secured prisoners from seven of his regiments and know that the 6th and 82d suffered severely in killed and wounded, yet these regiments were not upon duty.

Lieut.-Gen. Drummond broke up his camp during the night of the 21st and retired to his entrenchments behind the Chippawa. A party of our men came up with the rear of his army at Frenchman's Creek; the enemy destroyed part of their stores by setting fire to the buildings from which they were employed in conveying them. We found in and about their camp a considerable quantity of cannon ball and upwards of one hundred stand of arms.

I send you enclosed herein a return of our loss. The return of prisoners enclosed does not include the stragglers that came in after the action,

Report of the Killed, Wounded and Missing in the above Action.

Killed, 79; wounded, 216; missing, 216; total, 511.

C. K. GARDNER,
Adj.-Gen.

Return of prisoners taken in the above action:—Two majors, 4 captains, 4 lieutenants, 1 ensign, 1 assistant-surgeon, 4 staff sergeants, 19 sergeants, 17 corporals, 1 drummer, 332 rank and file. Total, 385.

J. SNELLING,
Insp.-Gen.

Names and Rank of Officers Killed, Wounded and Missing at Fort Erie, 17th September, 1814.

Killed—Lt.-Col. Wood, Engineers; Capt. L. Bradford, 21st Inf.; Capt. H. Hale, 11th Inf.; Capt. L. G. A. Armistead, 1st Riflemen.

Wounded—Brig.-Gen. Ripley; Brigade-Major Lieut. Crawford, 11th Inf.; 9th Inf., Lt.-Col. Aspinwall, Capt. Ingersol, Lieut. E. Childs, (bayonet wound); 11th Inf., Lieuts. W. F. Hale, I. Clarke, Stevenson, and Davis; 19th Inf., Maj. Trimble, Ensign Neely; 21st Inf., Ensign Cummings; 23d Inf., Lieut. Brown, Ensign O'Fling, (mortally); 1st Rifles, Capt. Ramsey, Lieut. Cobb, (dead); 4th Rifles, Col. Gibson, (dead), Lieut. Grant.

Missing—Lieut. Ballard, 4th Rifles, militia.

Killed—Brig.-Gen. Davis, Capt. Buel, (Crosby's Regt.), Lieut. Brown, (McBurney's), Lieut. W. Belknap, (Hopkins'), Ensign Blakely, (McBurney's).

Wounded—Maj.-Gen. Porter, (sword wound), Lieut. Frazer, 15th Inf., Riddle, 15th Inf., Capt. Bigger, N. Y. Vol., (Dobbin's Regt.), Capt. Knapp, Lieut. Bailey, (McBurney's), Capt. Hale, (wounded and prisoner, Hopkin's Regt.), Lieut. Gillet.

Missing—Lieut.-Col. Churchill, Major E. Wilson, Q. M., O. Wilcox, Capts. Crouch and Case, Lieut. Case, Ensigns Chambers, Clark, and Church.

General Brown to the Secretary of War.

H. Q., CAMP FORT ERIE, October 1st, 1814.

SIR,—Looking over my official account of the action of the 17th ultimo, I find that the names of the regiments which composed General Miller's command were not given. As I believe it even more important to distinguish corps than individuals, I am anxious to correct this mistake. General Miller on that day commanded the remains of the 9th and 11th Infantry and a detachment of the 19th. Of three field officers attached to them, two were severely wounded; Lt.-Col. Aspinwall of the 9th, gallantly leading his men to the attack, and Major Trimble of the 19th, who was shot within their works, conducting with great skill and bravery. A detachment of the 17th Regiment was attached to the 21st.

www.ingramcontent.com/pod-product-compliance
Lightning Source LLC
Chambersburg PA
CBHW020827230426
43666CB00007B/1127